MINING CAMPS

A Study in American Frontier Government

harper ✝ torchbooks

*A reference-list of Harper Torchbooks, classified
by subjects, is printed at the end of this volume.*

AMERICAN PERSPECTIVES

EDITED BY BERNARD WISHY AND

WILLIAM E. LEUCHTENBURG

* *in preparation*

MINING CAMPS

A Study in American Frontier Government

BY

CHARLES HOWARD SHINN

EDITED BY
RODMAN WILSON PAUL

Harper Torchbooks ▼ The University Library
HARPER & ROW, PUBLISHERS / NEW YORK, EVANSTON AND LONDON

Dedication

———

TO MY FRIENDS IN CALIFORNIA

MINING CAMPS

Introduction and Footnotes copyright © 1965
by Rodman Wilson Paul

Printed in the United States of America.

This book was originally published by
Charles Scribner's Sons in 1884.

First HARPER TORCHBOOK edition published 1965 by
Harper & Row, Publishers, Incorporated
49 East 33rd Street, New York, N. Y. 10016.

CONTENTS

PREFACE.

FEW undertakings of my busy life have brought me more pleasure than the group of studies linked together in this volume. They were begun and carried to completion while I was a student at this university; and if they possess any value, it is chiefly because of the spirit of original investigation fostered here in every department of knowledge.

Since I am about to send this volume to the press, I desire, with sincere respect and affection, to place on record my sense of personal obligations to President D. C. Gilman, Professor Gildersleeve, Professor Paul Haupt, Dr. H. B. Adams, and Dr. Richard Ely, of Johns Hopkins; to President W. T. Reid and Professor Cook of the University of California; and to Dr. Josiah Royce of Harvard, —all of whom have helped me by the loan of pamphlets, by advice, and by their cordial interest in the undertaking.

CHARLES HOWARD SHINN, A.B.

JOHNS HOPKINS UNIVERSITY, BALTIMORE,
December, 1884.

viii

INTRODUCTION TO THE
TORCHBOOK EDITION

by
RODMAN WILSON PAUL

In the early 1880's the Johns Hopkins University was one of the most exciting centers of learning in America. A new foundation, created by the will of a Baltimore financier, the Johns Hopkins University had opened its doors to students in 1876, at a time when American universities were just awaking into intellectual vigor after decades of confinement within a restricted classical curriculum. A stress on science, a beginning of true graduate work patterned after the German Ph.D. programs, and a demand for original thinking at both undergraduate and graduate levels—these were among the innovations that were arousing the academic world.

As a new university, Johns Hopkins had no inherited torpor to shake off and no traditionalist faculty to convert. Instead, under the leadership of President Daniel Coit Gilman, formerly head of the University of California, Johns Hopkins began energetically to develop America's first great graduate university and to nurture, in the shadow of the graduate school, a challenging, unorthodox, small undergraduate college.

Being unconventional, Johns Hopkins was prepared to admit some unusual students, especially if the applicants came from distant parts of the Union. In 1882 the authorities accepted Charles Howard Shinn of California, even though Shinn was then thirty years old and had had little formal college training. A native of Austin, Texas, where he was born on April 29, 1852, Shinn had been brought to a farm in Niles, Alameda County, California, in 1856. His father, for all that he was born in Ohio and tried farming in Texas, was of New Jersey Quaker stock, and married to a lady who claimed descent from New England ancestors, including one who came over on the Mayflower.

Young Charles Shinn grew up on the family farm at Niles and was a pupil in the local public schools before he, to quote his own abbreviated summary, "attended the old College School in Oakland—Then one year at the Univ. of Calif."[1] At that time the University of California had only just been established as the tax-supported successor to a privately-financed, church-inspired foundation that had been struggling to maintain at Oakland both the College School and what was known as the College of California.

Whether for lack of money or because the new state institution was not sufficiently challenging, Shinn dropped out of college to try school teaching and writing. During the next few years he taught in several rural California counties—San Luis Obispo, Monterey, Alameda, Trinity, and Shasta. Some of these counties were dominated by farming, some by livestock raising, and some by mining. In all of them Shinn found subjects for free-lance writing. For the newspapers and San Francisco periodicals he wrote essays on horticulture and

[1] Charles Howard Shinn to A. B. Nye, n.p., n.d., but in response to Nye's letter of inquiry dated August 3, 1905. Bancroft Library, University of California.

rural life, articles on California local history, and poems describing romantic California scenes.

He did well enough to win promotion in 1878 to the staff of the San Francisco *Bulletin,* for which he served variously during the next several years as reporter, telegraph and news editor, editorial writer, and special correspondent. With his characteristic energy and enthusiasm, Shinn found time also to edit the *California Horticulturist* magazine, and to publish in 1879 a successful manual that bore the lengthy title *Pacific Rural Handbook; Containing a Series of Brief and Practical Essays and Notes on the Culture of Trees, Vegetables and Flowers, Adapted to the Pacific Coast. Also, Hints on Home and Farm Improvements.*

Shinn was thus a veteran of a decade of school teaching and professional writing and editing before he sought permission to enroll in the new university at Baltimore. The authorities at John Hopkins accepted him as a special student (''extra ordinem'') and permitted him to step into what was essentially graduate work, although Shinn was a candidate only for the bachelor's degree. At Baltimore Shinn found himself in the company of a small group of intense, dedicated students of history and political science. Their mentor was Professor Herbert Baxter Adams (A.B. Amherst, Ph.D. Heidelberg), a stimulating teacher and energetic promoter who was determined to make Johns Hopkins *the* American center for the ''scientific'' study of history and politics along the lines followed at the great German universities of that day.

''The main principle of historical training at the Johns Hopkins University,'' Professor Adams declared, ''is to encourage independent thought and research. Little heed is given to text-books, or the mere phraseology of history, but all stress is laid upon clear and original statements of fact and opinion."[2] Fair enough, but that was not quite the whole story. The patron saint of historical studies at Johns Hopkins was Edward A. Freeman, the noted English student of political institutions, who believed that the key to understanding the history of the English-speaking peoples was to recognize fundamental political continuities that ran back to that ancient day when the ancestors of the Anglo-Saxons dwelt in the forests of Europe. The institutions of an American state, Freeman declared in an article written after a visit to the United States in 1881, are not simply local creations but rather "part of the general institutions of the English people, as those are again part of the general institutions of the Teutonic race, and those are again part of the general institutions of the whole Aryan family. . . . The history, in short, of a Massachusetts township or a Maryland manor becomes, if looked at in a scientific spirit, part of the general history of the world. Of course I assume that they are studied in a scientific spirit."[3]

Freeman's thinking, with its stress on Germanic origins, racial inheritance, and "scientific" research, accorded perfectly with the predispositions of American scholars like Herbert B. Adams, who had been trained in Germany and who looked with admiration at the nineteenth century German universities. Adams' own approach to American institutional history can best be indicated by citing the titles of the three papers he con-

[2] Herbert B. Adams, *Methods of Historical Study* (Johns Hopkins University, *Studies in Historical and Political Science*, 2nd series, I–II. Baltimore, 1884), p. 5.

[3] Edward A. Freeman, *An Introduction to American Institutional History* (Johns Hopkins University, *Studies in Historical and Political Science*, 1st series, I. Baltimore, 1882), p. 13.

tributed to the first volume of Johns Hopkins historical studies: *The Germanic Origin of New England Towns* (written in 1881); *Saxon Tithingmen in America* (also written in 1881); and *Norman Constables in America* (1882). The title of the Johns Hopkins series was equally revealing. These were to be studies in "Historical and Political *Science*."

Apparently, then, "independent" investigation of American institutions, when guided along "scientific" lines, would inevitably lead an historical researcher back from America, to England, to what were variously termed Germanic or Teutonic origins. The "scientific" element in this process implied in part a psychological attitude—specifically, a rigorous search for the truth, free from what were regarded as traditional or parochial biases—and in part, an attempt to apply Darwinian notions of biological evolution to the development of political institutions. Political institutions, according to this reasoning, were to be viewed as organisms that developed from inherited "minute germs."

Nor was Adams thinking merely of academic tasks when he urged his bright young men to seek the truth through "scientific" research. The motto on the wall of the seminar room at Johns Hopkins was a quotation from Freeman: "History is past Politics and Politics present History." Students at Johns Hopkins were encouraged to link their academic researches to issues of current importance. And in fact the intensity that marked their scholarly efforts was to characterize also the lifelong concern of many Johns Hopkins men for political and social reform. Woodrow Wilson was the greatest product of this Johns Hopkins inspiration of the 1880's; but he was not unique. Shinn's own later career in the United States Forest Service and his prominence in the conservation movement reflect the lasting influence of the Johns Hopkins stress on public service.

Shinn fitted perfectly into the atmosphere of dedication and purpose that he found at Baltimore during his two years' residence, 1882–1884. With a warm, friendly personality, and a rich store of enthusiasm and constructive energy, he was accepted at once into the little community of hard-working scholars. In a speech given at Johns Hopkins on November 17, 1882, Professor Adams specifically welcomed him:

> And now a student from California, bearing letters from the faculty of the institution at Berkeley, has come eastward to Baltimore, leaving an associate editorship of the San Francisco Bulletin, for the sake of discovering, for himself, an old world of science. And already in the light of Institutional studies he . . . is preparing to develop a veritable mine in the study of frontier law and of the wonderful evolution of self-government in California mining-camps, where old Saxon forms of associated families of *men* sprang full armed into life and law.[4]

It would appear, then, that from almost the time of Shinn's arrival in Baltimore, there was agreement between student and mentor as to what Shinn's special topic was to be. This selection of a subject that grew logically out of Shinn's personal background was in harmony with a scheme that Professor Adams had conceived. His plan for the seminar, Adams explained, was "for advanced students . . . to investigate in a sys-

[4] Herbert B. Adams, "Co-Operation in University Work," appended to Adams' *The Germanic Origin of New England Towns* (Johns Hopkins University, *Studies in Historical and Political Science*, 1st series, II. Baltimore, 1882), pp. 44–45.

tematic way the Institutional or Economic History of their own section or locality. Young men, with slight experience in scientific research, will see an obvious advantage in beginning work upon familiar ground and upon limited areas.''[5]

In Shinn's own mind there was no question but that his upbringing in California, and more particularly his observations while serving as teacher and journalist, had given him special qualifications for understanding the life of the California mining camps. As he later explained, while teaching school ''in the autumn of 1878 . . . in a little Mining Camp of Trinity County, California, [he had] witnessed the practical operations of 'rules, usages and customs' in regard to local government over well-defined areas known as 'Mining Districts.' ''[6] Similarly, while serving as traveling correspondent for the San Francisco *Bulletin* in the spring and summer of 1879, Shinn ''explored the mining region of the Sierra counties of California, became acquainted with pioneers, and visited many of the famous old camps,'' where he found abundant evidence of ''the institutions that American freemen created in time of need for the protection of life and property.''[7]

Mining Camps was, therefore, the product of two impulses: of Shinn's enthusiasm for Californian themes, and of the inspiration and guidance that the young Californian found in the seminar at Johns Hopkins. The book was really a seminar paper, prepared in a class whose thinking was directed in accordance with a very definite philosophy of history. If much of that philosophy

[5] *Ibid.*, p. 48.
[6] Charles Howard Shinn, *Land Laws of Mining Districts* (Johns Hopkins University, *Studies in Historical and Political Science*, 2nd series, XII. Baltimore, 1884), p. 5.
[7] *Ibid.*, p. 6.

appears grotesque today, in the 1880's it seemed a stimulating approach that offered new insights.

The influence of the seminar was apparent from the very first chapter, which Shinn opened with the declaration that "the episode known in the West as 'the mining-era' deserves to be called a stanza in the political epic of the Germanic race to which we belong," and which he closed with the hope that this study would reveal "the capabilities of our Germanic race" for improvising government under emergency conditions. One can almost see Professor Adams nodding approval, and quoting Freeman in support of his young protege's thesis.

With the loyalty of a convert, throughout the book Shinn strained for opportunities to point out parallels between ancient Germanic customs and the practices of nineteenth century western American mining camps. His insistence on referring to California miners' meetings as the "folk-moot of our Germanic ancestors" and the "folk-moot of the Sierra" (pages 125 and 176, and 105) strikes a modern reader as eccentric if not ridiculous. But there was at least some justification for this talk of British and German antecedents. Mining has always been a specialized and decidedly international occupation, in which customs, techniques, and individual miners have circulated quite independently of national boundaries. The mining lawyers whose manuals Shinn listed in his bibliography, such as Gregory Yale, had long recognized the debt western American miners owed to the legal customs developed in the Harz mountains of Germany and the tin mines of Cornwall. A similar case could be made in regard to technological precedents. Shinn's heavy emphasis was an exaggeration, but it was not a mere invention.

Nor did Shinn allow an enthusiasm for British and Teutonic ancestors to permit neglect of non-Germanic origins. Spanish, Mexican, and pre-Californian American practices all received consideration, especially in the introductory chapters. Indeed, one might well question whether too much space was not given to Spanish institutions that had little to do with mining, such as the missions and pueblos.

Against these shortcomings, how stand the book's strengths? First and foremost, *Mining Camps* was, as its author modestly claimed, "an attempt to break ground in a comparatively new field," that is, to reveal the western mining camp as an important source of enduring law and institutions. With vivid and pardonable exaggeration Shinn opened his book with the declaration: "To-day, over the western third of the United States, institutional life traces its beginnings to the mining-camp; that is the original contribution of the American pioneer to the art of self-government."

If Shinn had accomplished nothing else with this volume, he would still be remembered as the man who fixed the mining camp in the thinking of everyone who had a serious interest in the history of the American west. Shinn was as much a pioneer in enlarging our historical understanding as his miners were in expanding the limits of settlement. Many previous writers, chiefly journalists, had given elaborate descriptions of California and the Far West during the immensely varied and colorful mining era. Shinn surpassed them, because he lifted out of the crowded, confused mass of evidence the scattered bits of information that, when rearranged, fitted together, and interpreted by a scholar, revealed the central significance of the mining camp as the mechanism through which the boom-time crowd drafted their home-made rules for deciding ownership of claims and punished men accused of crime.

In short, Shinn did precisely what Johns Hopkins trained its students to do—he wrote a monograph ("a special treatise on a particular subject"—Webster). His book thus not only went well beyond journalistic reporting, but also made a much more decisive impression on the reader than even such important contemporary studies as the massive volumes on California history compiled by Hubert Howe Bancroft's staff in San Francisco, or the briefer history of California written in Cambridge by the Harvard philosopher Josiah Royce. For example, tucked into half a dozen of the 787 pages that constituted Volume VI of Bancroft's *History of California* (published 1888) was a very competent little summary of the rules regarding mining claims, while two huge volumes (published 1887) gave highly detailed accounts of the evidence Bancroft had found concerning extra-legal justice as enforced in the mines, San Francisco, the river towns, and "cow counties." Royce's book (published 1886) was more evenly organized, but even so, the discussion of what Royce termed "Self-Government, Good-Humor and Violence in the Mines" occupied only a hundred of the book's five hundred pages. More significantly, Royce's history became in large part a brooding, discursive essay on the American character as revealed in California during the decade that included the Gold Rush.

By concentrating on a single theme, Shinn made his point with a clarity, coherence, and decisiveness scarcely possible in the more comprehensive works of his two distinguished contemporaries. He deserves credit also for being the pioneer, since his book preceded Royce's by a year and Bancroft's by two to three years. (Both men cited Shinn's study in their texts.) *Mining Camps* had the further great virtue of being well written. Shinn was already an experienced author before he came to Baltimore, and in Baltimore he was encouraged to concentrate on a thoroughly congenial theme that enlisted all of his considerable enthusiasm and talents. The result is a liveliness and finish that make for pleasant reading.

This is particularly true after the first eight chapters. The first eight are essentially introductory and, typically of a seminar paper, are crowded with scholarly references to mining in bygone days. Starting with Chapter IX, Shinn tends strictly to the subject matter implied by his volume's title and sub-title. Comments about the habits of "our Germanic ancestors" become infrequent, and descriptions of what actually happened in California predominate. Here the author is thoroughly at home. Dramatically he describes the successive transformations of the ravines and river valleys, as miners overran them, built their camps, washed away the original topography, and then deserted them for newer and richer regions. Sympathetically Shinn describes the "decaying camps," and the "few old and trembling men" still to be seen in the diggings when he passed through in 1878 and 1879.

But Shinn's own travels in the gold region provided no more than the background—the "feel"—for his material. His research, according to his preface, was done entirely at Johns Hopkins, and yet it was remarkably comprehensive. The number of contemporary and reminiscent accounts consulted by Shinn was large. Not only did he read widely, but he anticipated the present vogue for "oral history." He crossexamined Forty-Niners whom he managed to meet on the Atlantic Coast, he wrote to veterans of mining life and received long replies, and by correspondence he persuaded Californian friends to interview "old-timers" who were still resident on the Pacific Coast. Like Bancroft's staff in San Francisco, Shinn did much to preserve for later generations the opinions and explanations of men who were soon to pass forever beyond reach of human interrogation.

The one obvious gap in Shinn's sources was newspapers. Both Bancroft and Royce made extensive and good use of California newspapers of the mining era, and Royce justifiably criticized Shinn for his failure to do likewise. Perhaps no files of journals were available in Baltimore; perhaps Shinn thought that he had enough material on most subjects without adding this further source. In his chapter on "Difficulties with Foreigners" he does speak of making "a close study of the newspapers of the time," although he gives no specific citations.

The question is of some importance, for Royce cited his newspaper files as the evidence for believing that Shinn gave too favorable a picture of the miners' attitudes and actions. Royce was impressed by the cruelty, injustice, prejudice toward foreigners, and general social carelessness shown by the crowds in the mining camps. Yet a reader who studies Shinn's book closely will find that all of these failings of the miners are acknowledged. For example (page 227): "We find, throughout the mining-era, sporadic cases of true mob-law; of men being hung without judge or jury, without fair trial, and perhaps without justification." Or again, when speaking of the attitude toward foreigners (page 212): "Sometimes, however, the Americans were unjust and overbearing, or were at least careless and indifferent to the rights of others."

Like Royce, then, Shinn recognized these evils, but having stated them as a warning to the reader, Shinn went on to complete his book with an optimistic message. Lacking legitimate government and statutes, the miners had nevertheless extemporized their own courts, juries, and codes of law, with results that made for the greater good of by far the greater number of people. In Shinn's opinion, the evil episodes were far fewer than the constructive actions. Perhaps this is equivalent to suggesting that Royce's earnest, intricate doubts led him to one emphasis, while Shinn's buoyant temperament led him to quite a different one.

The fact that California occupied so much of the space in a book whose title claimed coverage of all American mining frontiers was justified logically by Shinn on the unquestionable ground that California was the pioneer, that California practices became the precedents that were copied all over the Far West. Less logical but perhaps equally compelling was the simple circumstance that California was the area that most interested the author. By the latter part of 1884 Shinn felt sufficiently confident of his subject-matter so that he was prepared to publish parts of it not only in *Mining Camps* but also in periodical and academic form. Articles on ''California Mining Camps'' and ''Local Government in the Mines'' appeared in the *Overland Monthly* for August and December, 1884, and another entitled ''California's Golden Prime of Forty-Nine'' was published in the *Magazine of American History* for November of that same year. A collection of documents illustrating mining camp government, with a fifty page preface, came out in 1884 as a monograph in the Johns Hopkins historical series. All of these publications incorporated, almost verbatim,

sizeable chunks of the text that was soon to be published
in 1885 as *Mining Camps,* under the imprint of Charles
Scribner's Sons.

Shinn had helped to pay his way through Johns Hopkins by writing for New York, Baltimore, and California
newspapers, and while waiting for his book to appear, he
moved to New York City to try working as a newspaper-
man and contributor to American and British periodicals. His sister Millicent having become editor of the
Overland Monthly, Shinn was persuaded to return to
California to serve as business manager of that magazine from 1885–1890. This position he left when the University of California offered him an appointment as
Inspector of Agricultural Experiment Stations, an as-
signment that surely must have been more congenial to
one of Shinn's interests than serving as a business manager.

The rest of his life was spent primarily in work connected with agriculture and forestry. He shifted to the
United States Forest Service in 1902 and served in suc-
cessively higher administrative posts in the Sierra National Forest. For much of this latter time he and his
wife, the former Julia C. Tyler of Oakland, whom Shinn
married in 1888, actually lived in the forest, at a lovely
spot called Northfork, in Madera County, where Shinn
built a home that he named Peace Cabin.

Shinn wrote extensively about subjects relating to
agriculture, forestry, conservation, and California history. During Gifford Pinchot's terms as head of the
Forest Service, Shinn played a prominent part in the
crusade to preserve the people's heritage from predatory
interests. In the midst of all this responsible activity, he
found time on one occasion, soon after his return to
California from New York, to participate in a collabo-

rative research project sponsored by Johns Hopkins,[8] and in the mid-1890's he turned once more to his interest in mining, when the firm of Appleton invited him to write the volume on mining for Ripley Hitchcock's *Story of the West Series.* Published in 1896 under the title of *The Story of the Mine as Illustrated by the Great Comstock Lode of Nevada,* Shinn's new volume was a less original contribution to the history of western mining than *Mining Camps* had been. The new book, like its predecessor, revealed Shinn's admirable understanding of the habits and ways of thought of western mining people, but it borrowed extensively from a government-sponsored historical study, Eliot Lord's *Comstock Mining and Miners* (Washington, 1883).

In Shinn's twilight years he and his wife left Peace Cabin and went to live with their daughter and son-in-law at Ukiah, in the Russian River Valley, one hundred miles north of San Francisco. A letter written by Shinn from Ukiah starts with a contented exclamation that life is still wonderful and then goes on to summarize some of the associations that were uppermost in Shinn's mind in his closing years: "I am still in the Forest Service—which I entered in 1902," [and although at retiring age I] "am needed, and shall stay till July. . . . I hear often from my old classmates of J.H.U.—Albert Shaw, Woodrow Wilson, and ever so many more."[9]

He died at Ukiah on December 2, 1924.

CALIFORNIA INSTITUTE OF TECHNOLOGY,

PASADENA, JULY, 1964

[8] Charles Howard Shinn, *Coöperation on the Pacific Coast* (Johns Hopkins University, *Studies in History and Political Science,* 6th series, IX–X. Baltimore, 1888), pp. 443–481.

[9] Shinn, Ukiah, to Robert Underwood Johnson, December 30 [no year stated]. Bancroft Library, University of California.

MINING-CAMPS.

A STUDY IN AMERICAN FRONTIER GOVERNMENT.

CHAPTER I.

SCOPE OF THE PRESENT INVESTIGATION.

THE following pages deal largely with ancient, mediæval, and modern mining-laws, and with the life of mining-camps; but this is solely for their value as contributions to American political science and American institutional history. The proposed investigation is as far removed, on the one hand, from a technical history of mining, as it is removed, on the other hand, from a digest of mining-decisions. It is primarily a study of the mining-camp commonwealths; that is, of those States and Territories in the remote West whose development has been under conditions widely different from those that prevailed on the Atlantic slope and in the Mississippi Valley. It is also a study of the Spanish land-system in Mexico and in California, and of the relations of priest, alcalde, and commandante, in mission, pueblo, and presidio; for otherwise the place of the true mining-camp, as a nucleus of most effective organization, cannot be fully understood. It is an at-

1

tempt to break ground in a comparatively new field, and to examine the laws and customs, not of primitive pastoral nor of primitive agricultural communities, but of the workers in ores, and the toilers in auriferous river-sands.

The best thoughts of such writers as Maine, Seebohm, Nasse, the Von Maurers, Laveleye, Kovalevsky, have been devoted to studies of early land-tenure. Patiently they have examined the traces of village communities; of common lands, " *Wald, Weide,* and *Wiese;* " of the prehistoric "three-field system," whose rude crop-rotation the Teutonic farmers have followed, with various modifications, since the days of village moot assemblies by the Frisian Sea and on the Swabian Mountains; and of the Russian Mir, Swiss Landesgemeinde, and old Teutonic field meetings, — all of them primitive social organizations, and sources of such institutions as Saxon territorial tithings, English parish assemblies, and New-England town meetings. For men of our Germanic race this line of investigation is, doubtless, the widest and most important one that institutional history offers; but we shall do well to remember that all beginnings of government and society are valuable to the student, and that, since the days of Tubal Cain, the arts of mining have fostered peculiar independence, and developed a most distinctive organization.

Thoughtful Americans feel that they cannot too thoroughly understand our early civic communities, our towns, parishes, and counties, the germs of State and national growth, so firmly rooted in the past of our race. As Green, the "historian of the English people," wrote: "in the village moots of Friesland or Sleswick . . . England learned to be a mother of parliaments." Freeman, historian of the Norman Conquest, looking beyond our political and geographical separation, holds that "the English-speaking commonwealth on the American mainland is simply a part of the great English folk," and urges that the members of this mighty kindred should be to each other "at least as much as were the members of the scattered Hellenic settlements," — these all Englishmen, as those were all Greeks. In studying American colonial life, this sense of noble unity increases; and we are inevitably brought to studies of the European sources of that life. Virginia and Massachusetts lead us not only to the England of Shakspeare and Cromwell, but also to that older England of the Continent.

But, if our institutional studies cease at the summits of the Alleghanies, we have learned only a part of the lesson that America has to teach. In that New West beyond the rocky borders of Nebraska, and the remote sources of the Missouri, American pioneers have shown their hereditary fitness for self-government under exceptionally trying conditions. They have wrought out, and are still extending into new regions, local institutions in the highest sense their own. Their State life, growth of law, crystallization of society, largely came from small settlements known as mining-camps, and from a social organization presenting remarkable political and economic features. So strong, natural, and impressive has been the display in these camps of a capacity for organization of the highest order, that the episode known in the West as "the mining-era" deserves to be called a stanza in the political epic of the Germanic race to which we belong.

The influence of the Atlantic colonies prevailed without opposition in the early settlements of the Mississippi Valley; but there came a time when American frontiersmen of the third generation found a new environment, adopted a new occupation, and met alien influences from Moor and Saracen, from Spaniard and Mexican. Problems more difficult were nowhere else presented on the continent: nowhere else were they more triumphantly solved. To-day, over the western third of the United States, institutional life traces its beginnings to the mining-camp: that is the original contribution of the American pioneer to the art of self-government. Boone and his foresters, Carson and his trappers, Bent, Bridger, Beckwourth, and their "mountain-men," all melted away before the tides of civilization, without being forced by imperious necessity to the creation of any code of local laws, or to the organization of any form of permanent government; but the early miners of the Far West showed large and noble capacities for bringing order out of chaos, strength out of weakness, because they were a picked body of men, and also because the life they led fostered friendship, encouraged individuality, and compelled the closest social union.

Thirty-seven years ago the discovery of gold in California caused thousands of miners to assemble in the cañons of the Sierra Nevada; and soon they were forced, by lack of Territorial and State government, to organize for self-protection, and to enact and execute their own civil and criminal codes. The previous history of this region had been such that many foreign influences continued to act either directly or indirectly upon the rude but efficient system of the early mining-camps, until, with the formation of permanent government under a State constitution, all necessity for this local camp-law of the mountains of California appeared to have suddenly ended. Nevertheless, a large portion of this local law, created thus rapidly and under such unique social conditions, exhibited surprising vitality. It persistently kept its place, persistently extended itself to other Territories, persistently influenced township and county government. It found ample recognition from Territorial and State legislatures, from Congress, and from the Supreme Court of the United States; and it ultimately developed into what can safely be called the "American system of mining-law," — a system that is honored throughout the civilized world, and forms the basis of mining-jurisprudence in many of the newer gold-regions of other countries.

At the present time in the United States, over nine States and Territories, and throughout a rapidly developing region already peopled by more than three million persons, and extending from the silver-ledges of southern New Mexico to the frozen placers [1] of Cœur d'Alene, and even beyond, mining-property is still held in the main by customs of tenure originated by the early placer and quartz miners of California. Although the present laws allow mineral lands to be "patented," and purchased from the government, it is still true that only the well-developed mining-properties are so purchased, and that the vast majority of claims are held by simple possessory rights under the "land-laws" of the camp or district. Often the early "camp" grew into a "district," embracing several camps; and this district ultimately developed into a township of a county; while the original "camp" in many cases became a "county-seat," though still retaining strong evidence in local customs of its growth and previous history. The free,

---

[1] The word "placer" is from the Spanish. It means "content," "satisfaction." "Placers are superficial deposits of gold which occupy the beds of ancient rivers" (Decision in Case of Moxon *vs.* Wilkinson, 2d Montana Reports).

strong life of the mining-camp has been a factor of
prime importance in the social, literary, and institutional development of large and prosperous American
communities. The laws of the mining-camp, in modified form, still influence many of the newer States and
Territories. Nothing that is likely to happen will ever
take from the civilization of this imperial domain of
Pacific-Coast and Rocky-Mountain region certain characteristics due to the mining-camp era. Even when, a
century hence, it is, perhaps, divided into twenty States,
with a population of twice as many millions, the atmosphere and traditions of the mining-camp will yet linger
in the mountain gorges, and fragments of the miner's
jurisprudence will yet remain firmly embedded in local
and State law.

In order to better understand these camps of the Far
West, it has seemed proper, and indeed necessary, to
first investigate, though briefly, the ancient and mediæval mining-systems. Through legal sources, and by
means of history, chiefly Spanish, English, and German,
we must connect the mining-experiences of the New
World with those of the Old, sufficiently, at least, to
serve for purposes of illustration. We shall everywhere discover that, as Professor Stubbs says in his
"Constitutional History," "the roots of the present lie
deep in the past," and that "nothing in the past is dead
to the man who would learn how the present comes to be
what it is." The very kind of local law and self-government known to the miners of California has existed
in some degree among the miners of many other lands.
The mining-tribes of ancient Siberia, the mining-cities of
desert-guarded Midian, the Grecian "companies" that
"drifted" in the hill of Laurium, the Carthaginian
"prospectors" who "panned out" gold from the sands

of Tagus and Guadalquivir, — each and all contribute
precious material to our investigation. Above all, the
customs of Cornwall and Thuringia serve to define,
illustrate, and explain the workings of primitive law
on the Pacific Coast. We must also study the Spanish
civil and mining code, as developed under Mexican
skies, and as transplanted to the soil of Alta California.
In California itself we must trace Spanish-American
forces from the days of saintly Padre Serra and bluff
Governor Portala to the advent of the bold, restless
Anglo-Saxon trappers, farmers, and miners, with their
capacity for work, and their faculty for organization.

At the point of time when the military governors of
newly conquered California began to rule along the
coast, and when the eager, energetic miners first pitched
their tents beside the foaming Feather and Yuba, and
swung their mighty picks against the splintering bowlders, and hewed their "rockers" from the giant mountain
pines, century-old, overhead, our investigation, pursued
through so many preliminaries, broadens at last into the
study of American miners' courts, their officials, their
criminal and civil codes, their land-system, their forms
of procedure and government. Some of these forms
were adopted from Spanish law, some from primitive
forms familiar to the Germanic races from the times of
Tacitus, some were peculiarly a product of the men and
the emergency, but all are historically interesting and
important. From this point our studies are properly
confined to an examination into the growth of these
forces, and of their abiding influence upon later society
and government. We must not look upon this period
as merely a brilliant episode full of impetus and splen-
dor, dear to the heart of the Western pioneer, and
crowded with precious accumulations of material for

coming poet and novelist, but as including elements of permanent historical value, judged by a standard of utility, and as, in reality, an episode of great institutional importance, closely connected with a curious past, and still an influential fact in forms of local organization as yet incomplete.

One result of our labors will, perhaps, be that we shall more clearly comprehend the capabilities of our Germanic race for swift adaptation of the means to the end; for readiness in every emergency; for rapid, yet lasting, social organization; for acceptance and transformation of local institutions already at hand; for that sort of hearty, honest compromise which makes the best of circumstances, and continually evolves better and better conditions under which to act. Perhaps we shall thus gain a higher faith in that Republic whose children have wrought out, unknown, in silence, and under enormous difficulties, laws wise and good for the sufficient protection of life and property, adding, of their own will and choice, the majesty of government to the careless freedom of their frontier existence. On this higher level, as a humble contribution to the practical political experience of the race, this study of the hitherto undescribed institutions and unwritten laws of typical mining-camps must find, if anywhere, its reason and its justification.

In 1866 the chairman of the Senate Committee upon Mines and Mining closed his report upon a bill then before Congress, in the following language: —

"It is essential that this great system" (of local law) "established by the people in their primary capacities, and evidencing by the highest possible testimony the peculiar genius of the American people for founding empire and order, shall be preserved and affirmed. Popular sovereignty is here displayed in one of its grandest aspects, and simply invites us, not to destroy, but to put upon it the stamp of national power and unquestioned authority."

CHAPTER II.

MAN, as Aristotle remarks, is endowed with an instinct subservient to the ends of social union, and is led thereto by the commands of Nature. Through three great forms of productive industry, this instinct has been exercised and developed: first, by the life pastoral, — the keeping of cattle, the tending of sheep, reining of wild horses; second, by the life agricultural, — the wrestling with tangled forests, the breaking of the stubborn soil, the walling-in of "tun" and "burh;" third, by the life of miners, — the search for metals both useful and precious, the impetus thus given to commerce and the arts, the development of inventive skill, the closer organization akin to that of cities.

The value of the precious metals was understood in the earliest ages, as appears in the literature of ancient Oriental nations, the rent-rolls of Assyrian monarchs, and even the curious public libraries of that antediluvian race, the Accadians, who had collections at Sippera, Pantabiblia ("Book-town"), and elsewhere, and whose cylinders of baked clay speak of "gold weighed out for payment." The Egyptians are known to have had rich gold-mines in Nubia and Abyssinia, also in the deserts of Sinai and on the borders of Arabia, where they also

10

mined for turquoise, copper, and silver. A papyrus of the nineteenth dynasty still exists, containing plans of the workings of the Nubian gold-mines. Herodotus gives the annual product of the ancient Egyptian mines, as recorded upon the walls of one of the palaces of the kings of Thebes, as a sum equivalent to thirty millions of dollars. This was chiefly from quartz-veins, which Diodorus describes as "glittering with bright metals, out of which the overseers cause the gold to be taken." Egyptian and Assyrian methods were purely despotic, crushing and destroying the earlier freedom of the miner, which had in all probability existed, and substituting the doctrine that the ownership of all minerals was vested in the crown.

The Phœnicians mined copper in Kypros,* and gold in the mountains of Thasos, where, as Herodotus tells us, they had "overturned a whole mountain," even before the thirteenth century B.C. The Book of Job contains a realistic description of the early methods of mining extant in Arabia, and doubtless stimulated by Phœnician traders. When the merchandising of the Phœnicians began to assume world-wide proportions, their caravans developed the gold-searching instincts of many a semi-civilized nation and half-savage mountaineer tribe. Throughout Asia, the "Golden Continent," are the remains of ancient and extensive gold-workings on the Smejewka in Siberia, in the Urals and the Caucasus, along the Oxus and Indus, in Arabia, Persia, Tibet, Biluchistan, Japan, and at many other widely separated places.

The probabilities in regard to most of the prehistoric placer-mines in Northern Asia are, that they were worked by wandering Scythian tribes, who were, perhaps, on much the same intellectual level as the turquoise-miners

* The island of Cyprus.

of New Mexico, the mica-miners of North Carolina, and
the ancient copper-miners of the Lake-Superior region;
carrying on their mining-operations with rude appliances, and without other than a tribal organization. In
the same region, Gmelin, during the last century, found
upwards of a thousand small smelting-furnaces of brick,
evidently used for gold-ores many centuries ago by
miners of whom we have no further record. It is, however, an interesting reflection, that some portion of a
modern coin, ornament, or vessel of gold, may consist
of Siberian metal bartered for by Phœnician merchants,
sold to Persia, conquered by Alexander, offered as a
part of the annual tribute of one hundred million dollars which Gibbon estimates that the provinces sent to
Rome, paid by the degenerate Greeks to Harold Har-
drada when he stood among their Varingians, won at
Stamford Bridge, and lost at Senlac. Such is the permanence of gold, that, in the worn wedding-ring a starv-
ing woman offers to-day at a pawnbroker's counter in
New York, there may be particles that once shone in
the crown of Sestu Ra, the Grecian Sesostris, or helped
to cover the Ark of the Covenant.

Change and decay have ever been the fate of the
most famous of mining-regions. Mountainous Midian
furnished a hundred and thirty-five thousand fierce
Bedouin warriors in the days when her "captains and
mighty men of valor" for seven years overran Palestine
(thirteenth century B.C.), driving the people for refuge
to the mountain caves and fastnesses, until the greatest
of the judges of Israel arose, sifted his followers by the
"Spring of Trembling," and defeated the invaders in
the Valley of Jezreel. But this Midian, anciently so
populous, has now become a desert land, inhabited by
only a few nomads. On the sea-coast, and far inland

along the channels of perished rivers, are the ruins of large cities which were chiefly supported by mining-industries. The placers and rich gravel-mines, whose exhaustion caused the decay of once wealthy and commercial Midian, are fairly reticulated with old water-ditches; on the barren hills are vast reservoirs and ruined walls; the country was long ago denuded of its forests for mining-purposes; and so waste and desolate does the region appear, that its ancient prosperity is hard to understand, although the unimpeachable evidence is before the eyes of every traveller in the "land of Midian."

The historical and geographical link between Asia and Europe is Lydia. The broad, fertile, and easily tilled plains of the classic Kayster were encircled by mountains rich in mineral wealth. Among the Phrygo-Thrakians were mining-tribes whose chief occupation was in gathering gold and silver, learning to smelt the latter with great skill, and finally inventing a coinage. Strangely enough, the Lydian standard, the silver *mina*, afterwards used with slight changes by the Greeks, was truly the *mana* of the Accadians, given by them to the Babylonians, and so transferred, by way of Persia, to the mountaineers of Lydia. In this, as in so many greater things, Europe drew the sources of her knowledge from the remote, despotic, and mysterious Orient. But, as regards methods of mining, all the Oriental monarchies were alike in the use of the most cruel forms of slave-labor and in the greatest conceivable waste. From an institutional stand-point, they afford little that is worth study. The mere figures of gold-yields are astounding. Solomon, it is estimated, had a yearly income of twenty-three and a half million dollars in gold alone; and Calmet thinks that he spent on Jerusa-

lem and the temple the sum of four thousand million
dollars. Diodorus tells us, that, out of the ashes of Susa
and Persepolis, seven million dollars in gold was ex-
tracted. But treasure-houses such as these were filled
by forced labor and royal monopolies. In the case of
the early Oriental powers, the tribes upon their borders
who were developing local systems for the ownership
and working of mineral deposits were crushed and overwhelmed before those systems could take permanent
form. We must leave "the wide Asian fen," and turn
to the hills around whose heights "the first-born olive-
blossom brightened," to the rocky coasts that "sheltered
the Salaminian seamen," to "nodding promontories and
blue isles and cloud-like mountains," to the city "violet-
crowned," whose deathless memory moves like sunlight
about the broad earth forever.

In the Athenian state, we discover the first orderly
and effective system in regard to the management of
mineral resources, and the government of mines. The
famous silver and lead mines of Laurium in southern
Attica rose to prominence about the year 600 B.C., and
were worked with varying success till the second century
before the beginning of our era. In 1864, after nearly
two thousand years of neglect, the old shafts were re-
opened by a company of French capitalists. An estimate has been made, that, during the three hundred
years that the Athenians worked these mines, they procured two million one hundred thousand tons of lead,
and twenty-two and a half million pounds of silver.
According to the law of Athens upon this subject, the
mines were not freehold property. Although belonging
to the state, they were not leased or farmed out to the
highest bidder, as was the Roman custom: they were
granted to individuals to use as a permanent tenantcy.

A small sum was paid on taking possession, and only one twenty-fourth of the gross ore-yield of the mine was required as rent. The mine was then to all intents private property, unless neglected; when the state could bring suit, and recover. The statement, that before the time of Themistocles the mines were the absolute freehold property of certain families, rests upon slight authority, and seems improbable. Any and all members of the community were empowered to institute public suits against the mine-possessors in case of their violation of any statute, and suits of this sort were frequently brought. There is evidence of the existence of a "director of the mines," elected by those interested. The income which the state derived from the rents was annually distributed among the citizens, in much the same way as was the "Theoricon" in later times, every one whose name was in the book of the Lexiarchs receiving his portion. Themistocles, it will be remembered, persuaded the Athenians to devote this income to the building of ships.

From Xenophon's "Treatise upon the Revenues," and Demosthenes' speech against Pantænetus, we gather much about the Grecian system of managing the Laurium mines. Companies were organized to work one or more shafts, and many of the wealthier Athenians owned shares in several such enterprises. The size of each "claim" was strictly defined, and private enterprise was greatly encouraged to send out "prospectors." Secure though the tenure of mining-property was, it could be transferred only to a citizen, or to aliens capable of holding agricultural lands. Any person was allowed to dig for new mines in unexplored places; but, although richly rewarded, successful prospectors had no prior right: what they found belonged to Athens, and might be rented to any other person. The labor used in the mines was that of private slaves. Each shaft was registered by the mine-inspector of the state, who examined the supports of the various drifts and galleries, and saw that the bounds were not exceeded. Lessening the supports of a drift, and trespass, were punishable by fines, infamy, banishment, or death. Demosthenes addresses the tribunal as the "mining-court," set to try "mining-cases." Some of the island mines paid one-tenth of the ore to the shrine of Apollo at Delphos.

Spain, the Peru of Europe, and in minerals the richest country of the ancient world, developed slowly, and under enormous pressure, a system of mining-laws which once ruled the greater portion of the American continents, and still prevails in variously modified forms throughout Mexico, Central and South America. In that law, deeply embedded as fossils in a slab of limestone, there yet remain principles of widely differing origin, — Carthaginian, Roman, Gothic, Moorish, Castilian. But the traces of mining-institutions are few indeed under the dominion of either Carthage or Rome. Instead of many mine-owners, bound together, as in Athens, by a common law, having the same duties towards the state, and equal protection from it, we have in Spain, under Carthage, the almost uncontrolled authority of the proud family of Barca. Hannibal procured about three hundred pounds of silver each day from his Spanish mines. Pliny describes the method of obtaining gold from streams of Spain by using a pan, also a method of "ground-sluicing;" and he mentions the use of timber supports in drifts and tunnels, some of which extended fifteen hundred paces into the hill.

Even in Carthaginian days, the almost inevitable

destruction attending great mining-operations was going on with unusual rapidity in Spain; subsequent Roman methods wonderfully accelerated this ruin.   Their mines, farmed out to the highest bidders, were wastefully worked and recklessly destroyed.   For a time the Romans employed twenty-five thousand slaves at Carthagena alone, and the silver-yield was equal to ten thousand dollars daily.   The Spanish placers yielded large sums; and they also were farmed out, after the manner of the silvermines.   Inventive skill of a high order characterized the early miners of Spain, who greatly improved the Egyptian methods of grinding or smelting ores, and extracting the precious metals.   All this implies close organization, division of labor, and severity of discipline.   The later Roman emperors made reforms in the close military system, gave more sway to private enterprise, allowed some mines to be worked by associations, granted the "prospectors" permission to search for mineral, and introduced a sort of feudal service.   The Romans also knew of placer-mines in northern Italy, discovered by the Etruscans, who even brought iron from Elba; but, curiously enough, the Roman senate would not allow them to be worked.   The Salassians opened placers in Lombardy; and, as Polybius relates, the Taurisci found such rich placers near Aquila, that the price of gold fell one-third throughout Italy in the space of two months.

Thus far in our investigation we have seen, that, although the gold-hunger has ever furnished a stimulating element to early society, the ancient world afforded narrow opportunities for the development of valuable institutional forms among the classes engaged in mining. We read of rich placer-mines by the score, but not of their local legislation and self-government; such features being absent until the advent of miners of the

race whose "political instinct" has become a familiar
phrase.   Golden sands of the rivers of Tibet and India
set long caravans in motion past Babylon, past Palmyra,
to imperious, luxurious Tyre; golden nuggets from the
Chinese frontiers poured into stately Balkh, "mother
of cities," cradle of ancient kings, and greatest satrapy
of Persia; Grecian placers of Pactolus yielded their
treasures to Crœsus, and were still worked in the days
of Xenophon.   But waste and barren of constructive
energies were all the mining-regions of ancient Europe
and Asia.   As the mining-history of the mediæval
world shows, the Germanic races, and they alone, have
organized true mining-camps which developed into
higher forms of society.   Whatever elements other races
have contributed, the informing spirit of such camps
has been thoroughly Germanic.   The organization of a
Spanish mining-law began with the Visigothic kings, in
the days of Pelayo; the laws of the California camps
of 1849 were linked in spirit to the "mining-freedom"
and the mining-cities of the middle ages.

It is impossible to determine what influences from
the Roman mining-world, which even in its decadence
embraced all the rich mineral regions of southern
Europe, could have survived the chaos and wreck of
barbarian conquest.

After the fall of Rome, the Arabs, Franks, and Goths
in Spain, Gaul, and northern Italy, worked to some extent the abandoned and nearly exhausted Roman mines.
To northern Spain the Visigoths brought a new force;
and the *Fuero Juzgo*, or code of laws of the Gothic
predecessors of Alonzo the Wise, shows greater freedom
of the individual, greater respect for local institutions
and for self-government, than Spain had previously
known.   Hints of local mining-organizations in Thrace,

and along the Danube in the fifth and sixth centuries, make it evident, though definite records are lacking, that wandering miners existed in that region, and were slowly "prospecting" the mountain ranges to the north and west. Hungarian mining can be traced back to the year 750, begun by prospectors from Gaul, says Reitemeier.

But German mining-history* clusters about the Hartz** Mountains; and it is a significant fact, that mining began there, at the great Andreasberg ledges, in the midst of a political and national renaissance which profoundly stirred and influenced the whole of central Europe. It began there towards the close of the tenth century, in the reign of Otho the Great, second emperor of the Saxon line, who wore the iron crown of Lombardy and the imperial crown of Rome, reviving the glories of that holy empire, obscured since the mightest of medi- æval monarchs had sunk to rest with his paladins and his sword, — in the reign of that Otho whose father, Henry, had driven back the heathen in many a fierce battle, had quelled the wild Magyars at Merseburg, had taken the Mark of Brandenburg from the Sclavonians to become in after-time heart of Prussia and appanage of the Hohenzollerns, had built frontier fortresses, and posted his warrior *Mark-grafs* to protect the borders against Dane and Finn, Sclav and Hun. With a firmer government, a stronger national life, material enter- prises developed wonderfully ; the forest-ways began to be trodden by peaceful merchants, and explored by seekers for precious metals. In Saxony, in the tenth century, mines of vast richness were discovered by Bohemian salt-carriers, who found silver ore in the ruts worn on a steep hillside by the wheels of their rude cart. The early German miners soon began to make enactments to govern themselves. A law of mining-

* It seems strange that Shinn's summary of medieval German mining contains no reference to one of the great classics of min- ing history, Georgius Agricola's *De Re Metallica* (1556), which

claims, and rules of mining-life, prevailed among these first Thuringian miners who struck pick into rocks of Black Forest and Ḥartz, and unveiled the treasures of Freiberg, no less certainly than similar laws and usages prevail to-day among the organizers of the newest camps on the Rio Grande and Yukon. The *Mark* method of dividing lands was no more certainly a product of the thought of the Germanic race than are the customs which to-day govern freemen in distributing with fairness the auriferous soil of western placers. The spirit of the tribes of whose social and political organization Tacitus gave so vivid an account, lives at this hour in free "miners' courts" of Idaho and Alaska.

To Germanic sources we must trace the most important principles of mining-law. The local customs of the earliest Hartz miners have never since ceased to exert an influence upon civilization. The *Mark* system of common lands, annually re-distributed, was most likely the foundation of early German mining-regulations; but it took so long to make a mine productive, that the re-distribution plan could not be permanently adopted. The plan of making ownership depend upon actual use, and limiting it to small, well-defined tracts, was the obvious substitute. All the early German codes express the idea of mining-freedom, of a possible ownership of the minerals apart from the soil, of the right of the individual to search for and possess the precious metals, provided he infringed on no previous rights. This "mining-freedom" (*Bergbaufreiheit*) contains the essence of all frontier mining-customs ever since. The right to "prospect," "locate" a given claim, and hold it against all comers until abandoned, is the right guaranteed, in one form or another, by the newest mining-camps of Montana. This is the same right once possessed by

devotes Book IV to mining law, as applied in Germany. See the excellent translation from the Latin by former President and Mrs. Herbert C. Hoover (London, 1912; reprinted New York, the men of the "seven mining-cities of the Hartz," and by those of Freiberg, of Truro, of Penzance, and of other cities of the middle ages where mining guilds and organizations existed.

The first written document which embodies these rights is the mining-treaty of 1185, between the Bishop of Trent and certain immigrants from Germany. Other codes appear later; in 1250 one in Moravia, in 1307 one in Styria. All these, and others of the period, were founded on the unwritten custom, on those usages "which have lasted from time immemorial." The Moravian or Iglau code provides for the appointment of officials to fix mine-bounds, and defines conditions of ownership. The full size of a claim is set at four hundred and seventy-nine feet long, and one hundred and ninety-six feet wide ; a portion is set aside for the king, and a part for the town if on common lands, for the owner if on private property. Mining-courts are granted with special rights and jurisdictions (*Bergbehörde*). In later years the miners gave effective aid to burghers and artisans in their struggles against the robber barons. The precious "mining-freedom" asserted by the working miners underwent severe assaults from small land-owners, from petty princes, and from the emperor himself; but its broader principles were, as a rule, maintained intact. During the sixteenth and seventeenth centuries, German mining-jurisprudence grew exceedingly complicated, and covered a great range of topics. Associated mining-enterprises were frequent. Miners from the most famous districts of Germany had long been in demand in other mineral regions of Europe, and often offered their services to foreign kings. Everywhere they carried with them the customs, laws, experience, and superstitions of the craft. They worked

---

1950), which attaches to Book IV a four-page footnote summarizing mining law from classical times to 1912.
** Harz.

mines in northern Italy, in France, in Scotland and England, developing a strong professional pride and secrecy. They filled the place in the mediæval world that Cornish miners occupy in modern times. Theirs was the reputation for dealing with the most stubborn ores, and the most difficult engineering problems.

Speaking in the broadest sense, the true relationship which exists among the laws of all "mining-camps" worth the name, is not so much in the form of the laws themselves, as in the organizing capabilities of that race which works out similar results under similar circumstances, with surprising fitness of method and fulness of harmony, and with supreme and all-conquering self-confidence. No one is able to show that there has ever been any uniform theory of law for mining-camps, scarcely more than for caravans in the desert: but it has nevertheless happened, owing to this inherent political instinct, that whenever and wherever men of our Germanic race found minerals, they developed a satisfactory system of local government, based on a series of compromises, and differing in essential particulars from the sort of local government developed no less naturally by agricultural communities; their judgments grew swifter, and their justice surer, as was needed to counteract the volcanic passions and disrupting tendencies of their fascinating and hazardous pursuit. In the hands of the Germanic race alone, this fierce gold-hunger has been controlled, utilized, and made a force of primary importance in the shaping of civilized society. Communities created and built up by mining-industries have thus been transformed, without danger and without loss, into communities based on agriculture, commerce, and manufactures. With men of other races, the possession of wealth-laden placers has too often meant their rapid, reckless exhaustion, the washing-away of every particle of soil, the destruction of every forest-tree, the inevitable decay and desertion of towns, the absolute ruin and complete desolation of the entire region: with men of our race, the exhaustion of placer-mines has only hastened the development of more potent and permanent resources, has given us the wools of later Australia, the wheat and wines of later California.

The institutional history of modern mining-camps thus finds its proper place in the ever-broadening story of local self-government among men of our race, — the story which runs back to the days when rude, brave men lifted a chosen leader on their ringing shields, and swore allegiance; when the three judges, each with his twelve doomsmen, met in yearly tribunal; when " brothers of the sword-oath " (in Icelandic, *ver svorjum Bruderskaft*) bound their rune-cut, bleeding arms together, swearing eternal *freundschaft* over their naked war-weapons. You may find to-day, if you are able to recognize old types in new attire, the true descendants of the Germanic " sword-brothers " in the devoted " pards " of a raw mining-camp on the outposts of civilization; and closer resemblances than this lie thickly scattered along the course of our investigation. To those who have ears to hear, the free and unconventional yet sufficiently systematized life of mining-camps is able to tell a story of the beginnings of things, of forest meetings in Saxony, of freemen in isolated villages assembling to allot the common lands, of English folk-moots in England before the waves of conquest rolled over the wild heights of Exmoor, before the hill-fortress of Exeter passed from Keltic ownership, before Lindum Colonia became English Lincoln. Since Germanic mining began, certain vital principles have been asserted by the men of camp, district, and mining-town. The local mining-law whose sources are as old as the capitularies of Charlemagne, and probably far older, is a living force in the world to-day. Professor R. W. Raymond says of early Germanic mining-law, —

"In the form of a local custom, obtaining with remarkable uniformity in all the original centres of German mining, the principle of mining-freedom established itself, permitting all persons to search for useful minerals, and granting to the discoverer of such a deposit the rights of property within certain limits. This principle of free mining emigrated with the German miners to all places whither their enterprise extended itself, and the original local custom became the general law. In this existence of an estate in minerals, entirely independent of the estate in soil, lies the distinctive character of German mining-law. It is eminently a special law, not subordinate to civil law but co-ordinate with it." [1]

[1] Relations of Governments to Mining. United-States Mining Report, 1869.

CHAPTER III.

THE development of local legislation among some of
the miners of England furnishes most useful parallels
to the development of such legislation among American
gold-miners. Valuable gold-mines have existed in England, Scotland, Wales, and Ireland ; and mining excitements have several times occurred over the "auriferous
gossan" of Cornwall and Merionethshire. A Briton
tribe, the Trinobantes, coined gold, it is said, from the
"placers" of Essex. Edward III. issued a writ assert-
ing royal rights over a gold-mine in Salop County, and
Henry IV. did the same in several instances. During
the reign of James V. of Scotland, some three hundred
placer-miners worked for months at "Gold-scaur," near
Wanlochhead, and collected more than a million dollars.
The largest nugget found weighed thirty ounces ($480).
Many instances of alluvial washings for gold in the
British Isles might be given from the old chronicles;
the latest being those of Wicklow, Ireland, worked in
1796. But no trace of "local law" seems to have remained ; and we are forced to turn to the lead, tin, and
copper miners, for examples of successful organization.

Local customs of the utmost importance have long
existed in Cornwall, Devonshire, and Derbyshire, chiefly
in Cornwall, that land of folk-lore tales and strange

25

survivals. When, as legends declare, "St. Michael's wooded mount was six miles from the sea;" when the early Britons, or as modern Cornishmen call them "the old-men," were simple placer-miners digging up "stream tin" from alluvial channels, and leaving traces of their toil from Land's End to Dartmoor; when Beltane-fires were lit, and St. Piran became the miners' merry saint, — there was rude organization among the miners of Cornwall. They held great public assemblies under the open sky, upon chosen spots on the wild moor, surrounded by earthen walls, traces of which yet remain; and these meetings were called *Guirimears* or speech-days. Old smelting-furnaces of this Keltic period still exist, and the modern miners call them "Jews' houses." A curious old song, apostrophizing early Cornwall, says, —

> "Come old Phœnicians, come tin-dealers,
>   From Marazion come, ye Jews;
> Come smugglers, wreckers, and sheep-stealers,
>   Come tell the ancient county news."

Into this prehistoric drift, — to borrow a term from geology, — an adventurous element was brought from widely diverse sources. There was a wild freedom in the air of Cornwall; and outlaws sought its forests, sea-rovers the shelter of its cliffs. Literature, with its divine instinct, loves the stormy land where Tristram slew giants, and Hereward wrought deeds of prowess; and some of the greatest of living poets have made its shadowy legends as immortal as the tales of the Volsungs. Long ago the miners of "wild, bright Cornwall" chose their standard, a white cross on a black ground; until within this century they kept "Old Christmas," the 5th of January, and for twelve days suffered no fire to be taken from their hearths. So tenaciously does the past survive in the present, that even now a verdant branch is fastened on midsummer-day to the highest woodwork of the steam-engines, to mark the beginning of the Baal-year.

Early in the middle ages, miners from the heart of the Black Forest found their way to Cornwall.[1] They left numbers of mining-terms embedded in the language, and greatly modified the local laws and customs. The use of the divining or "dowzing" rod in England is not older than the advent of German miners, brought over by Queen Elizabeth to teach the Cornishmen how to work certain refractory ores. One of these, named Schutz, became warden of the stannaries. At this point, then, we discover the institutional link between English and German mining-law: we also understand how it has come to pass that the Cornish miners of Nevada and Montana still use a vocabulary some of whose terms are derived from phrases in use among the miners of Freiburg six centuries ago.

The former rights of the "free prospector" or "tin-bounder" of Cornwall have only recently fallen into disuse. The ancient stannary-courts, which we are now to describe, have only of late years received any serious modification; and, though shorn of many of their ancient dignities, they still remain as, historically speaking, the last representatives of older and far more powerful forms.

The local mining-courts, and the force of local custom,

[1] There was also some migration of Cornish miners to Germany. Camden's Britannia says, "After the comming in of the Normans the Earles of Cornwal gathered great riches out of these mines . . . sith that in those daies Europe had tinne from no other place." He goes on to state that in the year 1240 "was tinne mettall found in Germania by a certain Cornishman driven out of his native soil to the great losse and hindrance of Richard, Earle of Cornwal."

were authoritatively recognized by the organization of
the chief stannary-court, which long proved a most
valuable right and defence of the miners. It has been
modified into a court of records; but it originally existed
as an original court of equity, of the vice-warden of all
the stannaries of Cornwall.[1] At the present time it has
jurisdiction in certain matters over all companies engaged in tin-mining; but its local, representative, and
legislative character no longer exists. The stannary-
court is treated of at length in various Chancery and
King's Bench reports, and in papers published in the
British Geological Reports; and it was established, recognized, and enforced by numbers of ancient charters.

King John granted a charter to the tin-miners, giving them the right to mine on waste and unoccupied
lands. By a charter of 33d Edward I., all the working
tin-miners were given privilege of being sued only in
the vice-warden's court. According to this and subsequent grants, the "ancient charters, local customs, and
records of lower courts" were always to be received
as evidence. Henry VII. increased the powers of the
legal convocation, or "parliament of tin-miners," which
had settled disputes and made laws respecting tin-claims
since the days of Edward III. This stannary parliament consisted of twenty-four influential miners or

---

[1] Camden's account, in his Britannia, is as follows: "The whole
commonwealth of those tinners and workmen as it were one body hee
(King Edward Third) divided into four quarters . . . Foymore, Black-
more, Trewarnaile, and Penwith. Over them all hee ordained a Warden
called 'Lord Warden of the Stannaries and Stannum,' that is, tinne, who
giveth judgment as well according to equitie and conscience as law, and
appointeth to every quarter their stewards, who, once every three weeks
. . . minister justice in causes personall between Tinner and Tinner and
between Tinner and Forrainer. . . . . In matters of moment there are
general parliaments summonned whereunto jurats are sent out of every
Stannarie."

stannators, six chosen in each district. The last parliament was held at Truro in 1752. Here the men of Penzance and Carclaza, of Botallock, Carn Brea, and dozens of other mining villages and towns, met, and formulated Cornish mining-laws. They came from quarry-like mines on the barren moor, open to the sky; from shafts sunk deep in the earth; and from drifts extended half a mile under sea, where hammer-blows sounded beneath the keels of ships, with but ten feet of crumbling rock between. To-day the descendants of these men are among the boldest and most successful miners in America. At Eureka, on the Comstock, in the Black Hills, wherever one goes, in fact, the hereditary mining-lore of the Cornishmen is in demand.

The miners of the Mendip district, Cornwall, as late as the seventeenth century, punished those who stole ore from the drifts with banishment, and with burning of the offender's domicile; theft being considered, as in the Western camps of to-day, a crime of peculiar turpitude. These Mendip miners manifested a mingling of superstitious dread, and of faithful loyalty to each other, in their strict rule that the body of a miner who had been killed in a drift must be dug out, at any cost, and given Christian burial, before a stroke of work would be done elsewhere by a single miner. They also had local laws respecting the explorations of waste ground, and rights of discoverers, which were always respected.

Indeed, local mining-customs have existed in Cornwall " from time immemorial," as the King's Bench Law Reports tell us. Miners' rights and privileges were definitely settled centuries ago, and have been tenaciously held ever since by the descendants of those whom the varied mineral wealth of the Cornish land first attracted to its sea-girt cliffs and granitic moors.

The custom prevailed, even within the past twenty
years, that any person might enter upon the waste
land of another, mark out a plot of ground, send a
description to the stannaries' court, and lay claim to
it, provided that he proposed to work it himself "in
good faith." In the early part of this century, a written
description was required, just as in Western camps a
written claim-notice is necessary; but in still earlier
times a verbal statement was considered sufficient. The
written notice was read in the stannaries' court at three
successive meetings; when, if no valid objection was
raised by any person, the court accepted it, and proceeded to deliver possession to the "bounder," who
then had exclusive right to mine for tin and other minerals within the limits of his "bounds." The first act
of the owner was to define the corners of his property
by rearing piles of turf and stones, or by sinking small
square pits. It has always been the "custom" to mark
claims thus in Cornwall. When the earliest miners
of the region recognized "mining-claims" as property,
and began to ordain and enforce a general system of
obtaining them, they had taken a most significant step
towards organization.

The possession of this "tin-bound," thus acquired by
"taking it up," — to use the American expression, —
involved the payment of a tax known as "toll-tin" to
the owner of the land. This percentage varied according to the yield of the district, but not according
to the yield of that particular shaft. In other words,
the owner of the soil and the "bounder" of the mine
were both subject to the usual rule in this regard, and
no one need make a separate bargain unless they chose.
In Cornwall, and also among the miners of the "King's
Field" in Derbyshire, and in the "Forest of Dean," the

lord of the soil was usually considered as entitled to one-fifteenth of the gross ore-yield of each shaft sunk by a "bounder," said ore being "delivered at the mouth of the pit." As high as one-tenth of the ore, and as low as one-twentieth, have been given in the tin-mining districts.

The right to a "bound" was inheritable property, and might be transferred by sale; but neglect to work it caused forfeiture to the owner of the soil, or, by denouncement, to another miner. The landmarks of the "bound" must be renewed annually, and kept distinct and in good condition. This reverence and care for landmarks is a characteristic of all law-abiding and mighty races; and the varied customs by which the boundaries of districts and kingdoms, and changes in the ownership of tracts of land, were fixed in the memories of men, are highly curious and deeply interesting. In ancient times the "thoths" or tribal landmarks were often burial-mounds of wise chieftains and puissant warriors who still guarded the frontiers. On the border-land, national games, annual fairs, and public assemblies were held. And, of land transfers, we read in the Book of Ruth, "Now this was the manner in former time in Israel, concerning redeeming, and concerning changing, for to confirm all things: a man plucked off his shoe, and gave it to his neighbor, and this was a testimony in Israel." In the village communes of our Germanic ancestors, "field and homestead passed from man to man by the delivery of a turf cut from its soil." The annals of Salem, Mass., state that in 1695 a homestead there was transferred by "turffe and twigg,"[1] an unconscious survival of the customs of

[1] See Dr. H. B. Adams: Germanic Origin of New-England towns. Johns Hopkins University Studies, 1st series, Local Institutions.

those forest-villages whose freemen dwelt around their moot-hills, or gathered for council beneath the sacred oaks of the Odenwald. Other races, too, have transferred land with similar formalities: when, in 1670, the Raritan Indians made their final sale of Staten Island to Gov. Lovelace, they "brought a branch of every sort of tree and shrub that grew on the island, for a sign; reserving only two species used in their basket-work."

Transfers of mineral lands, since the dawn of history, have been accompanied with quite as much formality as that attending the transfer of agricultural property, or of holdings in tribal community lands. The miners of the California camps showed as much anxiety to have distinct landmarks and bounds as did the Cornish and the Thuringian miners of centuries ago; and at least once, as late as 1856, a transfer of mining-property in California was completed by the gift, before witnesses, of a handful of gold-bearing gravel from the claim. The man who did this was a miner, whom the writer met as prospector many years after. "Why did you do it?" we asked: "was not verbal possession sufficient?"

"Mebbe so: but my father, and his father before him, always gave a bit o' land away to wind up a bargain; an' the rule's good for a minin'-claim, I'll allow."

Leaving, however, for subsequent chapters, an analysis of the land laws and customs of modern mining-camps, we return to the customs of the tin-miners of Cornwall, in many particulars so similar to those adopted centuries later by the free miners of the Pacific coast. The size of their "tin-bounds," so carefully marked out and set apart, varied greatly according to the old Cornish rule. It must be "reasonable," but uniformity does not seem to have been thought essential; the point being to include sufficient surface to give space for proper workings. The entire system of "taking up claims" and securing them, in the Cornwall districts, during the sixteenth, seventeenth, and eighteenth centuries, was precise and effective, and "probably," as one of the English law-reports says, "was the law of an extinct kingdom of Cornwall."

The Cumberland silver-miners in the time of Elizabeth had special legal privileges, and the justices of assize went there in their circuit. This was one of the "royal mines," owing to its proportion of silver.[1] They do not seem to have had a court of their own for mining-cases; but the "smelters, refiners, and miners held public meetings," as recorded by Bushell in 1641. Their local customs were much the same as in Cornwall. Their "tolls" were paid, however, directly to the sovereign. In Cornwall such dues were paid to the duke, whenever such a nobleman existed.

The Duchy of Cornwall was created in the fifteenth year of Henry III. Edward III. made his son the first Duke of Cornwall, and gave him "all profits of the court of stannary and of the mines." Slowly, and with great difficulty, the ancient tenures and privileges of many of the tin and copper miners were lessened and abridged; and so it soon came to pass, that different degrees of tenantcy were recognized. In the most im-

---

[1] The well-known definitions of Blackstone and Plowden need not be quoted here. But that quaint and rare book, "A Just and True Remonstrance of his Majestie's Mines-Royall to His Majestie," published in 1641, contains a "declaration of learned lawyers what a Mine-Royall is, according to presedents," signed by the king's sergeant-at-law, and thirty other jurists. They say, "Although the gold or silver contained in the base mettall of a mine in the lands of a subject bee of lesse valew than the baser mettall; yet, if the gold or silver doe countervaile the charge of the refining, or bee of more worth than the base mettall spent in refining it, this is a Mine-Royall, and as well the base mettall as the gold and silver in it, belongs by prerogative to the crowne."

portant and numerous class, the bounds came to be fixed, or at least re-examined, each seven years, and re-allotted by an assession court. In the "Caption of Seizin" of the manor of Tewington, in the time of Edward III., there is a list of free tenants who hold "in socage" tracts of from five to twelve acres apiece, and pay "toll-tin" upon the product of all shafts they sink. Besides these miners, there were, so states this caption, "free conventionaries," or miners who held and worked much smaller tracts on the seven-year basis; and the sort of land-tenure system which prevailed in these peculiar "conventionary holdings" was a highly interesting "survival" of ancient Keltic forms analogous to those of Brittany. Concanen's special report of the English law case of Rowe *vs.* Brenton describes the system in full.[1]

In the lead-districts, the most interesting local institution was the bar-mote court, and its executive officer—called the "bar-master." It was his duty to do justice between miner and miner, between miner and "adventurer," and between all the miners and the lord of the manor. The "adventurers" were what the Western miner calls "prospectors;" and they have played a very important part in English mining-history, developing the richest of mineral districts by their skill and energy. Local law in the lead-districts awarded to the finder "the largest share" of a new mine. Disputes were tried at the bar-mote; and over this court the deputy stewards presided, and the bar-master was present. A

---

[1] Mr. Frederick Pollock, in "The Land Laws" (English Citizen Series: Macmillan & Co., 1883), speaks of ancient Cornish laws, and of these "conventionary" seven-year holdings (pp. 49, 204). He says that in 1844 certain conventionary tenants of the Duchy of Cornwall were enfranchised, and does not know whether or not other examples of this ancient tenure still remain.

jury was summoned, composed of miners, and questions were tried before them. Arrears of the duties of "lot and cope" were properly presented by the officers of the manor.[1] In modern times English law-reports show clearly the continued existence, and the recognition in mining jurisprudence, of most of the customs and local usages of tin, lead, and copper miners, alluded to in the preceding pages. Local customs, as modified by Acts of Parliament, are still in force in Cornwall, Derbyshire, and other mining-districts.

Throughout England the rule has held good, that mining requires much knowledge, skill, and special training; creating in the past a constant tendency towards separate courts, towards denial of the jurisdiction of the lower civil courts, and towards a more direct dealing with higher courts of appeal. The Cornish stannaries court of to-day is one of the survivals of this long-continued struggle, and so is the bar-mote court of the lead-districts. In the rocky and agriculturally worthless regions, where for many centuries the entire community was dependent upon mining for its livelihood, the miners evidently governed themselves long before there was any Duke of Cornwall or manorial claims: they recognized the liberty of the prospector and the sacredness of the claim-stake, in that remote past when "stream-tin" gathered from the river-channels was the chief mineral resource of the region, and the veins of ore were only superficially worked. To such conclusions, at least, the nature and evident antiquity of the mining-customs of Cornwall would certainly point. They seem to be fragments and remains of ancient laws adopted in meetings of freemen, for the

---

[1] Arkwright vs. Cantrell, 7 Ad. and E. p. 565.

purpose of securing equal rights, and imposing equal duties upon all within their jurisdiction. As a prominent California mining-lawyer once said to the writer, "Those old Cornish miners, with their local freedom and self-government, deserved to have been born four centuries later, as prospectors in the Sierra placers."

CHAPTER IV.

EARLY MINING IN THE UNITED STATES.

THE first English settlers in America hoped to find great mineral wealth; and the royal charters in most cases reserved "all mines," and claimed as rent one-fifth of all gold or silver ore, "to be delivered free of charge at the pit's mouth." Massachusetts, Connecticut, Virginia, Maryland, Pennsylvania, and others of the early colonies, had clauses of this kind in their charters.[1] But the "gold-ores" invariably proved worthless, much to the disappointment of the merchants in the Virginia and the Massachusetts companies, who had hoped for other resources besides those of fishing, trading, and farming. The "rights-royal" never amounted to any thing; and, in the process of time, mining-jurisprudence came to be founded upon common law merely, the mineral being held to belong to the soil, and conveyed by one and the same title with agricultural lands.

There is little of value for our investigation in the scattered attempts at mining in Colonial and Revolutionary days. The first on record appears to be that mentioned in Stith's History of Virginia, — the opening of an iron mine in 1622 at Falling Creek, near James River. The next was probably in New England, where Governor John Winthrop in 1657 obtained a license

[1] Bainbridge, "Law of Mines," chapter ii.

37

to work "mines of lead, tin, copper, or any mineral,"
and to "enjoy forever" said mines, and all woods,
lands, and things necessary for their workings, "within
two or three miles." He proceeded to prospect extensively; and in 1661 received a special grant of mineral
lands near Middletown, Connecticut, where he opened
and worked mines. President Stiles's Diary says, speaking of the "Governor's Ring," a mountain in East Had-
dam: "Governor Trumbull has often told me that this
was the place to which Governor Winthrop of New
London used to resort with his servant, and spend
three weeks in roasting ores, and assaying metals, and
casting gold rings." The mine was worked to a depth
of a hundred and twenty-five feet, with extensive drifts.
The abandoned shaft was discovered in 1852, and afterwards re-opened, though unprofitably. The first blast-
furnace in the New-England Colonies was built by Lam-
bert Despard at Mattakeeset Pond, Plymouth County,
Massachusetts, in 1702. The copper-miners of Simsbury,
Connecticut, received their charter in 1709. Arent
Schuyler began to work the cupriferous ores near the
Passaic, seven miles from Jersey City, in 1719. According to the centennial address of Mr. D. D. Field,
Middletown, Connecticut, in 1853, a lead-mine was
worked in that town long before the Revolution; and
from May, 1775, till February, 1778, this mine was
operated for the citizens "by a committee of three,
Jabez Hamlin, Mathew Talcott, and Titus Hosmer."

Such efforts, of which there were many, were merely
business or war enterprises, and had little or no organizing influence upon society. Somewhat more than this,
however, may be said with justice of some of the famous
gold-camps of the South, early in the present century.
In Spottsylvania County there were numbers of placers,

and from one claim twenty feet square ten thousand dollars was taken; in Louisa County, one placer-claim yielded seven thousand dollars; and near the Rapidan over forty thousand dollars was taken out by a miner from his placer property. These instances are noted in Mr. Taylor's report (1867) on "Gold-mining East of the Rockies." There were also some famous mines in Buckingham County, Virginia, and others in Abbeville District, South Carolina; but those of Rowan and Mecklenburg Counties, North Carolina, and particularly the placer-mines upon the tributaries of the Great Pedee, produced hosts of prospectors, who took up claims and worked mines according to a sort of local law, subject, however, to the jurisdiction of the county authorities. Wheeler's History of North Carolina gives interesting illustrations of this mining-era and its excitements; its crude organization, its "big nuggets" (that of 1803 weighing twenty-eight pounds), its culmination, and its decay. West of the Blue Ridge, along the famous French Broad River, a number of placer-miners worked for half a century on small claims held by possessory rights. The Georgia and Alabama gold-miners had a wider field; and the operations begun in 1799, in valleys that De Soto visited, have continued with greater or less energy ever since. None of the mining-districts of the South possessed any organization separate from that of the county, but some of them had simple local regulations in regard to the size of claims. In one case, that of the Hale mining-tract, Lancaster District, South Carolina, over fifty years ago, the system had fostered individual freedom, though to the great detriment of all the mines. The owner of the land allowed any persons to come in, and work where they chose, only agreeing to sell all gold found to him for

sixty cents per pennyweight, when it was really worth
ninety cents, thus paying a ground-rent of one-third
the gross yield. The alluvial deposits were, however,
so rich, that many prospectors accepted the terms.
They used "pans and rockers," dug holes in search
for "pockets," worked out the rich places, recklessly
stripped the mine, and then deserted it. Nothing permanent could come from such a wasteful and destructive
system. But as soon as gold was discovered on the
Pacific coast, all these old camps of the South sent well-
trained miners and prospectors to the new placers; and
there they found that larger freedom in which local
mining-institutions were rapidly developed.

The attitude of the state and national governments
towards mining-interests affords a much more important
theme than is offered by any of the Southern gold-dis-
coveries. Long before the Revolution, most of the Colonies had recognized the rights of land-owners over all
the contents of the soil; so that when, in 1785, the Con-
tinental Congress reserved one-third of the gold, silver,
lead, copper, and some other minerals found within
the States, the principle aroused the greatest opposition.
It was only an extension of the "crown-right" idea of
the civil law; but the rights so long recognized by immemorial custom and prescription in Germany, the Elec-
torates, France, Portugal, Spain, and other dominions
of Europe, seemed so "un-American," that their asser-
tion was soon abandoned.

The United States next tried the plan of attempting
to hold, and lease to the highest bidders, the salt-springs
and lead-mines. After the acquisition of Louisiana,
lands containing lead ores were reserved from sale; and
in 1807 the President received authority to lease them
for five years, in tracts of not more than three miles

square, afterwards reduced to one square mile, — the return of six per cent of the ores being required. Under this system the first lease was issued in 1822; but after 1834 many of the miners and smelters in Michigan, Wisconsin, Iowa, Missouri, and Arkansas positively refused to pay rents, because there had been a vast number of fraudulent entries of mineral lands as agricultural lands, and the system appeared unjust. By 1846 this lease-system became untenable, and was definitely abandoned.[1] Acts of Congress then restored to the several States the right to sell their salt-springs, and also opened to pre-emption as public lands the hitherto-leased tracts in the lead and copper mining-districts.

The history of the disputes, protests of pioneers, and litigations among rival claimants, which led at last to the abandonment of the lease-system, is long and highly interesting. It extends over nearly the first half of the century. The numerous complications which arose out of the entangled condition of Spanish and French land-titles in the provinces of upper and lower Louisiana, involved the best mining-districts of Missouri and Iowa, and test-cases were fought from court to court until

[1] The Annual Report of the Secretary of the Treasury for 1865 says, speaking of the Pacific Coast mineral lands, " A system of lease-hold, . . . after the lessons which have been taught of its practical results in the lead and copper districts, cannot, of course, be recommended."

The course of United-States legislation up to this point can be synopsized as follows: Ordinance, May 20, 1785, reserved one-third of the gold, silver, lead, and copper; Act of March 3, 1807, dealt with lead-mines; Act of March 3, 1829, authorized their sale in Missouri; Act of Sept. 4, 1841, excluded salines and mines from pre-emption; Case of U.S. *vs.* Gear, 1845, confirmed the previous act; April 18, 1846, mineral lands of Isle Royal, Lake Superior, reserved; July 16, 1846, lead-mines in Illinois, Arkansas, Missouri, and Iowa, offered for sale at two dollars and a half per acre; March 1, 1847, lands in Lake Superior district offered at five dollars per acre.

settled by the highest authority in the land. The lead-
claims of upper Louisiana introduced hitherto unknown
elements into our jurisprudence. Our government, acting in accordance with the law of nations, had agreed
to recognize all lawful titles to lands in the ceded
territory.[1]

Owing to these causes, it happened that American
lawyers who settled in New Orleans and St. Louis early
in the century found that a knowledge of French and
Spanish law was essential to success. As regards land-
titles, the courts of Louisiana have decided that the
colonial Spanish government of such rulers as Galvez,
Míro, and Carondelet, recognized verbal as well as written grants. The grants made by French officers during
the ownership of Louisiana by France were never contested, but most of the Spanish grants were. Land-
grants in some cases were referred for final decision to
the captain-general of Cuba, within whose jurisdiction
were Florida and Louisiana. The Indians were assigned
one square league about their villages, including the
town-site. A primitive land-title existing in any tribe
was never recognized. Absolute ownership in their
village-lands was not allowed, severe restrictions being
placed upon its sale and alienation. If all died or removed, the lands reverted to the crown. A simple order
from the governor was sufficient to establish these reservations. It thus followed that grants by Indian tribes

---

[1] Among the important decisions that bear upon Spanish and French
claims, Indian rights, mineral lands, and United-States title, are the
following: Sanchez *vs.* Gonzales, Louisiana Rep., 11 M., p. 207; Le Blanc
vs. Victor, 3 L., 47; Landry *vs.* Martin, 15 L., 1; De Vall *vs.* Choppin, 15
L., 566; Murdock *vs.* Gurley, 5 R., 457; Reband *vs.* Nero, 5 M.; Moes *vs.*
Gilliard, 7 N. S., 314; Brooks *vs.* Norris, 6 R., 175; Breaux *vs.* Johns, 4 A.,
147; Choteau *vs.* Molony, 16 How (U.S.), 203; Wilson *vs.* Smith, Yeager
5, 347 (Mo. Rep.); Delassas *vs.* United States, 9 Peters, 117.

to white men anywhere within the Louisiana territory required acceptance and confirmation from the Spanish authorities. A noted case which reached the Supreme Court in 1853 decided the ownership of the Dubuque lead-mines adversely to the claims of those who held under title from scheming Julien Dubuque, the old Indian trader and pioneer, who, in 1788, had received from the five chief villages of the Fox Indians in council assembled the gift of an illy defined tract of nearly one hundred thousand acres of land.[1] Albert Gallatin also made a report to the President upon the Dubuque claims, saying that the tract was undoubtedly government land. In 1832 there was trouble among the rival claimants to the mineral soil; and in 1833 troops were called into requisition, who drove off one party, and burned their cabins. The government then leased the land to the miners.

The St. Vrain concession of mineral lands was decided to have been perfected under the requirements of Spanish law; and so to be outside of the jurisdiction of the act of 1807, creating a board of commissioners for the re-adjustment of land-claims. The "inchoate title" of the descendants of "Pierre Charles Dehault, Knight, Lord of Delassus Luzieres, and Knight of the great cross of the royal order of St. Michael," covered a square league on St. Francis River, Missouri, containing valuable lead-mines, which had been worked by prehistoric miners, and were re-opened by the knight of many titles in the days of Baron Carondelet, who purchased, in the name of the Spanish Government, thirty thousand pounds

[1] Le Sueur, the French explorer, discovered mineral on this Dubuque tract in 1700 or 1701. The earliest notice of mines in the North-West, however, is contained in the report of Jesuit missionaries, who in 1660 found copper-ore in the Lake-Superior region.

of lead annually for five years. This title, legal as far as it went, but never made complete, was confirmed by the United States.

But while the courts and the lawyers were determining the status of hundreds of varying claims under Spanish and French titles, the region was being settled by hardy and energetic pioneers, long before the United-States Government had arranged to sell lands. The immediate result was the formation of "squatter associations," to take up, place on record, and hold land-claims. Professor Macy of Iowa College, in a paper upon "Institutional Beginnings in a Western State," read before the Historical and Political Science Association of Johns Hopkins University, Nov. 2, 1883, and since then published as No. 7 of the second series of the "University Studies in Historical and Political Science," has well described the claim-laws of these agricultural settlers, whose guiding principle was to give each man his fair and equal chance.

In the mineral region of Iowa, we find early organization. Professor Macy tells us, that June 17, 1830, the Dubuque lead-miners assembled, and appointed a committee of five to draught regulations, which were unanimously adopted. They agreed to live under "the code of Illinois," with the following additions: —

"ARTICLE I. That each and every man shall hold two hundred yards square of ground, working said ground one day in six.

"ARTICLE II. We further agree, that there shall be chosen, by a majority of the miners present, a person who shall hold this article, and grant letters of arbitration, on application having been made; and that said letters of arbitration shall be obligatory on the parties concerned so applying."

These simple laws, thus adopted by the lead-miners in public meeting, form the earliest, and for thirteen years the only, local code of Americans on the soil of Iowa.   In 1833 the Indian title to these mineral lands was extinguished, and within a year Dubuque contained two thousand inhabitants.   May 20, 1834, the miners tried and condemned a man for murder, and a month later policed the town, and executed him, after the Governor of Missouri and the President of the United States had been applied to for pardon by the prisoner's friends, and had replied that "the pardoning power rested with those who passed the sentence."

The early local history of this interesting mineral region shows most clearly the working of forces which reached their fuller development only in the comparative isolation of later camps.   Lead-miners of Iowa, tin-bounders of Cornwall, early silver-miners of Germany, all recognized the claim-stake, dwelt under equal laws of their own creation, and tried and punished their criminals.

Furthermore, as we have observed in the course of this chapter, the lead and copper miners west of the Mississippi came into contact, in many cases, with old Spanish grants and concessions.   Here, in the heart of the continent, midway between Lakes and Gulf, the American miner first met the Spanish influence that he was to find once more, in far stronger forms, on the shores of the Pacific.   Americans had no sooner controlled the lead-regions of Dubuque and St. Joseph, than they pushed westward, in the years preceding the great gold discoveries of California; there to meet a current of institutional development that had come from Spain by way of Mexico, not by way of lower Louisiana, and so had retained far more of its original characteristics.   It is to this Spanish-American realm that we must now

turn our attention, in order to understand the elements
underlying California life, and the conditions that
favored peculiar local organizations in the mining-camps
of the Sierra and the Rockies.

CHAPTER V.

SPANISH rule, and the first attempts of Spaniards to
mine in the New World, are of especial significance by
reason of sharp institutional contrasts to the forms of
Germanic development; also because of the influence
subsequently exerted upon the South-West, and the Pacific coast of the United States. The growth of the
Spanish system of government, and the complete separation of mining-courts from civil courts that for a time
existed in Mexico, form an essential part of our investigation.

The first Spanish colonists were lazy and lustful,
reckless and turbulent. They desolated the fairest
isles of the West Indies, they rebelled against their
governors, and they drove to suicide the unhappy race
they had enslaved. Everywhere under their system,
with its strange contrasts of stately indifference and volcanic energy, the Spaniards forgot their own Castilian
proverb of awful significance, *" Dios consiente pero no
para siempre "* (God may consent, but not forever).

The only judicial officer of these early colonists was
the alcalde, a district judge, who possessed a great
variety of powers, as will be shown in a subsequent
chapter. The first mention we find of this officer is at
Cuba, early in the sixteenth century. The first mili-

47

tary rule of Mexico brooked no interference from local officers of any sort; but Cortez soon developed great administrative skill and energy, and rapidly introduced the local institutions known to Old Spain.

It is, however, to a colony and a mining-camp that we must look for the best Spanish example of elected officers and local organization. Early in the sixteenth century, about a hundred Spaniards, led by Enciso, founded the town of "Santa Maria de la Antigua del Darien." The afterwards famous Vasco Nunez de Balboa, roused by some acts of petty tyranny, persuaded the colonists to depose Enciso, and elect himself chief alcalde, with an assistant and a *regidor*. A little later, in 1514 in fact, some rich gold-placers were discovered three leagues from "Santa Maria del Darien;" and a rush to the new mines was the immediate result. Almost at once the miners organized. They elected a mining-superintendent and a surveyor of claims, under whose supervision and authority plats of ground twelve paces square were measured off for each able-bodied miner; no one being allowed to hold or to work more than one claim at a time. They paid the royal demands; but, while the mines lasted, they managed their own local affairs with more skill and energy than miners of their race have elsewhere displayed. Here, in this little camp of Spaniards, a seed of local self-government had been planted; but it could find no firm root in national characteristics, and no abiding support from national institutions. Instead of springing up, bearing fruit, and extending itself to camp after camp northward along the Isthmus through Central America to the placers of Yucatan and Mexico, its blossom fell to the earth unfructified, its stem withered and perished in a single summer.

Permanent social order, and organized self-government, could not develop from the early Spanish placer-mining, any more than from the gold-lust of Spanish leaders like Cortez and Pizarro. Hither and thither through the New World, the freebooters of Spain had hastened, searching for traces of gold, as wolves follow the scent of smoking blood. Impelled by this passion, they hewed paths through tropic forests, crossed deserts, explored unknown seas, illustrated the utmost valor, cruelty, endurance, and fanaticism, and unfurled the intertwining standards of Rome and Spain at almost the same time in Amazonian and Floridian forests, in Patagonian and Oregonian wildernesses, and over hills of Arkansas, deserts of Arizona, and isles of the California pearl-coast. This breathless search was, happily, futile: the continents held no more semi-civilized kingdoms rich in treasures of gold. By the help of slaves, the baffled *conquistadores* then began to develop the mineral resources of New Spain. They still sent out expeditions by land to follow such mirages as the Golden Temple of Dabaiba, and fleets to search the North Pacific for the fabled Straits of Annian ; but the fever of exploration had nearly run its course. Silver and gold bearing rock soon began to be worked with system and success. Humboldt says that the annual gold-yield of America, from 1492 to 1521, was $250,000 ; from 1521 to 1546, it was $3,150,000. In 1545 Potosi began to pour forth its treasures, and the annual yield of gold and silver combined was $10,-300,000 for the sixty years after that discovery. The ransom of Atahualpa had been $20,000,000. Jacob, in his "History of the Precious Metals," says that the mining-industry of Europe was greatly stimulated by the mining done in America ; that, in fourteen years after 1516, there were twenty-five rich veins found in Bohemia; and that, between 1538 and 1562, over a thousand leases and grants of new mining-ground were made by the Bishopric of Salzburg.

The Mexican system of civil law, as transplanted from the overlordships of Castile and Aragon, lasted, with few changes, until well into the present century; and its more abiding local forms of administration still rule the land that Cortez conquered. The principles upon which the colonial possessions of Spain were governed, and even the details of that government, present remarkable parallels to the complex system of authority extended by Rome over her subject provinces. Under Spain, all titles, power, and dignity flowed from the royal throne, as, under the later Roman system, they all flowed from the emperor. The viceroyalties of Spain in Peru, Grenada, Mexico, corresponded with singular fidelity to the proconsulates and pro-prætorships of Syria, of Gaul, and of Spain herself under Rome. As, in the Roman world, hardly any two cities bore the same yoke, or occupied exactly identical relations to the central government, whether that of senate or of emperor; so, in the Spanish empire, hardly two viceroys had equal rank, or exercised identical powers. The most casual observer cannot but seize upon striking similarities and instructive contrasts between these vast and ultimately unsuccessful colonial empires.

The Spanish system had a feudal element, in that the land, and the Indians as attached thereto, were divided among the colonists. This royal gift of soil and people was called an *encomienda*, and first occurred in Hispaniola, extending thence to all the Spanish dominions. Cortez made a provisional *repartimiento*, or division of the natives; and this was re-adjusted by a royal *audien-*

cia, or council. Cruelty, disease, and hard work slew them so rapidly, that the greater part had perished before they were set free, and given land to cultivate in common, as in some of the modern pueblos.

The system of Spanish civil government extended upward from the alcalde of the village to the viceroy of the whole territory, all appointed or elected with such severe restrictions that matters were in practice kept under royal control. The detailed minuteness of the administrative affairs in even the most obscure provinces of Peru or the Indies, that passed under the eyes of the king himself, and were decided according to his wishes, is something that almost surpasses belief. Some choice in village and district affairs was all that was left in the hands of the people, until the mining-laws differentiated the powers of the system, and the local alcaldeship was thus enabled to gain a greater dignity and influence. Spiritually, Mexico was divided into provinces, sees, and parishes. The *visidados*, or special emissaries of the king, and the "legates of the pope," formed ambassadorial links between the Old World and the New.

Government of the towns (*pueblos*) was, in Spanish days, intrusted to a town-council, or *ayuntamiento*, whose head was either a *mayores* or an alcalde, assisted by several *regidors* (directors) and *syndicos* (clerks). The villages had only an alcalde. In the large towns of each district, the municipality chose two *alcaldes de mesta*, to preside over semi-annual councils of the live-stock owners. This pastoral custom was carried wherever Mexican colonists journeyed; in a modified form it survived in California until a few years ago, and still exists in New Mexico and the South-West.

Studying as a whole the civil government instituted

by Spain, we can safely affirm that no nation has ever possessed a nicer sense of the theoretical proportions of aristocratic rule, or brought to the difficult labors of colonial government a more dignified and stately administrative genius; but the fatal facility with which department was added to department, and wheel to wheel, made the whole cumbrous machinery break down at last beneath its own weight. It was an ingenious mechanical contrivance, not a vital organism. Pulleys, levers, and speaking-tubes, not arteries, nerves, and muscles, set the mandates of the central government in operation throughout the system. Hence its weight and increasing weakness, its decay and final failure, its giant wrecks rusting in solitude on the hills of every Spanish-American province, its mournful problems, as of misgoverned Cuba. This overloaded mechanism of government reaches its climax in the mining-laws of New Spain, more particularly of Mexico, which constitute the most unique, laborious, and complicated system of special jurisprudence ever developed on this continent.

In February, 1774, the miners of Mexico petitioned the King of Spain, by whose orders a perpetual corporation was established, embracing all the mine-owners, and ruled by a great tribunal consisting of an appointed president, an appointed director, and three elected deputies. Acting under this central organization were local tribunals, one in each province. The system proposed was to have jurisdiction in all cases which concerned the mines or the miners, and it was at first received with universal enthusiasm. One of the first things done was to found a college of mines on an immense scale in the city of Mexico. Alexander von Humboldt, in his "Political Essay on New Spain," describes this

Real Seminario de Mineria as it existed in the city of
Mexico in 1803. The director of the college had then
been collecting statistics from the thirty-seven *Depu-
taciones de Minas*, and from these reports he had perfected a mineral-map for the use of the supreme college
or head tribunal. A great banking-system, whose rami-
fications were to extend to the remotest mining-town,
was early organized. The tribunal, soon after its creation, had formulated a code of laws for the government
and regulation of mine-towns, mine-owners, and mine-
laborers. In 1783 this code received the full approval
of the king and the grand council of the Indies.[1] Thus
the mining-interests of Mexico were separated from
direct control of the civil authorities; and the powerful
corporation created in accordance with the petition of
the miners received rights of separate courts, and privileges and immunities almost royal in scope and nature.

No "mine-town" had a right to vote at any election
for a tribunal deputy, unless it contained "an inhabiting
population, a church, and a curate or deputy, a judge
and deputy of mines, six mines in actual working, and
four reducing-establishments."

Paternal government over the mines and the miners
was developed to such an amusing and exasperating
degree, that some of its manifestations seem almost
beyond belief. Supervision was never reduced to a

[1] This great Council of the Indies was created by Ferdinand in
1511, but was not fully organized till thirteen years later under Charles
the Fifth. It was a plan much favored by that wise statesman, Cardinal Ximenes, whom Sir Arthur Helps has compared to the English Earl
of Chatham. The *Recopilacion de las Leyes de las Indias* declared that
this council should consist of twenty-two councillors, presided over by
the king himself as perpetual president, and of four secretaries. It was
given supreme jurisdiction throughout Spanish America and the Philip-
pines. As a rule, the councillors were men who had seen service as
viceroys or captains-general in the New World.

more exact science. This royal ordinance of 1783 declares that all cases must be decided "without any of the usual delays, written declarations, or petitions of lawyers." It sets apart the refuse ore-heaps and "tailings" as "support for the widows and orphans, old and helpless." It forbids reduction of wages, fixes rations, commands registration of laborers with a view to prevent their leaving a mine, and orders that the price of articles used in the mines shall be fixed by law so that "no undue profit" shall be taken by any one. It also prohibits all persons from making demands of the workmen for alms, this being aimed at the beggars and the mendicant friars of the time. One of the most interesting provisions is to the effect that "persons going about to search for mines shall be allowed to have one beast to ride on, and one to carry their bedding and provisions, and shall not have to pay for their pasture, either on public or private property, whether it be customary or not to pay for the same." The reason for this provision is evidently to be found in the royal rights over mineral ground. Whoever discovered a new mine was an unofficial "king's messenger;" he was increasing the revenues of the crown. The prospector was, therefore, a more privileged characte1 in Mexico during the days of Washington, and under the rule of pleasure-loving Charles the Third of Spain, than he is at the present time in any spot on the American Continent.

The code ordained by the miners' tribunal further provided for certain local officers, called *disputaciones*, to reside in mining-towns as arbitrators in difficulties respecting mining-property, and also to discharge the very peculiar duty of "admonishing extravagant, wasteful, or gambling miners." If this warning was not heeded, the tribunal had power, which it often exercised, of "appointing a guardian for said miner, and of limiting his expenditures." In ways like this the mining-code of Mexico descended to the most minute particulars and trivial details of daily life, regulating the laborer's food, attire, and hours of labor; forbidding "dice, cards, and cock-fighting," still besetting sins of the Mexican miners; punishing idlers and vagabonds; and seemingly making some provision for every possible emergency.

The use of a *disputaciones*, or arbitrator, was a favorite idea of Mexican jurisprudence. The powers of this office were, at its abolishment, transferred to the alcalde-ships. The *disputaciones*, under this later form, was long in use in California. The same idea sprang up in the early "mining-courts" of the American mines, as we shall hereafter see; but the "arbitrators" of the miners had little historical connection with the Spanish *disputaciones*, except that this particular function of the early alcalde-courts might have aided to suggest the plan in some few of the mining-camps.

That section of the Spanish mining-laws which orders cases to be decided "without delay" is peculiarly characteristic of all mining-communities. Time is precious; every one is in haste; the poor are about to be made rich, the rich about to become extremely wealthy. The world over, all mining-codes in whose making the miners themselves have had a hand are certain to ignore technicalities, urge swift decisions, and laugh to scorn each fine-spun argument.

The laws of Mexico, as of Spain, recognized two distinct interests in land, — surface and mineral; interests not only legally distinct, but even transferred by separate and differently worded titles. One was *la propiedad del suelo*, the other was *la propiedad de la mina*.

The first, the right of pasturage and of agricultural use, was transferred or conveyed from the authorities of the province, by sale, by absolute gift, or by gift conditioned on settlement; the second, the right to dig for minerals, was obtained by special gift of the king himself, by registration of discovery, by denouncement of another mine for, "non-working" and its consequent forfeiture, or by purchase subject to special royal taxes and restrictions. An agricultural grant left the entire right to minerals in the hands of the Spanish Government, which right passed thence to Mexico at the Revolution. The right of miners to enter on private domains was absolute, nor was it conditioned upon payment of damages. The ideas involved in the system were, so far as regarded mineral lands, somewhat as follows: legal title complete in the crown; absolute right of the public to search for mineral, and work ungranted mines; right of eminent domain over mining-lands and mining-interests of every sort, such as in wood and water, vested in the government; rights of the crown to confer private ownership; ordinary mining-rights, valid only during the life of the reigning king, and a renewal necessary at his death.

Many of the agricultural grants made by Mexico to citizens of Alta California were found, after the conquest, to contain mineral wealth; and in some cases such lands were entered upon by prospectors, and claimed as being public lands, in the sense of the Mexican mining-law, and so having passed by conquest to the United States. A knowledge of the Spanish laws thus became necessary to every American lawyer in California, as once before to the lawyers of Louisiana and Missouri, and as now in Arizona and New Mexico. They were obliged to have some acquaintance with the codes and commentaries of the famous Spanish jurist Gamboa, with the ordinance of 1783, with subsequent acts of the *Tribunal de Mineria*, and with various decrees of Comonfort, Juarez, and other Mexican presidents, and acts of different Congresses.

The greatest alterations which have been made in the mining-laws were shortly after Mexican independence was established. The mining-deputations were brought more under the control of the government; mining-courts, consisting of a lawyer and two mine-owners, were established in each one of the States, to serve as a court of appellate jurisdiction; lastly, the rights of foreigners to purchase mines was recognized, though with restrictions. This was in 1823. At a later period, all "contentious jurisdiction" was transferred to the civil courts, and the separate mining-courts lost the greater part of their authority. Successive modifications of the laws respecting foreign miners, and the influence of English, German, and American capital and energy, have produced many changes, of late years, in the northern Mexican States. The local customs and district laws of that region are being superseded slowly but surely by American mining-usages.[1]

The condition of Mexican mining and civil law at the present time is, however, foreign to our investigation. Our inquiries have been only for the purpose of ascertaining to some extent the spirit of Mexican institutions, so as to understand more clearly the nature of their influence upon California, and the modifications they necessarily underwent. Before American pioneers

---

1 " This Province [Sonora] is beginning to adopt American mining-customs" (private letter from the late Manuel M. Corella, professor at the University of California, and afterwards an eminent Arizona lawyer; written in 1880).

captured California, before American miners had organized a single camp, three institutions of Spanish origin, the mission, the pueblo, and the alcaldeship, existed in the coast-region, and deserve our careful study. They serve as a background for the fuller activities of the American period, and they help to explain the local political difficulties that preceded the organization of State government. The pueblo and the alcaldeship were transferred, with slight modifications, from the limits of Mexico; the "mission" was an institution that gained for a time, in the provinces of California, an influence almost as overwhelming as that it so long held in parts of South America under the Jesuits.

CHAPTER VI.

THE MISSIONS OF THE PACIFIC COAST.

THE institution known in California as the " mission " was, from one stand-point, missionary and ecclesiastical; from another it was industrial and political. There was a decided flavor of worldliness, not to say greed of gain, mingled with the undoubted zeal and holiness of the early priests. In all the mountainous wilderness from Cape St. Lucas to Cape Mendocino, their missions occupied the choicest spots in the fairest valleys. They chose for soil, water, climate, sightliness, commanding position; and subsequent years have only confirmed their almost unerring judgment. The cash value of each convert to the gardens and pastures of the mission's broad domains was never overlooked: Christianized Indians meant laborers and vassals. The California natives of whom, in 1721, Collier wrote, " Every family hath an entire legislature, and governs at discretion," were brought into a subjection only paralleled in Paraguay. Students of economic subjects could not fail to find much of interest in the internal management of these famous missions of Alta (or Upper) California, the outgrowth of those established by the Jesuits in the peninsula of Baja (or Lower) California, where Fathers Ugarte and Salvatierra planted Loreto, Oct. 19, 1697. Within seventy years the priests had four flourishing missions and many minor settlements along the shores of the Gulf, then known as the Red Sea, or the Sea of Cortez (*el mar Cortez*). Soldiers under their command mapped out the surrounding region. Humboldt in his " New Spain " describes early conflicts of secular and ecclesiastical authority, terminated by the Spanish courts, which issued a *cedula real*, or writ, and put the entire detachment at Loreto under the orders of the priests. This famous shrine was soon enriched by pearls from the Gulf and silver from the mines : it possessed embroideries made by the hands of the Queen of Spain, and paintings by Murillo and Velasquez. In 1719 Father Ugarte built a missionary ship from timber dragged two hundred miles through the gray mountains and barren sand-dunes, there being no forests nearer to Loreto. At last, in 1767 the Jesuits were expelled, giving place to their successful rivals the Franciscans; and the following year they left the adobe-built missions of Lower California, the gardens, young orchards, and semi-civilized converts of their faith. The first settlement, the first church, and the first ship built in the California provinces were the result of Jesuit enterprise. The work they did was the direct means of attracting the attention of Spain to Upper California, and led to immediate efforts for its colonization. The leaders changed; but the movement which culminated at Mission Dolores on the Bay of San Francisco received its primary impulse when Fathers Ugarte and Salvatierra, with nine soldiers, set up their rude cross by the sheltered cove of sultry Loreto.

In July of 1769, — that fateful year which witnessed the birth of those mighty leaders of opposing armies, Napoleon Bonaparte and the Duke of Wellington, — Father Junipero Serra, the Franciscan apostle, a man of singular zeal, piety, asceticism, and administrative ability, founded San Diego, and began the mission system in Alta California.[1] His successors completed its ecclesiastical conquest, and brought the coast-tribes into full subjection.

The missions in their prime were little more than Indian reservations, managed, it is true, with great skill and marked industrial success, but entirely incapable of making citizens out of their Indian occupants. From the days of the good Las Casas, Spain and Mexico had honestly tried to do their best by the Indians. The laws of Mexico gave them many rights which in practice they were utterly unable to obtain. A decree of Philip II., in 1571, ordered that the property of Indians should never be sold except at public auction, before the alcalde, after thirty days notice. Later Spanish laws created additional safeguards against the loss of their common or other lands. The *Recopilacion de Indias* says explicitly that they cannot be sold nor alienated (" *Por ningun caso se les pueden vender ni enagenar* "). The royal *Audencia* of Mexico, adopted in 1781, enforced with additional legislation the same idea. The object of all these regulations was purely beneficent, — to interpose an insuperable barrier against all attempts of the whites to strip the newly emancipated Indians of whatever property they might receive from the government, or accumulate by their own industry. Their rights in the common lands of a pueblo could not be sold or rented; and this was good law in California, for some time after the American occupation.[2]

---

[1] Father Serra founded six mission colonies, gathered into strict discipline over seven thousand Indians, died Aug. 28, 1784, and was buried at San Carlos, Monterey, beneath the church-altar. Father Francisco Palou, his friend, associate, and biographer, wrote Serra's life at Mission Dolores, — the first book written in California.

[2] Sunol. *vs.* Hepburn, 1 Cal. Rep., p. 224.

But in California, as in Mexico, the actual rights possessed by the Indians were less than their legal rights, even during the sixty years of the missions' undisputed control. For these slaves of the soil, that civil authority represented by *commandantes*, *ayuntamientos*, and other officials of pueblo, presidio, or province, only existed as casual apparitions, gorgeous and stately as the bandits of an Italian opera. Very justly says quaint old Nicholas Mill, in his " History of Mexico," " In California the monks do rule the country." In the early mission days, they discouraged settlements and colonies of whites; and at a later period they still found means of controlling the Indian population far more absolutely than had been the intention of the civil authorities. Mexican laws enacted early in this century, and still in force in California after the American conquest, provided for Indian alcaldes, in these terms : —

"Mission Indians have the right to elect their own alcaldes, who, with the advice and assistance of the mission priests, shall make all the necessary regulations for their own internal government."

The Acts of 1833–34, secularizing the missions, pay much attention to the welfare of the Indians. From the point of view taken by the Mexican Government, the only good reason for the long-continued existence of the missions had been to train citizens. They were not intended to be permanent establishments; but would, it was hoped, change peacefully into prosperous parishes, and gradually lose their peculiar industrial, political, and communal features. But the laws relating to Indian alcaldes were practically a dead letter. Cooke, in his "Conquest of New Mexico and Cailfornia," mentions such an alcalde at "San Phillipi"

(Felipe); but otherwise, so far as we are able to learn, the right was unused and forgotten.

If the condition of vassalage in which the mission Indians were kept be considered entirely justifiable, their treatment was, on the whole, satisfactory. Few whites except priests and soldiers were allowed to live at the missions, whose tile-roofed buildings of black sun-dried bricks (adobes) surrounded a large court, cool with flowing streams of water and shade-trees. One side of the square was occupied by the great mission-church; while the remaining three sides were devoted to galleries, porches, workshops, barns, stables, grana-ries, kitchens, store-houses, cells of neophytes, and rooms of priests. The Indians were fed and clothed, taught trades, simple mechanical arts, and the system of agri-culture practised in Spain; passing their uneventful lives as humble servants of the Church, which was virtually independent of Mexico, owner of the soil, and master of the country.[1]

One might fill a volume with incidents of life in these quaint and curious missions before their hour of doom came. The people rose at sunrise, spent an hour at the chapel, marched singing to the fields, re-turned when the evening angelus rang, spent the even-ing in games and amusements, and retired to their huts of *tules* grouped under the mission's protecting shadow. They planted gardens, orangeries, vineries, and olivari-ums, — gardens in which the choicest fruits of Granada and Andalusia were grown; and they tended the fast-multiplying herds of the mission in the broad valleys and on the fertile foot-hills. California became almost a sanitarium and refuge for army veterans and worn-

---

[1] Paper on California. Harris: Maryland Hist. Soc. Pub., 1849; now a very rare pamphlet.

out priests; the missions where they dwelt were like highly cultivated oases in the midst of a wilderness. Catholic writers have strongly denounced the subsequent Mexican policy of secularization, marked as it was by the confiscation of the "Pious Fund," established for missionary purposes by wealthy Catholics in Mexico and Spain. De Courcy says that the Franciscan Fathers had seventy-five thousand California Indians civilized and converted before 1813. Another writer, Marshall, adds that in eight years the secular administration of the missions "re-plunged the whole province into barbarism," and utterly failed in every particular; reducing at the chief missions the 30,650 Indians to 4,450, the 424,000 head of cattle to 28,220, the 62,000 horses to 3,800, the 331,000 sheep to 31,600, and the annual yield of 70,000 *fanegas* of wheat to 4,000. (A *fanega* weighed 150 pounds.) This scattering of helpless, ignorant Indians over California has ever, and most justly, appealed to human sympathies. Even at this day the great adobe walls of the few mission-churches that yet stand, the rude sculptures, gaudy frescos, and square belfries, the neglected burial-grounds, the huge and rude crosses set sloping on the hillsides or crowning some seaward-overlooking peak, the mournful silver-gray olive-trees, large as those that look down the dark chasm of Sorrento, all appear sacred and deeply impressive features in the California landscape. Protestants and Catholics alike treasure these memorials of the dreamy, romantic childhood of California, of conditions of society that have forever departed from the American continent, and of an ecclesiastical rule more powerful and more exclusive than existed elsewhere in North America.

When the missions were first established, a tract of

about fifteen acres was allotted to each one; but their lands were never surveyed, and they gradually extended their bounds until they virtually laid claim to nearly the entire region. The term "mission," that once had meant only the church-town, with the gardens and orchards near it, soon came to include the extensive tracts over which the cattle, horses, and sheep owned by the establishment were allowed to roam at will. There were, a few years later, some separate private grants and presidio reservations. The priests never received any formal acknowledgment, from the Spanish Government, of their land-claims. The revolution of 1822 put the subject into the hands of Mexican Liberals, who four years later freed the Indian serfs from compulsory allegiance to the priesthood. The mission-lands were gradually alienated, and the decay and ruin spoken of in the previous paragraph followed as a natural consequence.

It appears evident that the missions in their best estate were triumphs of organization, and marvels of pastoral wealth. San Gabriel, for instance, once contained three thousand Indians, owned one hundred and five thousand cattle, twenty thousand horses, forty thousand sheep, and seventeen extensive ranches all well cultivated; it had fig, olive, grape, and orange plantations; and thousands of dollars were in its treasury. The twenty-one missions of Alta California in 1820 contained thirty thousand Indians, and owned a million head of live-stock. By 1833, when secularization began, the number of Indians had fallen to twenty thousand, there being great mortality among them, and little recuperative energy. By 1837 the missions held only about four thousand Indians, and less than sixty-three thousand head of live-stock. Seventeen years never wrought more complete ruin in a social system.

We have now to consider the legal aspects and methods of organization of the mission colonies. The Franciscan *padre* who governed each mission was at first its civil as well as religious ruler, and dealt directly with the viceroy of Mexico. He was called the *presidente*, or governor, and administered the law within his jurisdiction. Nominally it was the law of Mexico; practically it was frontier government, — few and simple rules, prompt and summary enforcement, and no appeal except to the city of Mexico. Thus they governed the Indians, the soldiers, the few white settlers in the villages that grew up near the missions. The province had its *commandante*, representing the civil and military power, but never interfering with the management of the missions, nor criticising the decisions of the priests. In Father Junipero Serra's time, there was a conflict of authority, which ended in a victory for the ecclesiastics, and the military authorities accepted the situation.

The first grant of land the priests allowed to be given in California was in 1774, to a Spanish soldier named Butron, who had married a baptized Indian girl from Carmel Mission, and received a tract in that valley.[1] By this time their claims embraced nearly the whole territory from sea-coast to sierra, and from Sonoma Mountain to San Diego Bay. It was difficult, even at a later date, when secularization was evidently an inevitable fact, to secure ownership of land "against the encroachments of powerful missions which discouraged immigration, and under a weak and irregular territorial government."[2] Despite these difficulties, and the almost constant opposition of the priests, the little pueblos, or free towns, grew, and received alcaldes. In 1813

[1] Tuthill's History of California, pp. 60-63, *passim.*
[2] Cooke's Conquest of New Mexico and California.

the Spanish Cortes granted right to form *ayuntamientos*, or town-councils. By various enactments between 1822 and 1833, the Mexican Government took secular authority from the *presidencias*, and swept away the irresponsible, undefined, and illegal power so long exercised within those jurisdictions. The *presidente*, or priest-president, became a simple prefect, and civil authority prevailed over ecclesiastical.

The mission-land claims were continued long after the American conquest. Priests in charge of missions attempted to sell or rent lands in the vicinity, and were prevented by Mason, the military governor. The noted case of Nobili *v.* Redman [1] decided the legal status of the missions, and aided greatly in settling land-titles in California. This decision was to the effect that "the missions established in California prior to its acquisition by the United States were political establishments, and in no wise connected with the Church. The fact that monks or priests governed them does not prove the ownership of the Church. The lands the mission held remained government lands; and the Church can only claim mission property under the Mexican decree of 1824, and subject to all its limitations." [2] This evidently refers to and includes the Acts subsequent to 1834, carrying into effect the original announcement of 1824.

The secularization of the mission-lands will be described more at length in discussing the pueblos, or free towns, into which some of the missions were converted. This secularization seems to have been amply justified

[1] 6 Cal. Rep., p. 325. Another interesting case is that of Santilan *vs.* Moses, 1 Cal. Rep., p. 92. The position of the priest was held analogous to that of " sole corporation " in England.

[2] " *Primafacie*, that the Mexican Government of California had the power to grant mission-lands as they chose." — *Den. vs. Den.*, 6 Cal. Rep., p. 81.

as a principle of public policy, though it was not wisely conducted. It was, so far as the descendants of the first Spanish settlers were concerned, an act of simple justice. As early as 1763, men had removed from Mexico to California under promise of becoming land-owners; and this had hitherto been denied them. It was also an act of patriotism; because the priests of Mexico and California had done all they could to prevent the success of the revolution, and whatever reduced their political and financial influence aided the stability of the new republic. The last of the missions the priests had established was that of Sonoma, in August, 1823; and between 1824 and 1834 the various decrees already alluded to stripped them all of their possessions. The civil officers put in charge were often dishonest; the mission-cattle were stolen, or else strayed off into the mountains; the Indians in many cases gladly returned to their savage life, or wasted their patrimony, and sank into beggary. These ten years represent a transition period from the era of missions to the era of pueblos, and in many respects the change was a trying one for the people.

The famous missions, with all their faults of theory and of practice, had been planted by men possessed of the true missionary spirit: they had done much to civilize the natives, and more to improve the country. They had often dispensed a genial and generous hospitality to strangers, and they ruled their servants with a firm and liberal hand. When the whole social fabric of the mission-system went to ruin, the suddenness of its downfall shocked all thoughtful observers. Yet it was but an artificial system, and its intrinsic worthlessness was plainly revealed the moment outside pressure and military coercion were removed. Moral suasion was futile to retain the thousands of Indian converts, who could no longer be persuaded to make soap, mould bricks, weave wool, sing Latin hymns, and repeat mediæval prayers. They returned to their hillsides, their grasshoppers, their camass-roots,[1] and their idleness; while many of the priests went back to Mexico. The missions' lack of economic success was by far the least part of their failure.

The population of Alta California, exclusive of Indians, was at this time (1834) about five thousand, of whom not more than forty were English and Americans. Some of these, however, occupied very influential positions; several were alcaldes, and nearly all had married wealthy señoritas. But, in order to obtain any political rights, they had been compelled to become Catholics, and were objects of suspicion and hatred. Don José Castro was heard, in 1837, to declare that "a California *cavallero* cannot win a *señorita* if opposed in his suit by an American sailor. . . . These heretics must be cleared from the land." Their numbers, however, were constantly receiving accessions. The foreign element grew stronger, despite all efforts to dislodge them. They held on, with the tenacity of men in whose veins the blood of many generations of Aryan pioneers was flowing. A few swaggering trappers came wandering through the mountain passes; a few runaway sailors, such as Gilroy, who married the Spanish heiress of vast possessions, became lords of inland valleys; a few keen-witted Yankee traders settled in the towns: and the end of Spanish-American domination was close at hand. Meanwhile the light-hearted, passionate, generous na-

---

1 " *Camass esculenta*," the most important food-bulbs of the Pacific-coast Indians. Described by the late Hon. B. B. Redding in American Naturalist, and in report to Smithsonian Institute.

tive Californians established their *ranchos* in all the
fertile valleys, and built their dingy, thick-walled adobe
mansions on points of vantage from San Diego to Sonoma; always choosing, with some hereditary instinct of
the race, the picturesque and beautiful outlooks, or
nestling in the most sheltered of vales, or in the wildest of ravines. The life they lived, in its freedom from
care, and its glorious physical healthfulness, was simply
perfection. Dana somewhere speaks of the Californians
as "a people on whom a curse had fallen, and stripped
them of every thing but their pride, their manners, and
their voices." But he had only seen them in their
pueblos near the coast: he had not visited their wide-
roofed homes, when all the descendants of the Castilian pioneer of 1763 gathered under one roof-tree in
harmony and affection. Horses could be had for the
asking; cattle were only of value for the hides, worth
two dollars apiece, and called "California bank-notes."
There were no fences anywhere, except hedges of
nopal (or prickly-pear), walls of brush, and ditches
formerly dug by the mission Indians about the adobe
ranch-houses. There were no roads, except, near the
towns, the occasional track of a slow, wooden-wheeled
carreta, or ox-cart. Every one rode on horseback, and
with an ease, grace, vigor, and fearlessness, which have
never been surpassed by any race. This was the people whose flocks and herds soon covered the plains
and hillsides once claimed by the missions, and into
whose untroubled life the American pioneers brought
elements of change and confusion. This was the era
of California's eventful existence, that coming artists
of language will delight to portray. Its saints are such
as that high-born maiden, Concepcion Arguëllo, of
whose faithfulness Bret Harte's poem tells; its shrines

are mostly ruined walls of sunburned clay, the oldest architectural remains on the Pacific coast of the United States; its heroes are dark and haughty *vaqueros*, storming across broad *mesa*, wild canŏn, and steep *barranca*. An old Spaniard dying in a rude hut near San Luis Obispo, in the winter of 1874, sprang to his feet in the delirium of fever, and cried out, "I hear the ringing of their spurs on the mountain, the trample of their horses!" and so, repeating the names of his companions of fifty years before, he sank back in an unconsciousness from which death soon released him.

CHAPTER VII.

SPANISH TOWN-GOVERNMENT. — THE PUEBLO IN CALIFORNIA.

THE pueblos of Mexico are simply towns, as the *pueblicitos* are simply villages. In Alta California, the first pueblos were so distinct from the presidios, or nominally fortified towns under military rule, and from the missions under ecclesiastical rule, that they well deserve the title of free towns. They alone had an alcalde chosen by the people; and they alone had common lands, and gifts of town-lots to all residents.

But there is an application of the word "pueblos" to the relics of an ancient, fast-fading, native civilization, which has perhaps become more familiar to most readers than is the Mexican or Californian usage. The pueblo of the south-west region of the United States is far different from those we have just described. Adventurous students such as Mr. Frank Cushing, explorers such as Major Powell, and archæologists such as Mr. L. H. Morgan, have made us acquainted with the rock-fortresses and the immense communal buildings of the race that reared Cicuyé, Quivira, Cibola, and the City of Mexico.[1] Even to-day the Moquis shape their

[1] The first of these was discovered by Coronado; the second was the city that Peñalosa saw; the third was the mystic and seven-citied realm that the Franciscan friar, Marcos de Niza, reported in his "Relations" (Hakluyt Soc., vol. iii. p. 438). For these pueblos, see Morgan's Homes of the Aborigines, Government Reports of Major Powell, Short's North

black and red pottery as they did before Martin Behaim
began to dream of a new world; the Zuni priests still
guard their sacred fires, and pray in their secret language for the fast-fading "children of Montezuma." It
is curious enough that this Spanish word "pueblo" should
have come to be applied to the "joint-tenements" of the
proud and brave people that drove Otermin out of New
Mexico, and for fifteen years governed themselves. At
the present time the pueblo Indians of the South-west
choose their own chief ruler, war-captain, and fiscal, as
they have done for years. The pueblos of California
had no essential relation to the Indians, and were only
modifications of the Mexican town-system.

In Alta California, the need of pueblos began to be
felt soon after missions were first established. The
presidios, where the soldiers and commandantes were,
required grain, vegetables, and supplies of various sorts.
Spanish vessels from the East Indies occasionally wanted
provisions. The viceroy of Mexico therefore wrote to
the commandante of San Diego and Monterey, under
date of Aug. 17, 1773, declaring that he "grants him
the power to designate common lands, and also allows
him to distribute lands in private to such Indians as
may most dedicate themselves to agriculture and the
breeding of cattle; but they must continue to live in
the town or mission, not dispersed on their *ranchos*."
The commandante is also empowered to grant lands to
any new and desirable settlers, and he "must give legal
titles without cost." Then follows the statement, clearly
opposed to the claims of the ecclesiastics, that he "may,
if he deems it expedient, change a mission into a pueblo,
and subject it to the same civil and economic laws as

Americas of Antiquity, Putnam's Archæology of the Pueblos; also, A
Pueblo Fête Day, in Overland Monthly for April, 1884.

govern the other pueblos of the kingdom." Nothing, however, seems to have come of this permission, except a few isolated grants, all under permission from, and with the full approval of, the priests.

Four years later, in June, 1777, explicit directions from the viceroy ordered the establishment of two pueblos, one at San José, the other at Los Angeles, on the Rio Guadalupe and the Rio Porcincula respectively. In 1795 the Marquis of Branciforte founded a colony, and the pueblo of Branciforte, near Santa Cruz. All the other pueblos of California were outgrowths of missions or of presidios. The regulations outlined in the letter of the viceroy, written in 1773, were adopted for the first two pueblos.

In June, 1779, additional regulations respecting the pueblos were issued, and were approved and emphasized by royal orders of Oct. 24, 1781. By these orders, each *publador*, or village colonist, was to be paid $116.44 yearly for the first two years, and $60 yearly during the next three: he was also to have the free use of horses, mules, cattle, sheep, utensils, and to be furnished with seed-wheat and other necessaries, of which a long list is given.

The officials are to lay out the streets and public squares, with which all Spanish towns are well provided; and are to choose and mark out the common lands (*egidos*), the lands for municipal purposes (*propios*), the house-lots (*solares*), and the separate sowing-lands of the colonists (*suertes*). We have here a four-fold and extremely interesting division of lands among villagers, — a division of very ancient usage among the Spaniards. All the details of the system point to its origin in a community where some of the land had to be irrigated on account of the uncertainty of the seasons, and where much of the wealth of the people was in cattle. The common lands of the pueblo were to furnish water, pasturage, timber, and firewood, and these privileges were free to all dwellers in the town. Those who received grants of building-lots were obliged to fence them, make certain improvements, and plant trees thereon, within a stated time; and this they promised in their petition to the alcalde, or to the town-council. The "sowing-lands" were granted in two parcels to each individual; one half being "capable of irrigation," the other half "dry ground," or upland (*de tierras*).

The object of establishing the California pueblos was set forth in a long preamble in the royal order of 1781. It was, "to forward the reduction of, and as far as possible make this vast country useful to the State;" and the union of white men, or "people of reason" (*gente de razon*), in close communities; also, the "better education of the Indians."

Each pueblo was furnished with alcaldes and other municipal officers (members of council, and *syndicos*), in proportion to the number of inhabitants. For two years these officers were appointed; the third year, and thereafter, they were elected. The titles to houses, lots, and water-rights for irrigation, were recorded in the "Book of Colonization," and kept in the pueblo archives. The council had many duties similar to those of the ordinary town-councils known to Americans: they ordered the laying-out of streets, the planting of shade-trees, the repair of roads.

In some cases the pueblo council established schools. Feb. 11, 1797, Felipe Goycochea, of the presidio of Santa Barbara, wrote to Governor Borica, saying, " I transmit to you a statement in relation to the schools, together with six copy-books of the children who are learning to write;" and these Spanish copy-books of this pueblo school are still in the archives of California, and likely to long remain, the only thing for which history takes note of these last-century officials. The missions had their schools, also, where some of the brightest Indians were taught to read and write, to keep accounts, and superintend laborers in the field. The hero of Mrs. Helen Hunt Jackson's pathetic and beautiful novel "Ramona" is in no wise an impossible creation: a few such men grew up under the training of mission and pueblo. "Ramona" gives information about the organization of the more progressive Indian settlements of southern California, after the secularization of the missions, before their common lands were wrested away by fraud and force, and shameful neglect on the part of the United-States Government.

In March, 1791, the viceroy wrote from Chihuahua, Mexico, to Governor Romeu of California, — the order reaching him in October, — ordaining that the extent of four common leagues measured from the centre of the square was sufficient for the new pueblos, into which the old presidios were transformed. The captains of the presidios were to grant and distribute house-lots and lands to citizens and former soldiers within these limits. The decree closed with the customary phrase used by the courtly hidalgos of Spain, "God preserve you many years."

President Iturbide in 1823 established new laws for the pueblos, but they were never put into practical operation in Alta California. The decrees of 1824 and 1828 of the Mexican Congress, however, set forth minute regulations regarding the colonization of the vacant lands, and the granting of town-sites to individuals who bound themselves to establish colonies. No person was allowed to receive more than one square league of irrigated land, four leagues of land dependent on the seasons, and six leagues of pasture. The lands granted must be "vacant," as the exact status of the mission-lands was declared "to be as yet undetermined," and "must not be within ten leagues of the coast." This last was evidently an attempt, which proved of little avail, to populate the interior valleys. Less than twelve families were not considered as forming a colony. The government, policy, and town-laws of Mexican towns were copied as nearly as practicable.

The spirit of the laws governing the granting of lands to the pueblos was manifestly liberal, as is shown in an Act of the governor and territorial deputation of California, Aug. 6, 1834. It is there provided, that when a settlement is made, and the people establish a council, that body may apply for assignments of land. This evidently contemplates the growth of free towns, not begun by formal colonies, or under large grants, but by a few settlers in the ordinary Anglo-Saxon fashion of planting communities. The municipal land so granted was rented, or given out by lot, subject to an annual tax imposed by the council, — "the opinion of three intelligent men of honor being first taken." Each house-lot of one hundred varas square [1] cost the grantee six dollars and twenty-five cents for fees paid to the alcalde. Land required for warehouses and other edifices was reserved by the authorities.

Aug. 9, 1834, the long series of efforts to secularize the missions, and convert them into pueblos, of which we

[1] The vara is the Mexican yard of thirty-two inches and four-tenths. It is still in use in real-estate transactions in San Francisco.

have previously spoken, and which had extended over so many years, culminated in the "provisional regulations" of Governor Figueron, providing for the secularization of ten of the missions.[1] The new pueblos were given alcaldes and councils. Appointed commissioners took charge of the mission-property, and made classified inventories. They explained to the Indians, "with suavity and patience," that the missions had been converted into pueblos; that they were only subordinate to the priest in matters spiritual; and that each one must work, maintain, and govern himself, "without dependence on any one." A few large Indian *rancherias*, distant from the missions, were allowed to form separate pueblos; but these were failures.

Thus, as we have seen, the system that prevailed during the early part of this century underwent many changes. Once the territory had been divided into four provinces, — San Diego, Santa Barbara, Monterey, and San Francisco, — each with a commandante,[2] and the seat of government of each being named a presidio. About it were tracts of land reserved for the use of

---

[1] The Cortes of Spain first mentioned secularization in a decree of Jan. 4, 1813, in reference to Buenos Ayres; saying, "Steps will soon be taken to reduce vacant and other lands to private ownership." Sept. 13, they ordered the Buenos Ayres Indians to choose representatives to meet the governor's agents, and distribute the mission-lands. In January, 1831, the governor of California issued a decree based on these Acts of 1813; but clearly illegal, and so at once recalled. Agitation continued till 1833, when appeared the general Act under which the regulations of 1834 were passed.

[2] We have before alluded to the commandante. He is a classic figure in early California life. Cases from alcalde-courts and from missions were often referred to him. He held his appellate court with great dignity, — a naked sword on one side of his chair, and a silver-headed cane on the other. The sword awed the simple Indians and Mexicans; the cane was a perpetual writ of summons, sent to a man's door to call him as witness, or carried through the village to bring young and old to the court-room.

the king's soldiers, and called *rancherias*.[1] The missions held all they chose of the remaining territory. By 1835 there were secularized missions, ruled spiritually by priests, temporally by government administrators called major-domos in the Act of 1840; free towns or pueblos, ruled by officers of their own election; and private estates, controlled with almost manorial powers by lordly Spanish dons owning *ranchos* or *haciendas*. When Americans began to acquire property in the pueblos, a knowledge of their laws was essential; and many land-titles long depended on the pueblo records and procedure.[2]

Historically, the most important of the pueblos was that of Yerba Buena, at first a mere *embarcadero*, or landing-place, for boats of fishermen and hide-drogers; which grew up near the Mission of Dolores and the presidio of San Francisco, absorbed both, took the name of the latter, and has since grown into the largest city on the eastern shores of the Pacific. San José and Los Angeles have also had great prosperity, and prove, in American hands, that "the ancient and honorable pueblos" from which they sprung were admirably located.

The early courts of the State of California recognized and confirmed titles received from the pueblos, and sustained their rights to common and municipal lands.[3] In the case of the pueblo of San Francisco,

[1] The word has fallen from its high estate. A *rancheria* is now only a collection of Indian huts.

[2] "Pueblos could be formed by discharged soldiers, or by a grant to a chief colonist, or to twelve or more families, or by a presidio being established, or by the secularization of a mission" (Welch *vs.* Sullivan, 8 Cal. Rep., p. 165).

[3] Case of Welch *vs.* Sullivan, 8 Cal. Rep. Also Hart *vs.* Burnett, 15 Cal. Rep.

the centre of the old presidio square was made the initial point for a survey of the four square leagues to which the town was entitled as successor to the rights of the pueblo of Yerba Buena.[1] It was decided, under American law, that the lands of a pueblo were not subject to seizure or sale under execution.[2] The power of granting pueblo lands was usually vested in the alcalde, as before stated, but sometimes needed the approval of the *ayuntamiento*, or sometimes of the people of the pueblo. If there was no alcalde, a justice of the peace, in American days, granted lots. In all these cases, specific rules and restrictions were observed. The authorities, for instance, could only grant or lease small house-lots, or garden-lots of two hundred varas square. Certain lands could not be sold, mortgaged, nor alienated, even to pay municipal expenses.[3]

Under Mexican rule, the petition required to be sent to the alcalde must set forth that the petitioner was a citizen of Mexico, a resident of the pueblo, desired to use and possess a certain unoccupied tract, and would proceed to make certain improvements. The land was usually granted at once. The expenses of the proceeding varied at different times from five to twenty dollars.[4] The opportunities and perquisites of the office of alcalde were fully appreciated in later times by some of the American incumbents, who granted tracts outside of pueblo bounds, and seriously complicated land-titles. The American military governors of California had various difficulties on this score with the

---

[1] Payne and Dewey *vs.* Treadwell, 16 Cal., 220.

[2] Fulton *vs.* Hanlon, 20 Cal. Rep., 450.

[3] 1 Cal. Rép., 306. Also cases of Redding *vs.* White, 27 Cal. Rep., 282; Branham *vs.* San José, 24 Cal., 585.

[4] Petition of Rosalie Haro, of Yerba Buena Pueblo, to Alcalde Padilla (before American conquest), 1 Cal. Rep., 323.

pueblos of San Francisco, Sonoma, San José, Monterey, and Santa Barbara. So far as was consonant with justice, the grants made during this period were sustained. The rights of San Francisco were continuously recognized from 1835 to 1850, except that certain grants made in 1849 by a justice of the peace were set aside as invalid.[1]

In the Mexican system as known in California after 1837, the alcalde was chief officer in all towns, and always presided over the town-councils when such existed. As late as 1850 he retained the right of granting town-lots.

The preceding notes upon the pueblos have thus led by natural steps to a full consideration of this chief office of the pueblo, — the Mexican-Spanish alcaldeship. Several times in the progress of this study, we have found it necessary to use the term, and allude to the office. Alcaldes ruled the Darien colonists and the Darien mining-camp; they found a place in Mexican mine-towns, and Mexican pastoral communities. Transplanted to Alta California, the office still preserved its unique character, and continued its development towards higher forms. At last the American miners for a time adopted the name and the institution, transferring it from the towns of the coast to the camps of the Sierra. We must, in a separate chapter, consider the historical evolution of this office in Spain, in Mexico, and in California. How was it that a local officer of the Spanish civil system became the most important of institutional contributions from Spanish America to Germanic America? How was it that the freedom of the people to choose their own alcaldes was often

[1] Cohas vs. Raisin, 3 Cal. Rep., 443.

greater in California than in Mexico? To answer these questions, we must consider the nature and scope of the office in its varied forms, and throughout its eventful career. We must turn to the caliphate of Cordova and the three Christian kingdoms of northern Spain.

CHAPTER VIII.

A STUDY OF ALCALDES.

THE heart of the Spanish local system is the alcaldeship. We must, however, turn to the fruitful Orient for the origin of the office: it is, in fact, the *kadi* of Persia and Arabia, the *alkaid* of the Saracens and Moors; it is also the village judgeship of Spain in its heroic age, when Aragon possessed the most liberal constitution in Europe.[1] Art, romance, and literature have loved to linger over the picturesque features of this office; tales of the East, and peasant-songs of the Spanish peninsula, alike describe the "judge of the village," whose power for good or evil was almost unlimited.

The very forms that the word has taken in the Spanish language are evidences of the universality and importance of the thing itself. An *alcaidia* is a town-warden, or governor of a town, or it is the district of his jurisdiction; his wife is the *alcaidesa;* the duty anciently levied on all cattle driven across the district

---

[1] In Aragon, the citizens of the free towns, or pueblos, had provincial laws, organized guilds, and elected alcaldes. They chose deputies to the *cortes*, or legislative council; and this council elected the supreme judge, or *justicia*, levied taxes, and appointed minor officers. Aragon, Valencia, Castile, and Catalonia held *cortes* of three estates, — prelates, nobles, and deputies. Leon in 1188 assembled the first council of elected deputies. Barcelona grew from the Spanish *Mark* established by Karl the Great, and became independent in the days of Charles le Chauve.

or through the town was the *alcaida;* the *alcaiceria* was
the market-place. These are earlier forms, and point to
wider sway, and even greater powers, than the modern
alcaldes ever possessed. The true alcalde was judge of
the town, and *ex-officio* mayor of the council. To be
given *alcalda*, was to receive the protection of some
powerful citizen or great nobleman; the office itself is
the *alcaldia;* the judge's wife is the *alcaldesa;* lastly,
as a term of contempt, anger, or sarcasm, applied to any
absurd or hasty action, we have the word *alcaldada.*

Pleadings before the Spanish alcaldes were oral; and
proceedings were summary, and in all ordinary cases
were final. Even in very important trials, an appeal
was infrequent; for to carry it farther meant to become
entangled in the Spanish courts of record, a worse fate
than to drift into the delays of the English chancery
courts. In one of the mediæval Spanish romances, a
peasant says, " Yonder stone wall will rot ere thy law-
suit ends."

Under the Spanish laws, the alcaldes were the con-
ciliators of disputes, and the head men of the village,
responsible to higher authority for the behavior of those
under their charge.

Wherever the descendants of Spain went, they took
the main features of the alcalde-system to which they
were accustomed : the silver-headed official staff of the
alcalde was planted beside the cross of the Jesuit missionaries and the Franciscan friars. We have previously
spoken of alcaldes in the colonies of Cuba and Darien :
alcaldes also accompanied the soldiers of De Soto and
Narvaez. When Cabeza de Vaca, afterwards pioneer
explorer of New Mexico, declined to accept command
of the fleet of Narvaez, it was an alcalde who took the
position. The alcaldes of that period were soldiers and

judges by turn, leaders of expeditions, and governors of new colonies. Don Diego Peñalosa, one of the most adventurous Spanish knights of the seventeenth century, was in succession alcalde of La Paz, alcalde of Cuzco, and provincial alcalde of all the La Paz provinces.[1]

So soon as Mexico was conquered, division into districts and the planting of pueblos began, to each of which an alcalde was appointed, vacancies being afterwards filled by election. The powers and duties of the office were probably much the same as at the present time; except that, so long as the mining-courts existed, no alcalde had any jurisdiction over mining-cases. He could not even give a title to mineral-lands; this right, as we have already seen, being vested in the "mining-deputation" of the provinces. In 1812 the Spanish *cortes* extended municipality privileges to all Mexican villages of fifty or more inhabitants, and provided that several hamlets could be united politically for town government; that is, under an alcalde, for no council was considered necessary in such cases.

One of the most interesting and primary duties of the Mexican village alcalde was that of arbitration in all minor disputes. *Conciliacion* was recognized as a part of the mining-law: it also belonged in the civil code. No trial could take place until the alcaldes (always known in this capacity as *hombres buenos*) had tried to settle it equitably, and to the satisfaction of both parties without expense to either. "Each alcalde," the law said, "shall have a book, called the 'Book of *Conciliacions*,' in which to keep a record of all cases, and of the means taken to prevent litigation." But "ecclesiastical, mili-

[1] Shea's Peñalosa Quivira Expedition.

tary, and municipal cases, and those that affect public revenues," were not subjects for *conciliacion* and compromise. The ceremony of arbitration as a necessary prelude to all lawsuits was first disregarded, in California, in February, 1850.[1] The Spanish principle of *conciliacion* is doubtless a gift of Roman jurisprudence. The eighth section of the fourth book of the Pandects lays down the principles almost exactly as now accepted in Mexico. Some of the old provincial laws of France provided for " arbiters." The principle is recognized as of great importance in international law, to settle difficulties and prevent war.

There was a form of local and special alcaldeship first known to Mexico during the sixteenth century, that has, in modified forms, become a part of Western life in the United States. Yearly the village alcalde and the council (if one existed) chose two or more *alcaldes de mesta*, who presided over the semi-annual assemblages of the live-stock owners. This custom was carried wherever Spanish colonists went. In California these officers were known as *jueces del campo* (" judges of the plain "). They were obliged to be present at all the annual *rodeos*, or meetings on horseback in the open fields, for the purpose of collecting and branding all the live-stock of the district. These *rodeos* were the most important celebrations known to the Spanish Californians. Every *ranchero* and *vaquero* was on hand with whirling *riata* and gayly caparisoned mustang. The *jueces* were often called upon to settle disputes about the ownership of cattle, the identity of brands, and similar matters ; and they were very useful and dignified officials. From the first, the Californians ap-

---

[1] Von Schmidt *vs.* Huntington, 1 Cal. 55.

pear to have elected their own *jueces;* and several
times Americans were chosen before 1846. During the
military occupation of the territory, the office of *jueces*
continued; Americans serving in Los Angeles, Monterey, and San José. When the first legislature of the
State of California met, it passed, on the last day of
its session (April 20, 1850), a bill repealing all the old
Spanish laws "except the laws of the *jueces del campo*."
For years after, and, indeed, as long as any *rodeos* were
held in the pastoral regions of California, local judges
to decide disputes were chosen. As late as 1870, a visitor to San Luis Obispo County saw American and
Spanish cattle-raisers holding *rodeos*, and submitting
peaceably to the decisions of three "judges of the plain"
chosen from among their number on the first day of the
rodeo. The great plains of California have all been
fenced, and are being sown with wheat and planted with
vines, so that the annual *rodeo* is now an extinct institution. But in Western Texas, New Mexico, Colorado,
and northward, wherever great cattle-ranges are found
to-day, the stock-men, in their picturesque and exciting
"round-ups," still follow the ancient Spanish plan; not
knowing that it is a heritage from a race they despise,
they choose "cattle-judges," to settle disputes, and up-
hold their decisions as final.

The strange vitality of that nomad institution, the
alcalde de mesta, is explained by the fact that it was
perfectly adapted to the needs of a pastoral community,
as much to cattle-owners and cow-boys as to *rancheros*
and *vaqueros*. But the fixed and permanent office of
the true town-alcalde has proved hardly less enduring,
and is certainly much more instructive to the student
of institutions.

The Mexican alcaldeship of to-day is much the same

office that the first Spanish colonists knew. It is a
good working combination of justice of the peace, town-
constable, town-recorder; it involves a sponsorship before the law; it possesses a sort of patriarchal authority.
In each village, the power of the alcalde is supreme: his
will is exercised over the in-coming and the out-going,
the eating and the sleeping, the toil and the recreation,
of every inhabitant. Each traveller visits him to make
inquiries, to secure bargains, or to settle disputes with
his servants or guides. Questions the most trivial are
asked in the same breath with questions the most stu-
pendous: to this Indian he quotes the market-price of
onions, and to that blushing señorita gives advice concerning rival suitors. He has social privileges and political power. He is the chief overseer of local interests.
If a travelling show wishes to visit the town, it usually
bribes the alcalde to permit it to exhibit there, and the
village priest to announce it from his parish pulpit. The
messengers of the king used to carry letters of commen-
dation to the alcaldes along their route. The simple
and ignorant peasants have personal dealings with few
other officials. Fear and reverence encircle the throne
of this little autocrat, the alcalde, to whom every conceivable difficulty is brought for solution. For these
reasons, the office is one of the most interesting, primeval, and romantic of yet surviving Spanish institutions
upon the continent. [1]

The rule of the alcalde in California was never so
firmly established or so despotic as in Mexico, but it
was always of greater importance than its nominal
rights and duties would seem to justify. The powers

[1] Books of travel teem with allusions. Mr. D. S. Richardson of
California, the private secretary of Minister Foster, in Mexico, writes to
me giving an account of the alcalde's importance in village-life.

authorized by the decree of March 20, 1837, were supplemented and increased by the weight of local custom; for alcaldes had existed in California since the first pueblo was founded.

This decree of 1837 re-organized the judiciary of California, providing for courts of *conciliacion*, or lower alcalde-courts, for courts of first instance, courts of second instance, courts of third instance, and final appeals to the Mexican supreme court. But the revolutions and political difficulties in Alta California, then and thereafter, prevented the practical adoption of any such system: it simply remained a dead letter. The powers which it gave the alcalde were less than that officer really exercised. An enumeration of these powers, though suggestive and useful, must therefore be accompanied with a statement of the alcalde's unwritten duties.

"Alcaldes," it is provided in this decree, "shall secure good order;" shall execute the laws of the prefects; shall call for a military force, or upon the citizens for help, when needed; shall see that the residents of the town live by useful occupation; shall reprimand idle, vicious, and vagabond persons; shall preside over council meetings, and vote there; and may impose fines of not more than twenty-five dollars.

Jurisdiction over mining-claims was expressly withheld from the California alcaldes, and was left to the mining-deputation of the nearest province, Sonora.

The large towns were given three alcaldes, six *regidors*, and two *syndicos;* the nine forming the *ayuntamiento*, and the senior alcalde presiding. These officers were to be elected yearly; but the office-holding power was not limited, and it was declared that "no one must refuse to serve without having the governor's permission to retire." Certain officers of the government were prohibited from being members of the *ayuntamiento*.

The same Act of 1837 defines the duties of this council. It was to have charge of the streets and the cemeteries, of sanitary affairs, of prisons and hospitals, of the inspection of drugs, liquors, and provisions. It was to act as a committee of charity in case of pestilence; was to keep a record of births, marriages, and deaths; was to provide for market-places, straight paved streets, bridges, parks, and public fountains. One of its duties was that of "making contracts for all sorts of diversions," such as public games and shows. It was empowered to establish schools, and pay the teachers out of the municipal funds. Lastly, it was required "to be impartial to all citizens, rich or poor," to protect the weights and measures, to expend public moneys honestly, and to report annually to the governor. Each member of the *ayuntamiento* was responsible for mal-administration or malfeasance. When elected, they were sworn in by the prefect, or by a former alcalde.

In some of the Mexican towns, the councils were doubtless burdened with most of the duties described in the previous paragraph. In California towns, the council seldom met, since the office was not salaried; and the alcalde performed most of its functions, perhaps ordering a "horn-burning" in the pueblo square as a sufficient sanitary measure when unusual sickness prevailed.

A subsequent Act of 1837 restored certain powers to the alcalde. In the departments of California, New Mexico, and Tabasco, he was empowered to perform the functions of judge of first instance in all districts

where there were no such judges; and this was afterwards sustained by the American courts.[1]

But in most instances the alcaldes were even more
than "judges of first instance." The disordered condition of California gave the office greater power, but at
the same time rendered its tenure more precarious, than
the Mexican Government had contemplated. We have
before alluded to these disasters in speaking of the
sudden wreck of the missions, and the scattering of
the Indians. Bands of wandering trappers descended
into the valleys; the Russians had settled at Bodega
and Fort Ross; and the Americans in the country
aided Gen. Solis in his unsuccessful rebellion of 1830.
Minor disturbances followed, and the Indians raided
outlying *ranchos*. American rifles decided the success
of Alvarado's revolution of 1836–38; and from that time
the American party began to organize, much as it did
in Texas, aided in the downfall of Alvarado, and the
success of Micheltorena in 1842. By 1845 the corrup-
tion of his government caused a new rebellion, headed
by Castro, Pio Pico, and others; and Micheltorena was
deposed. The American settlers in the Sacramento
valley, and near Sonoma, soon had reason to believe
that movements were on foot to drive them out; and
they organized the noted "Bear Flag" battalion, commanded by Captains Ide and Grigsby, which thrust
Castro from the Sonoma and Sacramento valleys, and
was on the eve of proclaiming a republic when Fremont
and Stockton came to their aid.

While such political changes were in progress, the
alcalde's tenure of office became precarious, because any
district or town that wanted an alcalde preferred to

[1] Mena *vs.* Le Roy, 1 Cal. Rep., 216; also Panaud *vs.* Jones, 1 Cal.
Rep., 448. See 1 Cal. Rep., 559, appendix, on general alcalde system.

choose him for an indefinite period. Since the alcalde made his own laws, and saw them enforced according to his own methods, an unpopular law or a disagreeable decision speedily caused discontent, and sometimes ended in an appeal to the governor, or even in a *pronunciamiento* and a public assembly, taking the alcaldeship away, and ordering a new election. This was done, in some instances, before the American conquest.

In practice, the only judge above the California alcalde was the governor of the province, who could grant tracts of agricultural or pastoral lands in much the same way as the alcalde could grant town-lots, except that the papers and applications had to be forwarded to Mexico for final approval. Castro, Alyarado, and Pio Pico granted so many "concessions," that, in some cases, a single tract was given several owners, each showing equal title to the whole. Nominally there was a veto-power vested in the governor's council, called by courtesy a "departmental legislature;" but, under the governors we have mentioned, large tracts were given away, unchecked even by Mexico. American courts sifted and tested these grants, refusing to confirm a large number on the grounds of illegality according to Mexican law.[1] After 1837 the governor held the only true appellate court in California.

We have spoken of the "Book of *Conciliacions*" that was kept by each alcalde. Besides this, he kept a "Book of Verbal Processes," recording his judgments therein; also, and of more importance, he was compelled, according to the "Plan of Pitic," a Spanish law of 1789, to record all the grants of lands made by him within the pueblo bounds, to have them signed

---

[1] Cases of Ferris *vs.* Coover, 10 Cal. Rep.; Berryessa *vs.* Schultz, 21 Cal. Rep.; Waterman *vs.* Smith, 13 Cal. Rep.; and others.

and attested (though without seals), and a copy delivered to the petitioner. These books of record kept by alcaldes during the Spanish era, and previous to the organization of the State, were received as evidence of land-titles on proof that the signatures of the alcalde and clerk (*syndicos*) were genuine.[1] An alcalde deed to land was not void because no consideration was expressed, nor were transfers of property which he made compelled to have a price mentioned.[2]

The old Spanish forms of wills were extremely simple; and an alcalde, though appointed as executor, could authenticate the document in his judicial capacity, if only he was not named in the will as heir or legatee, nor derived any compensation for administering it. The will of Anastasio Alviso of the pueblo of San José, dated Sept. 19, 1846, contains a list of "passive debts" such as, "I declare that I owe Señora Romero seven hides;" also a list of "active debts" such as, "I declare that Vicente Monez shall pay for the kitchen utensils whatever he in his conscience shall think proper to deliver over."[3] Primitive habits of life are manifest in every line of such quaint documents, in spirit centuries removed from the California of to-day, though written less than forty years ago.

During the military rule of the American officers, who governed California before it was yielded by treaty to the United States, the powers of the alcaldes were much limited in the coast-towns, though almost as extensive as ever in places where no military were stationed.

---

[1] Cases of Touchard *vs.* Keyes, 21 Cal. Rep.; and Downer *vs.* Smith, 24 Cal. Rep. Halleck says that Governor Pio Pico made antedated land-grants, and inserted them in the blank leaves of record-books.

[2] Merle *vs.* Mathews, 26 Cal., 455.

[3] Panaud *vs.* Jones, 1 Cal. Rep.

In 1847, before the close of the war, while General Kearney was military governor, he appointed alcaldes whenever vacancies occurred, exercised close supervision over their acts, and removed them whenever he saw fit. He directed the alcalde of San José, John Barton, to dismiss a suit that the Mexican courts had already decided; he advised John Nash, alcalde of Sonoma, that a writ of restitution he had issued in an ecclesiastical case was illegal; he sent word to H. D. Fitch, alcalde of San Diego, empowering him to fine, imprison, or both, certain unruly persons.

When Colonel Mason succeeded General Kearney as military governor of California, he announced that "the alcaldes are not authorities of the United States, nor are they Mexican authorities. They are the civil magistrates of California, and therefore the authorities of California within their respective jurisdictions, subject to removal from office by order of the governor." He authorized them "to continue in the practice and custom of the country," and to grant lots within the town-limits, but construed the word "grant" to mean "sell for the benefit of the municipality." The alcaldes were not to perform the marriage ceremony in cases where either of the contracting parties was a Roman Catholic.

About this time the spirit of change and uncertainty prevailed in many places, and there were numerous instances of violation of property-rights. Squatters were taking possession of lands near the missions San José and Santa Clara, where, the previous winter, they had been permitted to occupy some old buildings. The San José alcalde was ordered to remove them. Troops were sent to the disputed lands; but a compromise was effected, and the settlers agreed to pay a small rent until the true limits of the mission-property should be ascertained.

The authority of the alcalde, in all cases between citizen and citizen, was decided to be the same as under the Mexican law, and to include minor cases in which citizens and soldiers were involved. An officer was reprimanded in 1848 for interfering in such a case, and for "sending a file of soldiers to rescue a disputed saddle from the alcalde's *juzgado*."

Indian troubles occurring in September, 1847, regulations were issued that all peaceable Indians should procure protection papers from the alcaldes of their respective districts. In December a letter from Colonel Mason urges the Indian agent to have them appoint alcaldes among themselves for their own better government. A later proclamation imposed a fine of one hundred dollars on persons convicted before an alcalde of selling liquor to Indians.

During October, 1847, a sailor who had stabbed the mate of the ship "Vesper" was turned over to the alcalde of San Francisco for trial. "In the old alcalde courts of California," Colonel Mason writes, "the alcalde tried such cases; and when the sentence was death, the governor either ordered the execution, or sent the case to Mexico for further advice." Some time in November, one Anastacio Ruiz of San Vicente, San Diego County, charged with murder, was tried before a jury of twelve presided over by the alcalde, Colonel Mason authorizing them to inflict capital punishment. He was probably acquitted, as the case is not again mentioned in the California Documents.

Although the acting governor had appointed alcaldes to fill all vacancies, yet in most cases he asked the people of the district to signify by petition their preferences. In 1847 native Californian alcaldes were in charge in only four or five towns on the coast. Everywhere else Americans ruled. At Sonoma a town-council was elected, and the alcalde issued certificates of election. At San José the town-council of six was twice voted for, and considerable difficulty followed; but the matter was settled by the appointment of a committee of three to examine the returns.

Dec. 20, 1847, an American alcalde who applied for information was told by Colonel Mason, that, "in cases of horse-stealing, a fine, and hard labor on public works, and in aggravated cases fifty lashes in addition, is in accordance with the old California practice." A month or so later, a commercial case, tried in San José before an alcalde and a jury of six men, was appealed to Colonel Mason, who denied it on the ground that there was no higher court.

San José pueblo at this time had two alcaldes, the first being an American, the other a Spaniard. These two officers appointed a town treasurer, who gave bonds, and at once entered upon the discharge of his duties.

The alcalde of San Luis Obispo, early in 1848, organized a party of thirty settlers to check the depredations of Indians who had been stealing cattle, and acted as their leader. Colonel Mason offered to furnish them ammunition if called upon to do so.

In March, 1848, there was but one alcalde, Elam Brown, in all the "Contra Costa and San Joaquin region," a territory some hundreds of miles in extent. Stephen Cooper had just been appointed alcalde at Benicia, the new town north of Carquinez Straits.

The various alcaldes in California were notified by Colonel Mason, that "notes and accounts contracted in the United States cannot be legally enforced and collected in California until the United States shall organize a territorial government in this country, and extend her laws over the same." No debts made elsewhere could be collected in California until the State constitution was in full operation.

By the close of October, 1848, the evil effect of the immigration caused by the gold excitement began to be shown in some places. Several murders were committed. Three men were tried by an alcalde and jury at San José pueblo, for robbery and attempted murder of two returned miners, found guilty, and promptly executed. Colonel Mason wrote: "I shall not disapprove of this course, and shall only endeavor to secure to every man charged with a capital crime a fair trial by a jury of his countrymen." A Mr. Reed and his entire family, ten persons in all, were murdered at Mission San Miguel; and the perpetrators were captured, tried before an alcalde jury, and hung. Other murders occurred; and some of the accused were given jury-trial, some were tried before an alcalde without a jury, some were lynched.

The most important alcaldeship in California, and that which probably contains the most complete and valuable records, was that of San Francisco. Its history from the days of the marine pueblo or *embarcadero* of Yerba Buena, established in 1833, to the days when the last alcalde under the military governors resigned his position, and was re-elected as the first mayor under the State laws and legislative Act of Incorporation, will sufficiently show the continuity of the office, and the importance of its archives.[1] No order actually

[1] The Spanish archives kept in San Francisco are the basis of many valuable real-estate rights. They embrace the *expediente* or record of proceedings; the petitions, maps, decree, and *titulo* or title-deed of nu-

announcing the establishment of the pueblo was ever issued; but its existence was assumed through all the changes, revolutions, and confusion of the last years of Mexican rule, as amply shown in Hon. J. W. Dwinelle's argument for the pueblo land-titles.

Nov. 27, 1835, the people of Dolores Mission held their first election, and chose J. J. Estudillo as alcalde. There was then but one dwelling, the tent of an English trader named Richardson, on the Yerba Buena cove. An adventurous American, Jacob P. Leese, procured, after much difficulty, permission to lay out a new town, and by July 4, 1836, had built a shanty of rough boards as a trading-house for the *rancheros* about the bay. The only other building in the vicinity was an Indian *temiscal*, or sweat-house. The presidio contained no garrison, and only one resident, a superannuated soldier named Pina. The rule of Alcalde Estudillo extended over the entire peninsula; but he lived upon an extensive ranch on the southern shore of the bay, in what is now Alameda County, and spent little time at mission or pueblo. Extreme simplicity of life and manners prevailed among the inhabitants.

Several changes in the alcaldeship took place; and in 1839 the franchises, books, and papers of presidio, mission, and pueblo, appear to have come into the possession of J. P. Guerrero, the alcalde, who assumed jurisdiction over all except the immediate possessions of the Mission Dolores. All the grants made by this alcalde before the war have been held by American

merous grants; the formal books *Tamas del razon* of 1828; the Jimeno Index, or list of grants, and its continuation, the Hartnell Index; and the evidences of the approval of the departmental legislation. There are five hundred and seventy-nine complete Spanish grants, and three hundred and fourteen incomplete or inchoate ones, recorded in these archives.

courts to have been made in the course of his ordinary duties. After the American ships took possession, General Kearney appointed Washington Bartlett as magistrate and justice, and gave him the right to give away town-lots; also, a little later, ordered the sale of certain water-lots. These orders constitute the earliest American titles to real estate in San Francisco. The title of the United States to the public domain was held to relate back to the time of the occupancy of the country,[1] when Mexican laws ceased, except as re-established by military authorities, as they were in most cases.

Alcalde Bartlett, and his successors Hyde and Leavenworth, exercised control over San Francisco affairs at a turbulent period. As soon as the war closed, Colonel Mason, and his successor General Peter Riley, attempted to unite the civil and military functions of government; and an anomalous condition of affairs followed. There was, for a time, nothing to set things in motion; and neither law nor administration of justice existed except so far as exemplified in the alcalde courts, which had known no checks and had taken no vacations. San Francisco was growing rapidly; and the local customs and simple code of a rude Mexican population, known in written forms to but few, chiefly dependent on verbal processes and instantaneous decisions, were suddenly required to fulfil the complex and varying needs of an active and enterprising people, carrying on immense business transactions, and sincerely anxious to base them on the laws of the United States. Governor Mason by proclamation enforced the Mexican civil law in its main features, and set Messrs. Halleck and Hart-

---

[1] See Woodworth *vs.* Fulton, 1 Cal. Rep., 295; Reynolds *vs.* West, 1 Cal. Rep., 333.

nell at work to make a translation and digest of such
parts of the laws of 1837 as were judged applicable, and
still in force.[1] The people, accepting all this as a sad
but inevitable necessity, began to struggle towards
local organizations and a State government.

During this unsettled period, the "judge of first instance," or alcalde, sat each day in the little school-
room on the plaza of San Francisco, trying cases, and
rendering that speedy justice that was then more desirable than exact justice, since men's time, in those
early days of 1849, was worth from sixteen dollars to
one hundred dollars per day. The judge listened to
brief arguments, announced his decision, took his fees,
and called up another case: hardly once in a hundred
times was there any thought of an appeal to the governor at Monterey. Criminal jurisprudence, however,
was in decidedly a bad way: neither jails, district funds,
nor city organization existed; so that sheriffs, guards,
and other officers had to serve without pay, and seldom, until the community was fully roused, could a
trial be had in cases demanding capital punishment.
For lesser crimes, lashes or hard labor on the streets
could always be imposed.

The powers of the alcalde increased apace, and various difficulties between that officer and two rival town-
councils early in 1849 culminated in the formation of
an independent organization called "The Provisional
Government of San Francisco."[2] Its chief feature was a

[1] Ready for publication in July, 1849, pp. 40. Printed in the appendix to Debates in the Convention of California. J. Ross Browne, 1850.
Washington.

[2] Early in 1849 the citizens of Sonoma and of Sacramento had elected
similar district assemblies. In San Francisco, Feb. 12, the people to the
number of five hundred assembled, organized, adopted a plan of government, appointed an election-day, and asked the council and alcalde
to resign.

legislature of fifteen members. They met March 5, 1849, and swore "to support the Constitution of the United States and the government of this district." They organized for business, began to make laws, and took the records of the town from Alcalde Leavenworth, with whom there was great dissatisfaction, and who had refused to resign as requested. It was a government *de facto*.

March 10 they addressed a letter to Major-General Persifor F. Smith, in which they pointed out the fact that the civil institutions of California were "neither Mexican nor American," but nondescript; that many ministerial and judicial offices of the pure Mexican system had been allowed to sink into disuse; and that the only office retained was that of alcalde, which office "had been permitted to obtain and exercise a most extensive and unlimited jurisdiction, wholly incompatible with the dictates of reason and justice. The right of appeal to the military governor has been denied or evaded." "Undoubtedly," the committee added, "this office of alcalde was continued" (through the interregnum) "by the presumed consent of the people, and without any alteration, except that the right of appeal became inoperative. The jurisdiction, power, and duty of the office, partially limited by martial law, became, without it, unlimited and irresponsible. The tenure, duty, and property of the office, as existing under martial law, without any definite or prescribed rules, was continued so, and the people left without any law in the adjudication of every civil and criminal issue, except the mere will of this single officer," who is "elected by the people," and "has all public records in his hands," and "owns no superior tribunal," not even to "compel him to discharge his obligations with his fellow-citizens

as a private individual. . . . All the civil and criminal issues that come before him are determined according to his own notions of right and wrong, directed
and enforced by his mere will;" and, as this emphatic
document reiterates in closing, "without the right of
appeal." But Provisional-Governor Riley, to whom a
similar statement had been made, proclaimed the entire
proceeding illegal, and the legislature without authority,
forbade the payment of taxes to its subordinates, up-
held the alcalde, and ignored the complaints formulated
in the above letter to Major-General Smith. The alcalde
afterwards resigned; and a new election was ordered,
resulting in the choice of Mr. J. W. Geary. It was a
noteworthy struggle throughout, and the temper of the
citizens was admirable.

When a city government under the State Constitution was established, the alcaldeship, with its varied
powers, came to an end, and yielded up its ancient
authority. Alcalde Geary, the last of the San Francisco alcaldes, was re-elected Jan. 1, 1850, and in April
was chosen city mayor under its first charter. Thus
the institutional link was established : thus the office of
mayor of San Francisco derived its historical descent,
not from American and English sources, but from the
semi-despotic rulers of Spanish pueblos, and the trib-
ute-levying governors of mediæval towns of Castilian
frontiers. The term survives; and San Francisco, metropolis of the Pacific Coast, still cherishes the title
of "ancient and honorable pueblo."

The story of the alcaldeship in San Francisco was
repeated on a lesser scale in many other towns and
villages of California. Everywhere it was of fundamental importance during the transition era, and everywhere it presented remarkable minglings of Mexican and

American features. The alcaldes, whether elected or appointed, were usually honest and intelligent, anxious to deal out justice with an impartial hand, well sustained by the American settlers, and obeyed by the Mexicans. But the confusion of authorities was vexatious and amusing. Some offices contained only a few worn and smoky Spanish manuscripts, heirlooms of the last century; in some the codes of Iowa, Illinois, Missouri, South Carolina, and other States, were in constant use; in some were a few volumes of French, Spanish, German, or English law, that the new alcaldes had somehow obtained to add an air of impressiveness to the scantily furnished room.

Before leaving this subject, and passing to the broader field of the mining-camp, we must sum up and define the duties and powers of the typical alcalde. We have seen that he always wielded great power, and sometimes wielded sole authority throughout his district, in both civil and criminal cases; that he was the guardian of the common and town lands; that he summoned courts, and appointed minor municipal officers; that he exercised an almost parental supervision over the inhabitants of his pueblo. Studying his multifarious functions, we discover with admiration, not unmixed with awe, that one and the same person was often supreme judge, clerk of court, town-constable, sheriff, recorder, treasurer, justice of the peace, land-officer, government-agent in land deliveries,[1] superintendent of roads, town board of health, board of school-trustees, arbitrator in petty disputes, general advisory board for young and

---

[1] A petition for a land-grant was often, in Spanish times, referred by the governor to an alcalde to report on. The last of the steps in judicial procedure in land-grants was the formal delivery of the tract, along with a map, by the alcalde of the district in which it lay, after examining the bounds. This ceremony was akin to the "livery of seizin" of English common law. See also United States *vs.* Pico, 6 Wall. 536.

old, and even, near the coast, judge in admiralty to pro-
nounce upon all marine cases.　One and the same room
was often the police-court, probate-court, civil-court,
criminal-court, court of equity, court of appeal, land·
office, council-hall, and *conciliacion* court; it was also
bed-room, dining-room, kitchen, library, and drawing-
room of the busy, potent, and ubiquitous alcalde.　Stran-
gest fact of all in this unique combination, the lordly
alcalde palace which sheltered such an army of officials
was probably, in the mines at least, an edifice of canvas, with an empty nàil-keg for a chimney-top.　In the
pueblos of the coast, the alcalde assembled himself in
some old Mexican house, under yellow roofing-tiles
moulded years before by serfs of the mission, and beside priest-planted gardens of olive and orange.　One
American alcalde of the transition period lived and
held court in a house of zinc, whose outside measure-
ments were less than twelve feet in length and breadth.
The law in which these men dealt was as concentrated,
and free from waste and surplus, as were the houses in
which they dwelt.　The various functions of government were performed without clashing, by this happily
invented alcalde-system; judicial jealousies, and brow-
beating of lesser officers, were absolutely unknown.　In
the nature of the case, nothing could be less permanent
than such an all-containing office as that of the alcalde
in its prime; but nothing could well be more influential
and arbitrary while it lasted.　Its widest freedom and
its fullest development were not in the quiet pastoral
and agricultural districts of the coast, but in the midst
of the whirling excitements of the famous mining-camps
of '48 and '49.　The alcalde of the Sierra is the perfected American type; but so rich was the period, that
this forms but a small part of its institutional harvest.

CHAPTER IX.

CALIFORNIA CAMPS. — THE DAYS OF '48.

THE four preceding chapters have been devoted to a study of Spanish-American institutions, and their influences on early California. The remaining chapters of this work deal with the organization and government, by citizens of the United States, of large and isolated mining-camps; returning in some cases to primitive forms, sometimes using and modifying the Mexican alcaldeship, sometimes adopting methods suggested by New-England town-meetings, but always aiming to quell disorder, and protect property and life. They attempt to describe what manner of men these miners were, and with what customs, laws, and usages camp and district were ruled. They discuss the influence these miners exerted, directly and indirectly, upon the political organization of California; and the acceptance, in American jurisprudence, of principles originated by gold-diggers in the folk-moots of the Sierra.

One of the most entrancing chapters of this nineteenth century's eventful history is that which narrates the gold-discovery of 1848, the rush of anxious wealth-seekers to California, and the rapid growth of new institutional life among people thus assembled from all parts of the world. When American pioneers conquered the Mississippi Valley, they made it the stepping-stone to more difficult victories. The sons of the men who settled Kentucky and Ohio crossed the mighty river, and took possession of Iowa and Missouri: their sons, in turn, have made the term "West" no longer applicable to the great valley; they have even shattered the phrase into fragments, and so have given us the South-West of New Mexico and Arizona, the North-West of Idaho, Oregon, and the Puget-sound basin, the Central-West of Colorado, Utah, Nevada, and California. The all-compelling magnet which drew peaceful armies to these wastes and mountains of the western third of the continent, there to build great cities, there to organize prosperous communities and powerful States, was a flake of virgin gold found on a California hillside thirty-six years ago.

That was the year of revolutions in Europe; of barricades in Paris, Berlin, Vienna, Milan; of Louis Blanc's "ministry of progress," and Louis Napoleon's deceitful presidency; of students in arms, and petty princes abdicating in haste their pasteboard thrones; of liberal constitutions, national assemblies, and a Sclavonic congress; of Lombardy, Schleswig-Holstein, and Hungary in arms, the last, under the leadership of Kossuth, to make her death-struggle for freedom. On the Bourse, and in Lombard Street, the kings of the financial world were noting the signs of coming storm, even as the year began; but the event of most importance to the money-markets of Europe occurred unheralded before the "Revolution of February." Let us note the place and the manner of the occurrence. It was one hundred and seventy miles east of the Pacific Ocean; it was in the grizzly-haunted mountains of an obscure and neglected province only a few months before owned by Mexico, thinly populated by tribes of degraded Indians, idle Spanish-Americans, musical-tongued Kanakas, wander-

ing trappers, and a few Anglo-Saxon farmers and speculators; it was Jan. 19, 1848,* and about a fortnight before the actual signing of the Treaty of Guadalupe
Hidalgo, which gave the United States 522,955 square
miles of territory, including this obscure El Dorado, for
the trifling sum of fifteen million dollars. Some laborers,
on this California hillside, were digging a water-ditch to
supply a flour-mill** that was being built by the feudal-
like lord of a vast tract over which wild oats waved,
wild flowers bloomed, and herds of antelope roamed,
mingling undisturbed with bands of cattle and horses,
and even venturing at times within sight of the massive
oaken gates of the adobe-built fort where this active,
courtly, enterprising, and generous adventurer had
established his authority as lord of "New Helvetia."[1]

Captain Sutter, at that important era in early 1848,
swung his malacca cane, pulled his trim military mous-
tache, gave crisp orders to his Indian alcalde, his com-
mander of the troops, his general superintendent, his
manager of cattle, and his head farmer; paid his two
hundred laborers with pieces of tin stamped with numbers representing days' work, and redeemable at his
storehouses; kept open house for every traveller, explorer, or government official: he was, in a word, the
most vital, sinewy, and picturesque figure in all Alta
California, beside whose manliness the plotting, irasci-
ble, treacherous, dishonest governors who disgraced the

[1] Captain John A. Sutter in 1841 received from Governor Alvarado
a grant of eleven leagues in the Sacramento Valley, and built a fort
where the city of the same name now stands. He was commissioned
"representative of the government, and officer of justice on the northern
frontier." The comparison to the old courts palatinate is irresistible.
He purchased from the Russians their extensive claims on Bodega Bay,
and thus, perhaps, saved the United States from many subsequent diplo-
matic difficulties.

* Although James W. Marshall, the discoverer of gold, at one
time recalled the date of discovery as having been January 19,
most historians believe the true date to have been January 24.
The principal evidence for this is the diary of one of Marshall's

closing years of Mexican rule, sink into utter insignifi-
cance. His title appeared unimpeachable, his possessions
secure under the American flag, his colony enterprise
well managed and certain of success. But the discovery
of a flake of gold, lying concealed in the red hillside
soil twenty miles away, set forces in operation that
blighted and destroyed all his plans.

January nineteenth, while unconscious Sutter governed his little kingdom, the workmen at Coloma, having finished their ditch, lifted the water-gate; and the
clear mountain torrent leaped gurgling and foaming
along its new-cut channel, uncovering a piece of virgin
gold, — first recorded nugget of American California.[1]
This precious lump, smaller than the first joint of a
child's forefinger, gleamed in Marshall's mill-race, attracted human eyes, was tested in a locked room by
roused and excited men, and caused a rush that ended
Sutter's multifarious operations, bidding the hides rot
in his tanneries, his wheat fall to the earth ungathered,
his herds wander untended, and perish at the hands of
outlaws. The fame of this discovery drew to the spot,
with magic power, the population of the whole territory; so that, a few months later, but five men were
left in San Francisco, ships swung sailorless at anchor,
and soldiers deserted their colors. All Alta California
was concentrating in the mines. Thus the memorable
gold-rush began.

Soon the news went abroad to all the world. Piles
of California nuggets lay in the windows of banking-
houses, gazed at by thousands. The fact that in the
new placers unskilled, uneducated, and penniless men
were able to gather from fifty to five hundred dollars

---

[1] Small placers had been found by Mexicans near the coast in 1828,
1833, and 1838. See M. Castanare's letter to President of Mexico, 1844.

workmen, Henry W. Bigler. See Erwin G. Gudde, *Bigler's Chron-
icle of the West* (Berkeley and Los Angeles, 1962), pp. 86–98.
** It was a sawmill, not a gristmill that was being constructed.

in gold-dust, each day they worked, was calculated to produce a profound impression. Mockers were silenced, doubters were swept into the current. Before the close of the year, fifty thousand of the healthiest and most energetic young men of the nation were on their way to California. Meanwhile the five thousand men who were fairly at work in the mines in 1848 dug out over five million dollars in gold-dust. Numbers of small parties from Oregon arrived before July, but the vast body of gold-seekers known afterwards as the "Argonauts" did not reach the Pacific Coast until early in 1849. The organization of the smaller mining-communities of 1848 must be considered before we can discuss the more complex elements of later camps.

When, early in 1848, mining began at Coloma, near Sutter's Mill, Captain Sutter himself had alcalde powers over the region. That autumn Mr. Belt was elected alcalde at Stockton. The two thousand Americans who were living in California in February, 1848, were nearly all in the mines before the end of June; and most of them knew what an alcalde was, knew that they had no legal right to elect any other officer, and knew that Colonel Mason, the *de facto* governor, was the only other authority. But there was no general acceptance of Sutter as alcalde. Some of the very first miners attempted to own, hold, control, and rent to others, a large and valuable mineral-bearing tract. After paying rent for a short time, the new-comers, who were in the majority, began to equalize matters, and adopt laws respecting the size of "claims." Nothing in the early history of these camps is more evident than the unpremeditated and unsystematic nature of their first proceedings. Officers were never elected until they were needed to give an immediate decision. And, as we have

See California Historical Society, *California Gold Discovery. Centennial Papers on the Time, the Site and Artifacts* (*Special Publication* No. 21, San Francisco, 1947).

said, local customs in regard to the "amount of ground a man could mine" took form before officers were formally chosen. Every one knew that most of the land on which they worked was government land: the use of it belonged to all alike until such time as the government made other regulations. Equality of ownership was the only logical conclusion. Here, then, the laws of the camp had their beginning. Long before lawlessness and trouble with foreigners arose, long before the first California gold had reached New York, "claims" of a definite size were being measured out in the mining-camps for each gold-seeker. The ownership of land was the beginning of organization; its ownership in equal parts is significant of the form of society that prevailed, for an unconscious socialism it certainly was.

The mines put all men for once upon a level. Clothes, money, manners, family connections, letters of introduction, never before counted for so little. The whole community was substantially given an even start in the race. Gold was so abundant, and its sources seemed for a time so inexhaustible, that the aggrandizing power of wealth was momentarily annihilated. Social and financial inequalities between man and man were together swept out of sight. Each stranger was welcomed, told to take a pan and pick, and go to work for himself. The richest miner in the camp was seldom able to hire a servant; those who had formerly been glad to serve others were digging in their own claims. The veriest greenhorn was as likely to uncover the richest mine on the gulch as was the wisest of ex-professors of geology; and, on the other hand, the best claim on the river might suddenly "give out," and never again yield a dollar. The poorest man in camp could have a handful of gold-dust for the asking from a more successful neighbor, to give him another start, and help him "hunt for better luck." No one was ever allowed to suffer: the treasure-vaults of the Sierra were too near, and seemingly too exhaustless.

To a little camp of 1848 (so an old miner writes me) a lad of sixteen came one day, footsore, weary, hungry, and penniless. There were thirty robust and cheerful miners at work in the ravine; and the lad sat on the bank, watching them a while in silence, his face telling the sad story of his fortunes. At last one stalwart miner spoke to his fellows, saying, —

"Boys, I'll work an hour for that chap if you will."

At the end of the hour a hundred dollars' worth of gold-dust was laid in the youth's handkerchief. The miners made out a list of tools and necessaries.

"You go," they said, "and buy these, and come back. We'll have a good claim staked out for you. Then you've got to paddle for yourself." Thus genuine and unconventional was the hospitality of the mining-camp.

The early camps of California did more than merely to destroy all fictitious social standards. They began at once to create new bonds of human fellowship. The most interesting of these was the social and spiritual significance given to the partnership idea. It soon became almost as sacred as the marriage-bond. The exigencies of the work of mining-claims required two or three persons to labor together if they would utilize their strength to the best advantage. The legal con tract of partnership, common in settled communities, became, under these circumstances, the brother-like tie of "*pard*"-nership, sacred by camp-custom, protected by camp-law; and its few infringements were treated as crimes against every miner. Two men who lived together, slept together, took turns cooking, and washing their clothes, worked side by side in dripping claims, and made equal division of returns, were rightly felt to have entered into relationships other than commercial.

There soon were larger associations to work deep claims, or turn the channels of rivers; but each such association came into existence when it was needed, not a moment sooner. Nowhere in the mines was there any planning ahead: men were too busy, and time too precious, for that. The result was a degree and quality of unhampered, untroubled freedom, to which it is hard to find an historic parallel. Society, reduced to its original atoms, began to shape itself anew.

One of the elements in early camp-life consisted of "companies," or groups of associates who had come from the same place, or had travelled together for mutual comfort and protection. Many of these companies had organized, and made rules for their own government, before they left their homes. Some were from the coast-region, some from Oregon; and in 1849 many such parties arrived across the plains, or by sea. Sometimes these companies formed separate camps, sometimes only a group in a larger camp, but usually the bond of unity was preserved. The Oregonians "hung together" remarkably well, and exercised the best of influence. Some of them had helped to organize local government and a legislative body among the pioneer Americans in the Willamette Valley. Peter Burnett, who became the first governor of California, was one of the earliest to start from Oregon, where he had been a poor and hard-working farmer. He organized a large company among his neighbors, was chosen captain, and guided them to the mines.

Ryan, in his "Adventures in California," gives the

rules of a small mining-company of whom he was one. Slightly abbreviated, they read as follows: —

"(1) That we shall bear an equal share in all expenses.

"(2) That no man shall be allowed to leave the company without general consent till we reach the mines.

"(3) That any one leaving with our consent shall have back his original investment.

"(4) That we work together in the mines, and use our tools in common.

"(5) That each man shall retain all the gold he finds, but must contribute an equal portion of our daily expenses.

"(6) That we stand by each other.

"(7) That each man shall in turn cook, and do his share of the drudgery.

"(8) That any one guilty of stealing shall be expelled from tent and claim, with such other punishment as a majority of our company decide upon.

"(9) That no sick comrade be abandoned."

These rules, we observe, do not provide for an appeal to the general body of miners, nor do they recognize any higher court than the law of the majority of the company. It is the idea of family rule and family justice, as opposed to tribal authority or to the supremacy of the whole body of assembled freemen. But this tendency played little part in actual mining-life, though a few cases occurred where men were punished by their associates, no others interfering, not through indifference so much as because of acquiescence. The rule that "each man shall cook in turn" was probably supplemented by the unwritten proviso, still dear to Western camp-life, that "no man shall grumble at the cook's failures, under penalty of cooking for twice the usual period."

When we compare the rules of different companies organized to go to the mines, we find considerable variation. Quite a number provided for an equal division of all the gold found. This was certainly a spirit that many tendencies of camp-life developed, but there were opposing forces of much more powerful nature. That chiefly which in the "flush times" prevented any general acceptance of the idea of equal division of profits among all the miners of a group, or even of a camp, was the fact that men like to take risks, run chances, and have the intoxicating excitement of sudden gains. The miners of '48 believed with all their hearts that there was gold enough for all; that the turn of the poorest miner would come; but that, as they often said, "gold belongs to the finder, and to no one else."

Several of these companies formed to go to the mines provided for disbandment at the end of six months' labor. Quite a number forbade their members to use ardent spirits, except as medicine. Some arranged for a certain percentage of each member's gains to be paid over to the captain in trust for sick or unfortunate comrades. But enough has been said to give a general idea of their organization.

As soon as the great value of the mines was known, and crowds of persons began to hasten thither, the necessity for having "wholesome regulations and laws, with a view to the security of personal property and the prevention of disputes among those engaged in mining," began to present itself to the military authorities at Monterey. There were no disturbances in the mines, however: the only crimes reported were from the coast-region. But it was suggested that the entire mineral belt should be laid off in lots, by a public land-agent and a surveyor, and that they should then, under proper regulations, allow miners to occupy and work these lots, requiring them to pay a fee, or ground-rent, to the government. While this was under consideration, so many soldiers deserted, that the governor threatened to concentrate the remaining troops in the mining-districts, and take military possession. One company, stationed at Sonora, lost thirty-seven men out of sixty.

In July, 1848, there were about two hundred men at work on the American Fork, at " Mormon Diggings," twenty-five miles from Sutter's Fort. Colonel Mason and Lieutenant (now General) W. T. Sherman were making a tour of the mines; and the first official report about that region is dated at Monterey, Aug. 17, immediately after their return. Along the whole route, houses were vacant, and farms going to waste. At the lower mines, the hillsides were strewn with canvas tents and bush arbors. Some of the miners used tin pans, some used closely woven Indian baskets; but the greater part had a rude machine known as the cradle. This required four men to work it properly. A party thus employed averaged one hundred dollars a day. Mining-camps were fairly established on the American Fork, the South Fork, the Yuba, Feather, and Bear Rivers, and on various tributaries. Colonel Mason was informed that about four thousand men were at work in the entire gold-region. The labor was very hard, but all seemed prosperous. In many camps, two ounces was considered but an ordinary yield for a day's work. A small, shallow rock-channel, a hundred yards long and four feet wide, was pointed out, where two men had obtained seventeen thousand dollars in seven days. From another small ravine, twelve thousand dollars had been taken. The principal store at Sutter's Fort received, in payment for goods sold in nine weeks, some thirty-six thousand dollars in gold-dust. A company of seven miners hired fifty Indian helpers to carry gravel to the "cradles," worked seven weeks, and obtained two hundred and seventy-three pounds of pure gold; they paid off the Indians, and each of the seven partners had about thirty-seven pounds for his share. A private soldier who was given twenty days' furlough went to the mines, where in one week he made fifteen hundred dollars, with which he returned and reported himself for duty. The cash value of gold in the mines was twelve dollars per ounce; in trade, sixteen dollars.

These instances are from Colonel Mason's report to the Adjutant-General. He also relates an occurrence to which he was eye-witness. At Weber's brush-built store, a man picked up a box of seidlitz-powders, and asked its price; he was told that it only cost fifty cents, but was not for sale; he offered an ounce of gold, and was refused; but, promptly raising his offer to an ounce and a half, he bore off the desired article in triumph.

Colonel Mason gives the most decided testimony as to the good behavior of the community. Crimes were very infrequent: peace and order prevailed. He naïvely expresses his surprise that no thefts or robberies had been committed in the gold-district, although every one lived in tents, bush houses, or in the open air, and frequently had about their persons thousands of dollars' worth of gold. He makes no allusion whatever to any elected officers in the various camps.

It was a matter of serious reflection to him, how the rights of the government in the land could best be secured. Considering the character of the people engaged, he resolved not to interfere. He suggested two plans: one, to grant licenses to work tracts of ground of a hundred yards square, at rents of from a hundred dollars to a thousand dollars per year, at the discretion of an appointed superintendent; the other, to survey the district, and sell to the highest bidder, in tracts of twenty or forty acres. The latter plan he preferred, but no steps were ever taken to carry either of them into execution. In a later letter, he proposed levying a percentage on the gold found.

In August, Indian troubles led to the establishment of a small military post in the Sacramento region; but it exercised no supervision or authority over the camps of the miners, though it was situated on Bear River, near some of the richest placers. The next year troops were sent to Taylor's Ferry, on the Stanislaus, partly to quell Indian difficulties, and partly to prevent an apprehended collision between the Americans and the foreigners along the Tuolumne; but "the reports of hostilities had been greatly exaggerated." Throughout the various letters, proclamations, and official actions of the *de facto* governor of California in 1848, nothing is more evident than the complete way in which the mining communities were left to their own devices. Even General Riley in his visit, a year after Colonel Mason's, told the miners that "all questions touching the temporary right of individuals to work in particular localities of which they were in possession, should be left to the decision of the local authorities," meaning alcaldes and other officers by that time installed in many camps.

Letters from pioneers, and all printed accounts, agree in the general features of mining-life in the later months of the summer of 1848. Scattered over a large territory, the men of the various camps dwelt together in peace and good-fellowship, without any representatives of the United-States Government in their midst. Legal forms and judicial machinery were as nearly non-exist-

ent as it is possible to imagine in a civilized country.
The "social-contract" ideas of Rousseau and his followers seemed to have suddenly found a practical expression. The unwritten, unformulated law that ruled
each camp was the instinct of healthy humanity to mete
out equal justice to all. There was no theft, and no
disorder; few troublesome disputes occurred about
boundaries and water-rights. The miners assembled to
discuss in open meeting the size of claims that should
be allowed, and the will of the majority was cheerfully
accepted by the entire camp. The size, however, varied
materially: most of the early camps thought that ten
feet square was quite enough, or, in some cases, ten feet
in width on the stream, extending from the base of the
ravine to the centre of the channel; fifteen feet square,
twenty feet square, and more, were allowed in later
camps. Ardent prospectors used to tell stories of new-
found placers "where four by four was enough for a
claim," but no camp ever adopted so small a standard.

Definite bounds for the separate camps that afterwards became mining-districts did not at first exist.
No surveyors went out from the camp to mark its subject territory. The district grew simply and naturally
about the most convenient assembly-place, gulch, or
camp; so that, when fully organized, it conformed to
purely physical boundaries. A relief-map of the Sierra
region, with all the deposits of auriferous gravel accessi-
ble to the rude appliances of the early miners marked
in yellow, would show, at a glance, how imperious the
physical reasons were. One district must, by reason of
its position, include the half-dozen camps of a circular
valley girt round about with rocky peaks; another must
extend itself along a narrow ravine, and be five miles
long and hardly an eighth of a mile in width.

The miners needed no criminal code. It is simply and literally true, that there was a short time in California, in 1848, when crime was almost absolutely unknown, when pounds and pints of gold were left unguarded in tents and cabins, or thrown down on the hillside, or handed about through a crowd for inspection. An old pioneer writes me, that "in 1848 a man could go into a miner's cabin, cut a slice of bacon, cook a meal, roll up in a blanket, and go to sleep, certain to be welcomed kindly when the owner returned." Men have told me that they have known as much as a washbasin-full of gold-dust to be left on the table, in an open tent, while the owners were at work in their claim a mile distant. Of course this condition of affairs was partly due to the ease of acquiring gold. Men, in some cases, pulled up bunches of grass from the gulches and hillsides, shaking them into buckets, thus obtaining many pounds of gold; one miner gathered sixteen thousand dollars thus in five weeks of work. Another miner "cleaned up" eighteen thousand dollars in one day's labor with pan and pick. Certainly it was easier to earn money than to steal it, but it was infinitely safer also. In later days, for a man to be caught sluice-robbing was to sign his own death-warrant; with the miners of '48, whipping, banishment, or hanging was likely enough to have been inflicted upon the robber of claim or tent. For the criminality of theft was brought squarely home to each man's conscience, and to the entire community. Considering all the circumstances, a man capable of stealing from his comrades in these busy, friendly camps, was hopelessly hardened, was capable of all the crimes of the Decalogue.

Throughout this Arcadian era, there was not only no theft, but the bonds of fellowship were strong and sincere among all the miners of the camps. In some districts where the American element kept strongly in the majority, the entire "flush period" from 1849 to 1853 was marked by such unity. But in most camps disturbances increased; human leeches and parasites lowered the healthy tone of the community; and the miners drew farther apart than in the days when their first tents were pitched beneath the lofty Sierra pines, in clumps of chapparal and manzinita.

The miners themselves noticed how rapidly disturbances increased in number a few years later. "We needed no law," writes an old pioneer, "until the lawyers came;" and this idea is repeated in a thousand forms. "There were few crimes," says one correspondent, "until the courts with their delays and technicalities took the place of miners' law." This is, in truth, the persistent prejudice against lawyers that has existed among frontiersmen (nor among them alone), in every age of the world. Poetry and fiction have always been severe upon the "cozening, cheating, subtle-tongued lawyers." Dr. Johnson, as a withering and overwhelming assault, once said of an opponent, "Although I should be sorry to calumniate any man, yet, sir, I believe the gentleman in question to be an attorney." But it is pioneers who give the most frank expression of this time-honored opinion. And, although the fact is not generally known, there was a time when one-half of the world tried, but of course unsuccessfully, to live without any lawyers. When Spain established her colonies, every one of them petitioned the king, in the most earnest and anxious terms, to allow no lawyers to sail for America; because they desired to live in peace and prosperity, freed from the malice of men and the malign presence of attorneys. As loyal Catholic subjects they

prayed to be protected from the whole "lean and rascally" legal fraternity. The gallant soldier of fortune,
Vasco Nunez de Balboa, wrote to the king, saying, —

"One thing I supplicate your majesty: that you will give orders,
under a great penalty, that no bachelors of law should be allowed
to come here; for not only are they bad themselves, but they also
make and contrive a thousand iniquities." [1]

Pioneers of New Spain, and pioneers of golden California, were equally in earnest in their denunciation of
lawyers, and were equally at fault in the analysis by
which they reached such conclusions. In views of this
sort, we have a curious confusion of ideas, a curious
substitution of effect for cause. The conditions of society do not change because of the lawyer's arrival: he
comes because the conditions of society are already
changing, and there is, or is about to be, a demand for
his labor. Though we grant all that the pioneers say
respecting the Arcadian simplicity, and total freedom
from difficulties, of the camps of the earlier gold-period,
we must not conclude that this absence of lawlessness
was necessarily due to the absence of lawyers. There
were plenty of them, working as quiet citizens in their
claim-ditches, and waiting until there was a demand for
attorneys and the machinery of courts. How could
there be much lawlessness where so few temptations to
crime, and so few opportunities for its commission, existed? Men could quarrel, could steal, could kill each
other; but nine out of ten of the misdemeanors and
crimes that appear in the docket of an ordinary criminal court were impossible in the mining-camps, while
ninety-nine hundredths of the ordinary civil cases were
equally out of the question. Land-titles all similar,

[1] Helps's Spanish Conquest, p. 338; note, *Carta el Rey*, Jan. 20, 1513.

transfers verbal, commercial transactions for cash, borrowing and lending simply a matter between individuals — the best of lawyers would have starved in such a community. As society grew more complex, temptations and opportunities increased; and by the time the machinery of a State was set in operation, California presented, as regards land-titles, mining-cases, and a thousand other subjects, so many legal complications, that for a time it became the paradise of lawyers.

By the close of 1848, mining was actually in progress for a distance of two hundred miles along the axis of the Sierra. Colonel Reading was at work with his Indians on Clear Creek, Shasta County; and General John Bidwell, in like manner, on Feather River. When winter came, most of the miners returned to their homes in the valleys, in San José, Monterey, Sonoma, or San Francisco. Before the summer of 1849, the pioneers of 1848 had been overwhelmed and lost in the gold-rush of that eventful year. The peace and freedom of the early camps gave way to a new order of things; and, out of chaos and confusion, the organizing faculty of the race began to bring settled government. But so marked, so characteristic, so different from all later types of miners, was the pioneer of 1848, that it has even been said, that with that year "all that was staid and primitive in or about the mines of California vanished; with it ended the old civilization and the old scenes." [1] This, however, is only true from the stand-point of a general observer: from the institutional stand-point, the camp-organizations of 1849-53 had their beginnings in the camp-organizations of 1848.

[1] Henry de Groot: Recollections of California Mining-life. Pamphlet, pp. 16. San Francisco, 1884.

CHAPTER X.

THE general features of the organization of the "mining-courts," that were in many cases found necessary towards the close of 1848, can easily be described. There were no permanent officers, except where the alcalde plan was adopted, as in instances hereafter described; neither were there any written laws, or any records of proceedings. Any one who desired could call a meeting. A person who thought himself wronged would tell his friends, and they would tell others, till the miners of the region would assemble if they thought the cause sufficient; but, if not, would ignore the call. Some important meetings grew out of informal discussions, among groups of miners, as to the best regulations for mutual benefit and protection. As soon as "mining-districts," so called, began to be laid out, they assumed exceedingly definite boundaries as regarded the actual gold-bearing territory, but were very indefinite regarding size and shape. Each district included certain gulches, ran to the top of certain divides, took in certain flats and ridges, and would have presented a very irregular appearance on a map. The district might include several camps, or but one, according to convenience. The term "camp" is properly used to express the nucleus of the district, the tent town to which the miners returned at night. The discovery of new mines might at any time create new camps, but not necessarily new districts, until its miners in camp assembled made new laws, and separated themselves from the jurisdiction of their former laws.

At the first meeting called to organize a camp in a recently discovered mineral belt, the boundaries of a district were drawn so as to include not only the claims of all the miners present, but also all the unclaimed ground that seemed easy of access, and likely to be valuable. If, however, the district proved too large for convenience as a political unit, the dissatisfied miners would post up notices in several places, and call a meeting of those who wished for a division of territory, and a new district. If a majority favored such action, the district was set apart and named. The old district was not consulted on the subject, but received a verbal notice of the new organization. Local conditions, making different regulations regarding claims desirable, were the chief causes of such separations. In most of these earlier cases, district and camp were one and the same: the camp was the unit. Disagreements between two camps, as camps, were never heard of. Cases of lesser camps uniting themselves for governing purposes with larger ones were of later occurrence.

There were no county lines to consider, for this was before the organization of the State. A number of districts were therefore laid out, through which county lines were discovered to pass when surveyed a few years later; but they retained their organization as separate political units. There are in northern California, at the present time, several mining-districts that include within their boundaries territory under the jurisdiction of two counties. The State of Nevada, in its laws of 1866, ordained that previously created districts, through which county lines passed, should be allowed to retain their autonomy, and continue to enact local laws. In facts like these we find evidence of the institutional nature of the early camps, or districts, which thus created a local government area long before counties were established, and were able, when they chose, to maintain it intact. The decay of placer-mining was perhaps the only thing that prevented the later adoption of districts as universal divisions of the township, or rather as areas of local authority that should disregard township and county lines much as English parishes, unions, school districts, and various local government areas, intersect and overlap at the present time.[1]

The "mining-court" of the camp, in its earliest form, was simply the assembly of the freemen in open council. All who swung a pick, all who held a claim, boys of sixteen and men of sixty, took part in its deliberations. It was the folk-moot of our Germanic ancestors. If the citizens had been summoned to try an important case, they elected a presiding officer and a judge, impanelled a jury of six or twelve persons, summoned witnesses, and proceeded to trial forthwith. Sometimes there was no jury; and the case was submitted to the assemblage without argument, and irrevocably decided *viva voce*. Had A trespassed on B's claim? Was C's possessory right forfeited by absence, or neglect to work? and could D assume it, or was D a "claim-jumper"? Such were the questions usually brought before the "folk-moots" of the Sierra. Changes and

[1] See Local Government, Chalmers, chap. ii., English Citizen Series, Macmillan & Co., 1883.

developments in this method of procedure occurred a year or two later, but the earlier camps seized upon the "folk-moot" plan with a true race-instinct.

Two things there were, that no camp-assemblage ever attempted to regulate: no mining-court ever collected debts either for or against any individual, nor did it ever take cognizance of minor personal difficulties. As regards the first of these, the miners felt and said that it was disgraceful to dun a man for money. They held that honor between men, and the strength of social and business relations, is a far better protection to the lender than bond of Shylock and execution of sheriff. In one case, in one of the camps of '48, a miner, dunned for a small debt at an unseasonable hour of the night, took a lantern, went to his claim, washed out more than sufficient, tied it up in a shot-bag, and, returning to the tent, flung it in his creditor's face with all the force of a sinewy arm. Men had to settle their financial affairs and their petty quarrels among themselves: that was mining-camp doctrine. Of course friends would interfere to separate drunken men, or to prevent a fight: but the camp as an organization set out to protect life and property, not to meddle with what seemed trivialities; so it winked at pugnacious tendencies, and possessed the most liberal definition of eccentricity conceivable. How else should it secure its Sunday-afternoon amusements, and maintain its clowns and oddities?

Crimes against society found swift enough punishment. The thief, for instance, was publicly flogged, and expelled from camp; forfeiting, of course, whatever mining-ground he had occupied. But the thieves were usually the hangers-on of the camp, the idle Mexicans, or South-sea Islanders, not the men who owned and worked claims. Stealing, as we have previously stated, involved a greater degree of crime than it possibly could in a more highly organized commonwealth; because the social compact was simpler, and more clearly understood by all men.

Late in 1848 the foreign element began to find its way to the mines, and compelled better organization on the part of the Americans. When Mexicans settled the noted "Sonoranian Camp," now the town of Sonora, in Tuolumne County, nineteen white men — twelve of them Americans — followed, and, a little later, held a miners' meeting, elected R. S. Ham as alcalde, and agreed to support his authority. This district, Jamestown, was known as the "American Camp." The Mexicans and Chilians were greatly in the majority in the region, and their numbers increased during the next year. Many of them were men of the worst character, and only the closest organization prevented a reign of lawlessness. The real struggle for control of the southern mines was, however, at a later period than '48. "Sonoranian Camp" obeyed the mandates of Alcalde Ham with reasonable cheerfulness, and the few miners' meetings held were devoted to making laws regarding claims. There was no official communication between Alcalde Ham and Colonel Mason, then acting governor of California : the camp was left to govern itself.

In the camps of '48, Americans learned what strength there was in organization; but systematic development of mining-courts, alcalde-courts, and other forms of camp-government, can hardly be said to have existed until the next year. The work of the better class of miners, during the winter of 1848–49, was closely connected with the beginnings of that larger life, — State organization. The miners returning to their homes, forced by winter storms to desert their camps in the mountain gulches, began to seek for a remedy for certain no longer endurable evils that were afflicting the body politic. American miners who had lived in peace and friendliness all summer in their camps, had formed new bonds of fellowship, had more closely cemented former bonds, and had proved their ability to protect and govern themselves, were now to take the initiative in several remarkable organizing efforts.

A "memorial," at a later period presented to Congress, reviews the political history of California.[1] It says, in effect, that, "as early as 1847," many Americans in California advocated the establishment of a civil Territorial form of government; that, in October of that year, the military contribution tariff was established in Californian ports, and rigorously enforced, but never once resisted though extremely onerous; that the overland immigration of 1847 strengthened the desire for a more American form of government; that the military power continued taxation without representation, and afforded inadequate protection to life and property; that the gold-discovery occurred, and in April the towns were deserted, all industrial pursuits were abandoned, and "a pall seemed to settle upon the country;" that in August the news of the treaty with Mexico was received, but the existing order of things was nevertheless continued. It describes an unsettled and unstable order of things, and a dissatisfaction and even a profound discontent as existing along the California coast in the summer and fall of 1848. It then

---

[1] Memorial presented March 12, 1850, by Messrs. Gwin, Fremont, Wright, and Gilbert, senators and representatives elect from California. App. to Debates in Convention, Washington, 1850.

proceeds to use the following remarkable language regarding the influence of the miners: —

"Upon the coming-on of winter, the great majority of the miners returned to their homes in the towns. They came rich in gold-dust; but a single glance at the desolate and unthrifty appearance of the territory convinced them that other pursuits than that of gold-digging must receive a portion of their care and labor . . . They felt, as all Americans feel, that the most important step they could take, and that most imperatively called for by the wants of the inhabitants, was the establishment of a stable system of government, which would command the respect and obedience of the people whose property it protected, and whose rights it preserved. Congress had adjourned without providing a Territorial government; and the public had settled into the firm conviction that the *de facto* government was radically defective, and incapable of answering the public wants."

This ample recognition of the important place in State-organization taken by the returned miners appears to be fully borne out by the facts. A large public meeting was held at San José, Dec. 11, 1848, at which the people of California were asked to organize in districts, and elect delegates to a convention for the purpose of forming a "provisional Territorial government," to go into immediate operation, and remain in full force until superseded by Congressional action. The plan was heartily welcomed and indorsed at mass-meetings held in San Francisco, Dec. 21 and 23; in Sacramento, Jan. 6 and 8; in Monterey, Jan. 31; and in Sonoma, February 5. Returned miners were prominent men in all these meetings. The very inclement weather, and impassable condition of the roads, had caused nearly two months to intervene between the San José meeting and the Sonoma meeting, and had prevented proposed meetings in other districts; but the five districts mentioned comprised more than three-

fifths of the whole population of California, and they
elected delegates to a convention to be held early in
March. Part also of this movement, was the election, early in the year 1849, of "district legislative
assemblies" for Sacramento and Sonoma. The legislature elected in San Francisco, for local reasons, was
of a somewhat different type, and was chosen at a
later date. The earlier assembly of Sacramento, which
aimed to govern the entire surrounding region, was
more directly the result of mining-organizations than
were the Sonoma and San Francisco assemblies. But
all three of them disbanded peaceably in obedience to
Governor Bennett Riley's orders. By the time the
Territorial Convention assembled, the majority saw
that California was too wealthy and populous for a
Territorial government; and they at once issued an address to the people, recommending a Constitutional Convention, which took place in September, 1849, at the old
pueblo of Monterey.

In all the important political events which began
with the San José meeting of December, 1848, and
ended with the adoption of a State constitution, the
men who had toiled, struggled, suffered, and "stood by
each other" in the mining-camps were leading spirits.
Some of them returned to the mines; some engaged in
other and more profitable occupations in the valleys and
coast-towns, for few of the pioneers of '48 had accumulated fortunes.

The preceding pages have in no wise exaggerated the
intrinsic value of the work done by the "men of '48"
in settling the foundations of society. Throughout
our examination into the methods of later camps, and
the laws made by various districts, we shall be constantly finding traces of earlier institutional organi-

zation. The debt of the Pacific Coast to the few thousands of miners who first explored the Sacramento and El Dorado placers is greater than historians have heretofore acknowledged. They were the pioneers of the pioneers: without their brave and loyal work as American citizens, the greater and more dazzlingly successful work of that strange and complex era which followed could never have been accomplished.

CHAPTER XI.

A KNOWLEDGE of the characteristic features of the mining-days of 1849 is essential to a full appreciation of the good sense and political wisdom shown by the miners as a class. Merchants, mechanics, farmers, existed but to supply the miners; and the gold of the mines was the chief resource of California. Four-fifths of the able-bodied male population were living in the mineral belt, or were on their way thither, when the working-season of 1849 opened. Only four years before, in the summer of 1845, there had been but five hundred Americans in California; in February, 1848, but two thousand; by December, 1848, this number had grown to six thousand; by July, 1849, to fifteen thousand; and by December, 1849, to fifty-three thousand. Chiefly owing to the gold-rush of 1848–53, the centre of population of the United States moved eighty-one miles farther west. Within four years after the spring of 1849, the population of the new State was three hundred thousand; and more than two hundred and sixty million dollars had been dug from the gold-fields. The gold-product of California for all the years from 1848 to 1883 inclusive has been over twelve hundred millions of dollars, or three-fourths of the entire gold-product of the United States during the past century. But, great as this total is, it would have seemed little to

132

the minds of the excited Argonauts of 1849. Only the stories of the fortunate wealth-seekers had gone abroad to the world, and men were prepared to believe any thing about California.

Dr. Stillman, in his "Seeking the Golden Fleece," says that at the close of January, 1849, "sixty vessels had sailed from Atlantic seaports, carrying eight thousand men, and seventy more vessels were up for passage." Bayard Taylor, speaking more particularly of the land-journey, said that "it more than equalled the great military expeditions of the Middle Ages, in magnitude, peril, and adventure." John S. Hittell writes: "From Maine to Texas there was one universal frenzy."

One of the "pilgrims" wrote a song, which was soon heard on every street-corner of the Atlantic cities, in which he proclaimed, —

> "Oh! California, that's the land for me!
> I'm bound for the Sacramento,
> With the washbowl on my knee."

As in the excitement of '48, so again in '49 a nucleus of camp-organization often began in these companies of pilgrims, by land or by sea, who became acquaintances and friends, who decided to proceed to the same district of the mining-region, and who often formed associated bodies of workers. The men who crossed the plains together, or were for months in the same ship, hold annual re-unions at the present time, on the Pacific Coast. Each year their numbers lessen, but the survivors cling to the observance with ever-strengthening affection.

There were many interesting features about this great onset, all the world seeming to be in haste to occupy this hitherto neglected region. Armies of emigrants were attracted by the magic of its name, and toiled wearily in wavering lines across the continent. Many a mountain valley was thus settled long before it could have been reached in the natural course of agricultural progress, and the entire frontier of the West was borne forward: the immemorial race-impulse of the Aryan had re-awakened with all its ancient force. In vain the elders of lonely Deseret, and the dupes of the Book of Mormon, tried by falsehood and crime to roll back or turn aside this dreaded and hated advance of American civilization. Some of the "Latter-day Saints" joined the current, but most of them were faithful to their shrine.[1] But the fierce, impetuous, resistless human torrent swept on its way to the Pacific Coast: it ran in haste, it fairly leaped over obstacles, as one sees mountain rivers curl down into hollows, and curve over bowlders, till, in the rush of its advance, the smallest inequality of the channel is reproduced in its surface.

The mining-camps, whose white tents and rude cabins rose so rapidly beside these rivers of this new Colchis in early '49, have found an enduring place in literature. The Argonaut himself has become one of the heroic figures of the past, and is likely enough to survive, as real and strong a type in the story of America as Viking or Crusader in that of Europe. But it is the place held by the Argonaut as an organizer of society, that is most important. He often appears in literature as a dialect-speaking rowdy, savagely picturesque, rudely turbulent: in reality, he was a plain American citizen cut loose from authority, freed from

---

[1] The Mormon leaders told their followers, that gold was to pave streets and cover houses; and, if they were faithful, they should have more than sufficient in their own territory when the proper time came.

the restraints and protections of law, and forced to make the defence and organization of society a part of his daily business. In its best estate, the mining-camp of California was a manifestation of the inherent capacities of the race for self-government. That political instinct, deep rooted in Lex Saxonum, to blossom in Magna Charta and in English unwritten constitution, has seldom in modern times afforded a finer illustration of its seemingly inexhaustible force. Here, in a new land, under new conditions, subjected to tremendous pressure and strain, but successfully resisting them, were associated bodies of freemen bound together for a time by common interests, ruled by equal laws, and owning allegiance to no higher authority than their own sense of right and wrong. They held meetings, chose officers, decided disputes, meted out a stern and swift punishment to offenders, and managed their local affairs with entire success; and the growth of their communities was proceeding at such a rapid rate, that days and weeks were often sufficient for vital changes, which, in more staid communities, would have required months or even years.

The gateway to the mines was San Francisco. In January, 1849, when Rev. Dwight Hunt, who had for several months preached to the returned miners thronging the streets, organized the "First Congregational Church," the population of the city was less than fifteen hundred. A little later, the first ship-loads of immigrants began to arrive; and, though every newcomer felt obliged to visit the mines to see for himself, yet many persons soon returned to enter into business; and San Francisco had fifteen thousand inhabitants before the close of the year.

A San-Francisco pioneer of '49 writes: —

"Gold-dust, provisions, and tools were safe without police. We had no disturbances at first, no rows, and no murders. Men gambled, for that was an old California vice;[1] but they did so as honestly as it can be done. We had no poor men, and labor was at a premium everywhere."

Before very long, however, an organization called "The Hounds" began to rob Spanish-Americans, and committed other outrages; and, July 16, the law-abiding citizens, who had in vain complained of the inefficiency of the alcalde, met, organized a court, elected a judge and attorneys, and by fines and imprisonments put an end for some years to ruffian supremacy.

The harbor of San Francisco became populous with ships of every nation. When scholarly Richard H. Dana, Harvard graduate, adventurous sailor before the mast, had visited Yerba Buena harbor, while the Mexican "eagle and *nopal* flag" yet drooped from the presidio staff, there was not a single vessel in the harbor, not a single boat on the broad bay, and but one house where San Francisco now stands. Herds of deer came down to the water's edge; and, as in Kotzebue's time, sea-otters swam within easy gun-shot.[2] Soon after, a Russian vessel entered the harbor, but in a few days

---

[1] Gambling in California was permitted under Mexican rule, and under the military government of '46-'49. It was even a source of revenue to the *ayuntamiento* of San Francisco in August, 1849. It was a legalized and important pursuit, followed with zeal by Mexicans, French, and Americans. See Hittell, Hist. San Francisco, p. 236.

[2] Lieutenant Kotzebue visited San Francisco Bay in 1816, when Arguello was Spanish commandante, and Kuskoff ruled in the Russian settlement at Bodega, thirty miles northward. Twenty Russians and fifty Indians captured two thousand sea-otters that season. Count Adelbert Von Chamisso, that sensitive genius, author of "Peter Schlemihl," and Eschscholtz the botanist, were members of this expedition. The latter's consonantal name is perpetuated in the most brilliant flower of the Pacific-coast flora, — the rich orange-scarlet wild poppy of field and hillside.

sailed away, and left the solitary hide-droger to its work. Less than fifteen years later the summer of 1849 saw no less than five hundred and forty-nine sea-going vessels in the port. In the month of August four hundred large ships were idly swinging at anchor, destitute of crews; for their sailors had deserted, swum ashore, escaped to the gold-fields. Thirty-five thousand men came by sea, and forty-two thousand by land, during the year. Australia, the Asian coasts, Africa, and South America contributed to the motley host that thronged the roads to the placers.

Society was masculine, and most of the men were under forty. In the spring of 1849, there were but fifteen women in San Francisco. As one writer says, "Women were queens, children were angels." Bearded and weather-bronzed miners stood for hours in the streets to get a glimpse of a child at play. At a little later period, there were plenty of women who were "vile libels on their sex;" but the reverence that Californians of the gold-era paid to respectable women has received a tribute of admiring praise from all observers. Men often travelled miles to welcome "the first real lady in camp." A New-England youth of seventeen once rode thirty-five miles, after a week's hard work in his father's claim, to see a miner's wife who had arrived in an adjoining district. "Because," he said, "I wanted to see a home-like lady; and, father, do you know, she sewed a button on for me, and told me not to gamble and not to drink. It sounded just like mother."

New towns were laid out in the valleys to supply the camps, and those already established grew with astonishing rapidity. Stockton, for instance, increased in three months from a solitary ranch-house to a canvas city of one thousand inhabitants. Sacramento also became a canvas city, where dust-clouds whirled, and men, mules, and oxen toiled; where boxes, barrels, bales, innumerable, were piled in the open air, no shelter being needed for months. For the City Hotel, Sacramento, thirty thousand dollars per year was paid as rent, although it was only a small frame building. The Parker House, San Francisco, cost thirty thousand dollars to build, and rented for fifteen thousand dollars per month. Speculation in promising town-sites soon reached as extravagant heights as it ever did in the Mississippi Valley or in the Pennsylvania oil-region. Every cross-road, river-landing, and ferry had its "corner-lot speculators," who prophesied its future greatness. The "town of Oro," near the mouth of Bear River, had but one house, and soon lost even that. Linda, Eliza Featherton, Kearney, and dozens of others, paper towns of the lowlands, are familiar to all pioneers.

The conditions under which business had to be conducted in San Francisco and at the interior towns were extremely trying and difficult. The only supply-markets were so remote, that the greatest fluctuations in the stock of goods on hand were constantly occurring, against which no human foresight could guard. New York was nineteen thousand miles distant by the sea-route; and about six months were required to send an order from San Francisco, and get the goods delivered. Oregon's few thousand pioneers had little to sell. China sent only rice and sugar; Australia and Chili supplied some flour. Every thing else came from the Atlantic seaports. Lumber, worth four hundred dollars per thousand one month, would not pay for the freight four months later; tobacco, once worth two dollars a pound, was tossed in the streets. Saleratus fluctuated between twenty-five cents and fifteen dollars per pound. The entire community was dependent for food and clothing upon other communities thousands of miles distant. And the rate of interest was ten per cent per month.

By the time goods reached the mountain camps, their cost was so enormous that most of the miner's gains went for necessaries of life.[1] Those who were very fortunate often indulged in curious and expensive whims and "extravaganzas," feeling sure that their claims would continue to yield treasure. They bought the costliest broadcloth, drank the finest wines, and smoked the best brands of cigars. "A wild, heedless, wasteful, dissipated set of men," is what one of the "forty-niners" calls his old comrades. Men who had been brought up to keep sober, and earn sixteen dollars per month, and save half of it, went to California, found rich claims, earned several hundred dollars a month, — of which they might have saved three-fourths, — but spent every cent in riotous living. Men who had been New-York hod-carriers paid out ten dollars a day for canned fruits and potted meats. But only a few years later, when the surface placers were all exhausted, these same unkempt sybarites returned to beans and pork, strapped up their blankets, and made prospect tours to other regions, taking their reverses more placidly than one could have thought possible.

To many cheerful, impetuous, and intelligent men, the ups and downs of mining-life seemed full of wild fascination. To be there was to be a part of a scene that each thoughtful miner knew in his heart was as

[1] Mr. George F. Parsons, for many years editor of the Sacramento Record-Union, and author of the Life of James W. Marshall, the discoverer of gold in California, copied the following prices from the books of the Sutter Fort store: "Two white shirts, $40; one fine-tooth comb, $6; one barrel of mess pork, $210; one dozen sardines, $35; two hundred pounds of flour, $150; one tin pan, $9; one candle, $3."

evanescent as it was brilliant, — an episode whose intensity corresponded accurately to its briefness. And, to many persons of this type, it certainly seemed as if the way to make the most of the era was to take a hand in every thing that came along. Reports filled each camp, almost every week, telling of new diggings where from a hundred to a thousand dollars might easily be collected in a day. Down came the tent-ropes, the claims were abandoned; the epidemic gold-rush fever had seized each Argonaut in the camp. They went to Gold Lake, Gold Bluffs, and a hundred other as loudly trumpeted regions, till the habit of following with swift feet each new excitement became as much a part of the Argonaut's nature as the habit of running after a fire is a part of the healthy boy's organization. The Argonaut was well enough aware that the blaze is very apt to be only a bonfire, or else to be over long before he arrives. But he could not bear to stand by, and see others run and hurrah: so off he started at the best of his speed, to come back, a few months later, "dead broke" financially, but wealthy in experience.

Fortunately there were men of quite another type, whose clear brains and steady habits enabled them to lay aside a part of their gains, afterwards to push larger enterprises, to organize mining-companies, to dig great water-ditches extending for miles in a magnificent system of engineering. Some of them bought farms in the valleys, or entered into business in the towns and cities, retaining to the fullest degree their affection for the wild mountain realm where they first obtained a start in life. Even in the earlier fever-heats of the gold excitement, there were numbers of men who had come to California to remain, and make homes, who recognized vast resources other than mineral, and by whose unswerving fidelity to justice the best elements of camp-life were evolved. The returned miners of 1848, and the home-hungry, home-creating few of the thousands of 1849, formed the nucleus of safety-committees and camp-courts of law.

A fine example of this was afforded in what were called the Southern mines, the camps of Tuolumne, whose organization late in 1848 has been described in the preceding chapter. The several hundred dwellers in and about the Mexican or "Sonoranian" camp were re-enforced as early as July, 1849, by fully fifteen thousand foreigners,* chiefly from Sonora, Chili, and the Isthmus. Many of them came in armed bands, and made the country unsafe. Some of them were outlaws and desperadoes of the worst types. They brought degraded women with them, had fandangos and bull-fights, and were a thoroughly alien community. Opposed to them was the little camp of Americans who had elected their alcalde the previous autumn, and several other American camps, well organized for self-protection, founded early in 1849. The foreign invasion (for it can be termed little else) was held in check, and finally turned back, only by the energy and "inborn capacity for creating order" displayed by some of the Americans. The methods taken by the Americans were not always wise or just: in many individual cases, cruelty was practised towards weak and inoffensive Mexicans, and their claims were taken from them, as has been done in innumerable cases along the south-west frontiers within the past few years. But the central fact of the necessity for organization on the part of the Americans remains undisputed. Men had been robbed, horses stolen, and the roads rendered unsafe for travellers. In some camps "good and true men" were at once

* This seems much too large. Bancroft's estimate of 5,000 as the total population of Sonora in 1849 seems more reasonable. Hubert Howe Bancroft, *Works* (39 vols., San Francisco, 1882–1890) XXIII, 469.

elected as alcaldes; in others there was the direct inter-
vention of "miners' courts," such as adopted by some
of the miners of '48; still a third form was the election
of a committee of justice. Under all these forms, supported by public opinion, the work of purification was
done rapidly and well. Suspicious characters, both
Mexican and American, were notified to leave; criminals were followed, captured, and punished. Although
the camps southward from Placerville (then Hangtown)
were undoubtedly more turbulent than the northern
mines, they struggled against greater difficulties, not
only in 1849, but at several subsequent periods, as we
shall see in a later chapter.

The mountain land over which mining became the
chief industry of men, and to which all sea-roads and
trails along the Sierra passes seemed to lead, was a region fitted by nature to attract and secure the affections
of a hardy and energetic race. Its physical features
are most noble and inspiring, even at the present day
when the valleys and foot-hills are subdued to agricultural purposes, and brought under a high state of
cultivation. But when the miners of '49 began to
pitch their tents in the wilderness, it was unfenced,
unclaimed, and almost unexplored; for the work of the
previous year had only mapped out the leading features
of the mineral belt. The unsurpassed wealth of what
is now Nevada County was as yet undiscovered. Everywhere the land had a charm that no language can describe. Flowers of new species and wonderful beauty
bloomed on slope and crag, trees of unparalleled grandeur
stood in the forests, the climate of the foot-hills was like
that of Italy. From the great and sea-like valley of the
Sacramento, eastward through rolling, oak-clad hills to
the broad plateau of the Sierras, and through wild forests

and dim gorges to the granite heights and the pointed peaks covered with eternal snow, the ardent miners searched every gulch, traced every stream to its source, and in five years of eager, reckless toil did the work that in other communities would have taken a generation. They spread out in every direction from the Sacramento and Feather-river region, searching ridge and ravine southward to the desert sands and borax deposits of Mojave, northward to the barren lava-beds of Modoc. They crossed the westward valley to explore the wildest and most difficult recesses of the Coast Range; established Redding Springs, afterwards Shasta City; rifled the Trinity basin of its riches; and discovered the placers of Klamath, Siskiyou, and Southern Oregon. They went waist-deep into the ocean, and brought back tales of beaches gold-spangled by

> " All the storms
> That hurled their ancient, white-topped, weary waves
> On California, since the world began."

The flickering, beckoning will-o'-the-wisp that ever led them on was the hope of new diggings, of nuggets gleaming from the moss of mountain lakes, of

> " Beds of streams that evermore
> Washed down the golden grain, and in a year
> Paid to the treasury of the insatiate flood
> More than the subjects of the richest kings
> Yield to their despots in a century."

But of all the writers who have attempted to express the splendid virility, the impetuous battle with nature's forces, the healthy outdoor atmosphere of happy, hearty toil, that the " miners of '49 " knew so well, none have said the right word in a better way than Fitz James O'Brien, poet, romancist, genial Bohemian, loyal friend, knightly soldier. Listen to the song of his "Sewing-bird" lyric : —

> "Up in a wild Californian hill,
> Where the torrents swept with a mighty will,
> And the grandeur of Nature filled the air,
> And the cliffs were lofty, rugged, and bare,
> Some thousands of lusty fellows she saw
> Obeying the first great natural law.
> From the mountain's side they had scooped the earth,
> Down to the veins where the gold had birth;
> And the mighty pits they had girdled about
> With ramparts massive and wide and stout;
> And they curbed the torrents, and swept them round
> Wheresoever they willed, through virgin ground.
> They rocked huge cradles the livelong day,
> And shovelled the heavy, tenacious clay,
> And grasped the nugget of gleaming ore,
> The sinews of commerce on every shore."

I have visited the mining-region, the realm of the "Argonauts of '49." Titans have been at work there. The land for miles is like a battle-field where primal forces and giant passions have wrestled. Rivers have been turned aside; mountains hurled into chasms, or stripped to the bed-rock in naked disarray. I have seen wild and steep ravines where each square rod once had its miner; where stores, theatres, and banks once stood in the flat, and gold-dust ran in the streets, and every man carried his pistol, and a day of life contained more of healthy out-door existence and passionate energy than does a year of life in a metropolis: and in those ravines — once so populous — a few old and trembling men, worn out before their time, and pitiful to look upon, creep down from their cabins to pick and moil among the crevices for the little gold left by the gallant "forty-niners;" and creep back to brood over memories,

while year after year they watch with feelings of pain
and almost anger the approach of gardens, vineyards,
orchards, slowly re-subduing, in far more durable manner, the lost conquests of the Argonauts.

Even to-day the smallest of these decaying camps is
worth patient study. In the hollows, grown over with
blossoming vines, are acres upon acres of bowlders and
débris, moved, sifted, and piled up by the hands of
pioneers; on the hill's sunny slope are grass-covered
mounds where some of them rest after their passionate
toil, their fierce and feverish wrestle with hard-hearted
fortune. Once this was Red Dog Camp, or Mad Mule
Gulch, or Murderer's Bar:[1] now it is only a nameless
cañon, the counterpart of hundreds of others scattered
over a region five hundred miles long by fifty miles
wide, each one of them all once full to the brim and
overflowing with noisy, beating, rushing, roaring, masculine life. Go down and talk with those ghostly inhabitants of the ancient camp, and they will set your
blood tingling with tales of the past. Twenty years,
thirty years, ago? Why, it is centuries!

The saddest of all possible sights in the old mining-
region is where there are not even half a dozen mmers
to keep each other company, but where, solitary and in
desolation, the last miner clings to his former haunts.
He cooks his lonesome meals in the wrecked and rotting
hotel where a quarter of a century before, then young,
gay, prosperous, and in his prime, he had tossed the
reins of his livery-team to the obsequious servant, and

---

[1] Names of California camps, given in books of travel, are not always
to be trusted: visitors expect an eccentric title for each ravine. But the
real names were remarkable enough; such were the following: Loafer
Hill; Slapjack Bar; Chicken-thief Flat; Git-up-and-Git; Rat-trap Slide;
Sweet Revenge; Shirt-tail Cañon; You Bet; Gouge Eye.

played billiards with the "boys," and passed the hat
for a collection to build the first church; he sharpens
his battered pick at a little forge under the tree on
which he helped hang the Mexican who had stabbed
Sailor Bill (how famous Bill was for songs and horn-
pipes in the El Dorado saloon whose roofless posts slant
in the yielding earth!); he looks down in the cañon
where vines and trees hide all but the crumbling chim-
ney of the house where the "Rose of the Camp" lived,
sweetening their lives with a glimpse of her girlish grace
and purity as she tripped over the long bridge to the
little schoolhouse, and waved her pretty hand to her
friends toiling waist-deep in their claims. But that
was long ago: she married, and went to Europe, and
is famous, he has heard; now the bridge has fallen into
the torrent, and snow-storms have shattered the schoolhouse, and the end of the story is very near.

Not one of all the thousands who hurried into the
new camps of '49, who developed and over-crowded
the old camps of '48, ever paused to consider how these
camps would look if deserted; nor, if some prospector's
tale carried them on a frenzied gold-chase, did they
glance back at the camp they left. The record of the
gold-returns is sufficiently suggestive. In 1849 the
miners took out, by official record, twenty-three million
dollars; in 1850 they increased this yield to fifty million
dollars; and the probabilities are that twenty-five per
cent of the gold discovered was not reported at San
Francisco. By the summer of 1850, there was forty
million dollars in taxable real estate in San Francisco,
and as much more in the way of personal property,[1]
most of which had grown directly or indirectly from the

---

[1] "Gold in California." International Review, October, 1880.

mining-interest. Yet, only four years before, Webster had said, in the United-States Senate, that California was worthless except as a naval station.

The typical camp of the golden prime of '49 was flush, lively, reckless, flourishing, and vigorous. Saloons and gambling-houses abounded; buildings and whole streets grew up like mushrooms, almost in a night. Every man carried a buckskin bag of gold-dust, and it was received as currency at a dollar a pinch. Every one went armed, and felt fully able to protect himself. A stormy life ebbed and flowed through the town. In the camp, gathered as of one household, under no law but that of their own making, were men from North, South, East, and West, and from nearly every country of Europe, Asia, South America. They mined, traded, gambled, fought, discussed camp affairs; they paid fifty cents a drink for their whiskey, and fifty dollars a barrel for their flour, and thirty dollars apiece for butcher-knives with which to pick gold from the rock-crevices.[1]

"They talked," as one who knew them well has written, "a language half English and half Mexican. They learned to wash and mend their own clothes, and bake their own bread, and cook their own pork and beans. They were hardy, generous, careless, brave: they risked their lives for each other, and made and lost fortunes, and went on lonely prospect tours on foot among the snow-peaks, and grew old and feeble, and found that a new race that knew them not had arisen in the State they created. They died lonely deaths, or perished by violence, pioneers to the last."

As about the typical camp there were too often loss, decay, and final desertion, so about the typical pioneer there were too often loneliness and sorrow, pathos and heroism. A few camps were germs of towns and cities.

[1] This sum was paid for a time by the miners in some districts of Tuolumne.

A few pioneers prospered greatly, and settled down into leading positions in the State their labors had helped to create.   But the vital waste and destruction of the struggle overwhelm the observer with pity.   The mines were no place for weaklings; even strong, healthy, and earnest men often sank beneath the wearing excitement of that fervid life.   But these rough and busy men, whose lives were so often only the saddest of tragedies, established and enforced a code of ethics governing their relations with each other and their property rights, enforced justice though without written law, and in the end created a system of jurisprudence that has won the approval and indorsement of the highest courts of the land.   Sturdy, keen-witted, courageous, independent, they left the impress of sterling natures upon all their primitive institutions.

As we have seen, there were times in almost every camp when the rowdy element came near ruling, and only the powerful and hereditary organizing instincts of the Americans present ever brought order out of chaos. In nearly every such crisis, there were men of the right stamp at hand, to say the brave word, or do the brave act; to appeal to Saxon love of fair play, to seize the murderer, or to defy the mob.   Side by side in the same gulch, working in claims of eight paces square, were, perhaps, fishermen from Cape Ann, loggers from Penobscot, farmers from the Genesee Valley, physicians from the prairies of Iowa, lawyers from Maryland and Louisiana, college-graduates from Yale, Harvard, and the University of Virginia.   From so variously mingled elements, came that terribly exacting mining-camp society, which tested with pitiless and unerring tests each man's individual manhood, discovering his intrinsic worth or weakness with almost superhuman precision, until at last the ablest and best men became leaders.   They fought their way to the surface through fierce oppositions, and with unblenching resolution suppressed crime, and built up homes in the region they had learned to love.

CHAPTER XII.

EVIDENCE CONCERNING LAW AND ORDER IN THE CAMPS.

LET us now examine the testimony of visitors, travellers, and government officials, and of miners who have since published their observations upon the condition of the camps during the flush period. Were these camps orderly and well-governed? What impression did they make upon impartial strangers?

Ryan, in his "Personal Adventures in California," says, —

"The miners dwelt together in no distrust of one another, and left thousands of dollars' worth of gold-dust in their tents while they were absent digging. . . . A determination to punish robbery seemed to have been come to, by all, as a measure essential to security."

This was written of the camps of 1850, as a result of wide observation; and he elsewhere alludes to the admirable manner in which the camps had been conducted from the first.

We have before alluded to Colonel Mason's report on the mines of '48. Governor Riley, deciding to see the mines for himself, left Monterey, July 5, 1849, with Major Canby, Captain Wescott, Captain Halleck, Lieutenant Derby, and others, proceeded to Sacramento, and thence to the principal camps. After his return he wrote to Washington as follows : —

"Order and regularity were preserved throughout almost the entire extent of the mineral district. In each little settlement or tented town, the miners have elected their local alcaldes and constables, whose judicial decisions and official acts are sustained by the people, and enforced with much regularity and energy."

In another place he says, —

"The alcaldes have probably, in some cases, exercised judicial powers never conferred upon them by law; but the general results have been favorable . . . to the dispensation of justice."

The alcalde system, as adopted and modified by the miners, was all that fell under Governor Riley's observation: but there were camps in the region he visited which were governed, perhaps quite as well, though in a much more primitive manner, — camps ruled by a chosen committee, to whom all authority was intrusted; or governed only by the irregular assemblage of the miners, which we have before compared to a folk-moot. Governor Riley did not inquire into the minutiæ of organization. He only knew, that, copying after the system of the old Spanish pueblos of the coast, the miners in the longer-established camps had chosen, and were obeying, alcaldes; and, to assist these alcaldes in the discharge of their duties, had ingrafted upon the system the town-constableship of New-England villages.

Bayard Taylor was an appreciative observer of the camps. In his "Eldorado" he describes their political organization. "There was," he says, "much order and regularity. The miners had elected one of their number alcalde (this was on the Mokelumne), before whom all culprits were tried." He says that several persons had been severely punished; some had their ears cropped, and others were whipped soundly. "It was a Spartan severity of discipline," all of which Mr. Taylor fully approves.　In another place he says, —

　　" The disposition to maintain order, and secure the rights of all men, were shown throughout the mining-districts.　In the absence of law, the people met, and adopted rules for mutual security. . . . There had been," he said, "previous to 1849, twelve or fifteen executions for murder and for large thefts. . . . Alcaldes were elected, who had power to decide all disputes or complaints, and summon juries.　When a new placer was discovered, the first thing done was to elect officers.　In a region five hundred miles long, inhabited by a hundred thousand people, who had neither locks, bolts, regular laws of government, military or civil protection, there was as much security to life and property as in any State of the Union.　The rights of each digger were definitely marked out and observed."

These words of Bayard Taylor's were written of the camps of 1850 and 1851, but apply with almost equal force to the camps of 1849.　Everywhere in southern, central, and northern camps, he reports a reign of order, under laws of their own creation ; and the sight fills him with admiration.

One of the speakers before the First State Constitutional Convention addressed that body in October, 1849, upon the permanent character of the towns built up in the mining-region, of which he was a resident. He added, —

　　" Every glen, every ravine, every cañon, almost every hill-top, is lined and covered with the thousands and tens of thousands that are scattered over the whole country."

He proceeded to speak of their peaceful prosperity, and the constant investment, in the larger towns, of capital dug from the mines.　Other speakers before the convention alluded to the quiet and order preserved in the placer-region.

Governor Peter H. Burnett, in his "Recollections," says: —

"The miners were engaged in a common pursuit, and exposed to common dangers. Property was almost held in common, — a practical socialism of a very interesting type."

Burnett says further, —

"We [the miners] had the right to establish a *de facto* government which would rest on the same basis as the provincial government of Oregon. We held a meeting at Sacramento City in January, 1849, and elected Henry A. Schoolcraft first magistrate and recorder for Sacramento District."

Mr. Burnett had then just left the mining-camps, where he worked during the summer and autumn of 1848, and had opened a lawyer's office in Sacramento. The leadership of ex-miners was unquestioned in politics and in society.

A vivid account of life in the early days is furnished by Mr. Frank Marryat's "Mountains and Molehills." He speaks of "Murderer's Bar," with the swift river, the black obstructing rocks, the village of sun-bleached canvas; the miners, waist-deep, toiling to turn the course of the river, others in pits digging to bed-rock; some alone, some in companies; all life, vigor, and determination. He says in one place, that —

"In most mining-villages, indignation [over theft] was confined to ordering the offender to leave, or take the consequences. . . . The mining-population was allowed to construct their own laws relative to the appropriation of claims, and the system worked well. There was no interference on the part of the Legislature."

This observation of Mr. Marryat's was made a year or so after the organization of State government, and, as we shall hereafter see, remained true of the mining-districts for many years.

"Every digging," Mr. Marryat continues, "has its fixed rules and by-laws. All disputes are submitted to a jury of resident miners. In some cases, twenty men or so from one camp are met by an equal number from another camp."

He proceeds to say that disputes sometimes arose, and even demonstrations with fire-arms, but that good sense always prevailed. He speaks of the by-laws of each district as recorded in the county office, and as sometimes being stringent, ill-defined, and conflicting. His own experience of their practical workings, however, was as follows : —

"I have had my placer-claim of ten feet square encroached upon. I appealed to the crowd; and a committee of three, being at once chosen, measured it from my stake; and, being found correct, the jumper was ordered to confine himself to his own territory, which he always did."

Mr. Marryat's observations are particularly interesting on several accounts. He was an English university man, and adept with both pen and pencil. He entered heartily into the spirit of life at the placers, studying mining institutions with trained intellect; and the time he visited the camps was after California had been divided into twenty-seven counties, and county government nominally established. Thus his statements regarding the amount of local government which each camp retained by tacit consent, and exercised whenever necessary, are of great importance. Committees from different camps still met in consultation : informal appeals were still made to the crowd to right or prevent a wrong. In all essential particulars, the camp was still the "camp of '49."

As late as 1857, "Blackwood's Magazine," reviewing books on California, and speaking of the entire gold-era, says, —

"It is an agreeable and unexpected feature in the mines themselves, that order, justice, and courtesy reign there." . . .

And again : —

"Patches of a few square feet, teeming with gold, are as sacred as if secured with title-deeds."

J. D. Borthwick's "Three Years in California" is full of choice material for studies of this era. He describes the daily life of the gold-miners; tells us of heaps of gold-bearing gravel piled up in some camps to lie unguarded but safe until the rainy season, having been made personal property by the labor performed in heaping them together; pays a hearty tribute of praise to the universal spirit of hospitality, — the careless liberality such as led the Downieville miners to give fully five hundred dollars in gold-specimens to a lady who sang ballads for them at one of the first concerts ever held there. Mr. Borthwick speaks in many places of the ample security afforded by the mining-regulations. He also seems to have been struck by the sharply contrasted social instincts and methods of organization displayed by the American miners and the French miners. He says, in effect, that the Americans wandered about the mountains, often as solitary as grizzly bears, working like demons, and keeping their own counsel regarding their prospects or claims with all the stolidity of Turkish mutes. Sometimes the American miner worked in silence and loneliness upon a single claim, going back and forth night and morning, a truly dangerous, resolute, and deliberative animal. The Frenchmen, on the contrary, were never seen alone : their social instinct was irrepressible; they went in groups to their work, and clustered together like buzzing bees. But when our solitary and reflective Americans found quartz or gravel that they thought would pay better to work in associated bodies, they came together at once in a way for which the sociable Frenchman showed slight aptitude. The Frenchman's bond of union was dependence, not mutual confidence: the American's reserve was really the source of his power, and the secret of his supremacy in every camp. Their loneliness meant resolution: therefore their organizations always meant business, and accomplished their appointed work.

One of the interesting bits of evidence upon the condition of the camps of '49 is afforded by Dr. J. B. Stillman's "Seeking the Golden Fleece." He says there was "no government, no law;" but "more intelligence and good feeling than in any country I ever saw. . . . Men are valued for what they are. . . . One feels that he has a standing here that it takes a man until he is old and rich to enjoy at home." This ignores the camp-laws, as unauthorized, but tacitly acknowledges the good order and peacefulness prevalent in the mining-region. On the subject of miners' generosity, Mr. Bacon, now an Idaho journalist, and an old California miner, writes me as follows: —

"I have never lived in any community where there was less crime, or where people were more charitable, than they were in the early mining-camps of California. No one was ever allowed to suffer for necessaries of life, and nowhere were the sick neglected. I remember many instances where a miner with a broken constitution, who had become discouraged or unable to work, and desired to return to his family, was sent home by the miners, and, in addition, was given one or two thousand dollars for a 'home-stake.'"

Theodore Winthrop, that bright, generous poet and novelist, saw the same characteristics in the hearty pioneers of the Pacific Coast, and rejoiced over "the rough sincerity impressed upon people by the life they lead in new countries."[1]

Some of the darker portions of the picture are shown by Theodore J. Johnson, in his "Sights in the Gold-Region;" and his views deserve careful consideration.

" The thirst for gold, and the labor required to procure it," he says, " overruled all else, and absorbed every faculty. Complete silence reigned among the miners. They addressed not a word to each other for hours."

He says, further, that although enduring great hardships, exposure, and often disease, the miners as a class obtained only a moderate remuneration. The average yield per miner was, he thought, only three or four dollars a day; and not more than one man in a hundred made a fortune, and invested it safely away from the mines. Out of one hundred and twenty men who went around the Horn, and were at the same camps, "not one had great success." These views regarding the average yield of the mines to each toiler are well sustained by the official reports. The five thousand miners of 1848 averaged one thousand dollars apiece, though many of them did not reach the mines till very late in the season; but the hundred thousand miners of 1850 dug out only half as much proportionately, working a longer season, and with far better appliances. The gold-product of the State reached its culmination in 1853, then sinking year after year to a point below the total of 1849, but varying little during the past ten years. The introduction of capital and machinery has rendered it impossible to estimate the amount that each man's labor now produces. The annual gold-yield of the

[1] Theodore Winthrop, "Life and Letters." See also his description of the "appalling activity" of San Francisco, then the chief outfitting point for all the mines; p. 134.

State has been, for a number of years, something over sixteen million dollars; in 1883 it was $16,500,000.

Another very strong statement upon the nature of life in the mines comes from Mr. George F. Parsons, in his Life of Marshall, to which we have previously alluded. He says, —

"It was a mad, furious race for wealth, in which men lost their identity almost, and toiled and wrestled, and lived a fierce, riotous, wearing, fearfully excited life; forgetting home and kindred; abandoning old, steady habits; acquiring all the restlessness, craving for stimulant, unscrupulousness, hardihood, impulsive generosity, and lavish ways, which have puzzled the students of human nature who have undertaken to portray or to analyze that extraordinary period."

He says that a true account of those times would be " so wild, so incredible, so feverish and abnormal," as to remind one rather of a description of a Walpurgis Night than of an era in real life. In another place we have this graphic picture: –

"Take a sprinkling of sober-eyed, earnest, shrewd, energetic New-England business-men: mingle with them a number of rollicking sailors, a dark band of Australian convicts and cut-throats, a dash of Mexican and frontier desperadoes, a group of hardy backwoodsmen, some professional gamblers, whiskey-dealers, general swindlers, or 'rural agriculturists' as Captain Wragge styles them; and having thrown in a promiscuous crowd of broken-down merchants, disappointed lovers, black sheep, unfledged dry-goods clerks, professional miners from all parts of the world, and Adullamites generally, stir up the mixture, season strongly with gold-fever, bad liquors, faro, monte, rouge-et-noir, quarrels, oaths, pistols, knives, dancing, and digging, and you have something approximating to California society in early days."

Statements such as these concerning the overpowering excitement of the gold-search, and its evil effects, undoubtedly reveal a deep psychical truth. Evil men became more evil, miserly men more miserly, in the

Sierra camps. There must have been many to whose souls this "yellow, glittering, precious gold" was a "most operant poison," making "black, white; foul, fair; wrong, right; base, noble;" and over whose wretched lives the spirit of the exiled, ill-starred, man-hating Athenian's terrible mockery prevailed in ghastly earnest, until they lived and died in the bitter faith that "this yellow slave" of the exile's scorn could —

> "Knit and break religions; bless the accursed;
> Make the hoar leprosy adored; place thieves,
> And give them title, knee, and approbation
> With senators on the bench."

All in all, the most unfavorable and rabidly pessimistic account of California and of life in the mines, that has fallen under my observation, is Mr. Hinton R. Helper's "Land of Gold." [1] Writing as late as 1855, he says that the country had "no redeeming features;" the land was "a desert;" the customs of the people were atrocious; murders were of daily occurrence, and men were lying sick and uncared-for in the streets of the towns; it was the Nazareth of States, from which nothing except evil could come. To further prick the "California bubble," Mr. Helper offers such items as the following: —

Loss by fires, 1849–54	$45,870,000
Loss by freshets, 1849–54	1,500,000
Shipping lost on the coast	5,060,000
Total	$52,430,000

This certainly seems to show an astonishing degree of waste and loss. But the table is entirely unreliable.

---

[1] Land of Gold: Baltimore, 1855. Printed for the author. An intensely interesting work, chiefly by reason of Mr. Helper's unexampled talent for persistent pessimism.

It furnishes the separate items of the fire-losses which go to make up that total of over forty-five million dollars, and by these items we can test its accuracy. The San Francisco fire of May 3, 1851, is stated to have caused a loss of twelve million dollars: Hittell, a most cautious writer, gives it as seven million dollars. The Sonora fire of 1852 is stated to have destroyed property worth two million five hundred thousand dollars: the Tuolumne County official directory places the loss at seven hundred thousand dollars. From a multitude of equally reliable sources, the grand total of over fifty million dollars appears to be at least one-third, and probably one-half, too great.

From the fact of Mr. Helper's temperamental bias towards gloomy views of Pacific-coast life, manners, and institutions, his unexpectedly favorable evidence regarding the miners gains a peculiar importance.

"There is," he remarks, "more real honesty and fairness among the miners than among any other class of people in California. Taken as a body, they are a plain, straightforward, hard-working set of men, who attend to their own business without meddling with the affairs of others; and I have found as guileless hearts among them as ever throbbed in mortal bosom.

"Almost every bar," he continues, "is governed by a different code of laws, and the sizes of the claims vary according to locality. In one place a man may hold twice, thrice, or quadruple the number of feet that are allowed him in another. One-fourth of an acre is an average-sized claim."

Governor Richard J. Oglesby of Illinois was one of the pioneers of Nevada County, in "the days of '49 and '50." In a letter, published in the history of that county, he says, —

"There was very little law, but a large amount of good order; no churches, but a great deal of religion; no politics, but a large

number of politicians; no offices, and, strange to say for my countrymen, no office-seekers. Crime was rare, for punishment was
certain. I was present one afternoon, just outside the city limits,
and saw with painful satisfaction, as I now remember, Charley
Williams whack three of our fellow-citizens over the bare back,
twenty-one to forty strokes, for stealing a neighbor's money. The
multitude of disinterested spectators had conducted the court.
My recollection is that there were no attorneys' fees or court-
charges. I think I never saw justice administered with so little
loss of time or at less expense. There was no more stealing in
Nevada City until society became more settled and better regulated."

Among the men who "prospected" in the Nevada
mines, during 1849, was the late Benjamin P. Avery,
afterwards editor of "The Overland Monthly," and for
some time United-States minister to China. Mr. Avery,
and the late Samuel Williams, long literary editor of
"The San Francisco Bulletin," were two of the noblest,
purest, and best-loved men ever connected with Pacific-
coast journalism; and their memories are kept green
throughout the State they did so much to develop. A
letter from Mr. Avery printed in Bean's Directory of
Nevada County, in 1867, recounts his adventures in the
mines, and gives a graphic picture of "the childhood of
California." "I started from Mormon Island," he says,
"late in October, 1849; rode a little white mule, with
pork, hard-bread, and blankets packed behind me."
He heard of "pound diggins" (two hundred dollars
per day) near Caldwell's Upper Store, and at Gold
Run, in the famous basin where Nevada City and
Grass Valley now stand. There were about a dozen
parties working the bars with dug-out cradles and
wire and rawhide hoppers. A few tents were scattered
over the flat. The "store" was a square canvas shanty,
where mouldy biscuit sold for a dollar a pound, pork

for two dollars, flour one dollar, and boots for six ounces of gold-dust per pair. He found good prospects, and returned for his comrades. Evidently there was as yet no organization by which he could secure a claim, and hold it during his absence. He seems to have posted no claim, driven no stake; and, when the party returned, the ravine Mr. Avery had prospected "was occupied from end to end by long-haired Missourians who were taking out their piles." They had organized, and staked out claims of thirty feet along the ravine; and found them so profitable that "many a long-tom party took a quart tin pail full of gold-dust to their camp at night." The isolation of the place is sufficiently shown by the fact that "it cost two dollars and a half to get a letter to or from Sacramento." Mr. Avery afterwards prospected "in the savage wilds of the Middle Yuba, where only the grizzly and wildcat roamed the lofty purple ridge, four thousand feet above the sea." Eight years later he was editor and proprietor of a newspaper published there, in the midst of villages, churches, schoolhouses, gardens, vineyards, and hydraulic mines.

An unvarnished account of pioneer experiences is to be found in Lawson B. Patterson's " Twelve Years in the Mines of California." Arriving in canvas-built Sacramento, July 29, 1849, the author set out, on foot, for Mormon Camp, where the early miners had taken out over a million of dollars. He afterwards prospected far into the wilds of El Dorado. " Georgetown Camp" contained several hundred tents, but there was not a single woman in the district. " Hudson Gulch," in the same region, " is only three hundred yards long, but the first time it was worked it paid over fifteen hundred thousand dollars," and has been worked over and over perhaps a dozen times since. American miners began to find the need of business organization; and in 1850 and 1851 a "company of one hundred members tunnelled in Cement Hill." They did most of their own work, and ran four distinct tunnels far into the solid rock before they pierced the basin of auriferous gravel whose existence they suspected. Their association was reduced to six members, then rose to twenty, before success came. The total expenditure was one hundred and twenty-five thousand dollars, and yet the results paid well. Associations of miners ran twenty different tunnels into "Mameluke Hill," and sank many deep shafts, taking out over thirty-five hundred thousand dollars. The organization of the placer-camps was already leading to personal association for working the deeper deposits.

We find notes from a careful observer of mining-life in E. S. Capron's "History of California." He tells us that the miners are mostly "persons in the humbler walks of life," yet there are "no inconsiderable number connected with the learned professions. Whoever attends one of their miners' meetings will be convinced that neither the fools nor the drones go to the mines. Let the visitor wend his dark way into the mountain drift, or clamber over heaps of rocks and earth, and leap wide artificial drains, or go to some river where a deep, broad eddy has allured the hopeful miner, or travel over miles of upturned earth to where a solitary toiler is at work under the exhausting sun, and he will meet the grave divine, the skilful physician, the shrewd lawyer, the professor, the philosopher, the gentleman of leisure, and the student, as well as the farmer, mechanic, and common laborer. . . . Their time is esteemed too precious to hunt, fish, or cultivate the soil.

. . . Vagabond Mexicans, outlawed at home, make the miners their frequent victims."

Of mining laws and customs, Mr. Capron gives a tolerably accurate account. He says that the miners in public meetings had established courts "summary and signal in their proceedings;" and that "their jurisdicion embraced all actions and proceedings, civil and criminal. In most cases, the presiding officer was an elected alcalde, aided by a sheriff." The spectators constituted the only court of appeals. Annual meetings of the miners regulated all laws regarding claims. The size of claims averaged sixty by one hundred feet, and they were numbered and registered. In earlier times meetings were held much oftener than once a year, and the great body of "local mining-law" had been thus created. The "imperious necessity for these enactments" was universally recognized.

Quotations might easily be made at much greater length, and from many more writers. Everywhere we find, among observers of mining-life, testimony to the success of the system of self-government adopted in the camps; and, in no less degree, testimony to the energy and simplicity of the miners themselves. Some few among these observers give instances of abuse of mining-courts, of camp-justice that had for the moment degenerated into mob-rule. Cases are given where men's lives were saved by the prompt and cool courage of a few persons who insisted on another trial, or pointed out defects in the evidence. But we shall hear more of these things hereafter, in studying the local history of some of the notable camps. The main point to remember, so far, is the favorable impression made upon so many different writers, English, German, and American.

CHAPTER XIII.

ILLUSTRATIONS FROM EARLY AND SUCCESSFUL CAMP ORGANIZATIONS.

REMINISCENCES of the pioneers of California often drift into print. Many a book, justly famous, has been hammered out of the virgin gold of stories told around the camp-fire by men who were a part of that eventful period. A number of pioneers, some of them leaders, some of them of the uncounted thousands who only followed, have written me, giving, to their best ability, accounts of the organization of various mining-camps. Their recollections are often hazy upon definite points; but they all agree as to the informality and celerity of early proceedings, and the high degree of good order secured in every camp, without exception.

A gentleman, once a pioneer citizen of Marysville, before the famous Briggs orchard was planted, or Yuba County organized, writes, saying that he was among the first of the miners "in quite a number of migrating camps which proved evanescent, and disappeared with the swift current of events," but "were well governed while they lasted." In one case he and a companion "found pay-dirt in a cañon which sloped to the rushing Yuba," then a clear and beautiful river. Here they toiled for several days, and were doing well, when, one morning, they were suddenly visited by a delegation of miners from a neighboring camp, where the report of lucrative discoveries in the new gulch had been circulated by men who had climbed the hills in search of a stray pack-mule. The visitors, six or eight in number, proposed to organize a new camp, and share the "find." A consultation was held; and it was decided that each miner should be allowed to own and mine a strip of land ten feet wide on the river, and three hundred feet deep. Our friend and his companion were in the minority, and could not have objected had they wished; but the plan was so entirely in accordance with the usual custom, — the unwritten law of older camps, — that they yielded a ready and cheerful acquiescence. In view of the fact that they were the discoverers of the mineral wealth of the gulch, it was unanimously agreed that they should have first choice of ground; that is, the privilege of abandoning the location already made, and of taking up any other claim on the gulch. In many districts, they would have been allowed two claims apiece in acknowledgment of their rights as prospectors, but first choice was quite as often the rule. In closing his narrative, this gentleman says that "there was seldom or never any difficulty, because such a spirit of fair play actuated the miners of '49." [1]

Another gentleman, a graduate of Yale,[2] says, in the course of a highly interesting letter, that he "ought to know something about it," for he "began to work at mining when there was not even a custom, so that a man hardly objected to your digging close beside him so long as you left him room to swing a pick."

---

[1] This pioneer was Mr. William C. Dougherty, now (1884) deputy postmaster of San Francisco. He was once sheriff of Yolo, and was well known throughout the northern mines.

[2] Mr. C. T. Blake of San Francisco.

"A little later," he goes on to say, "I was present at a miners' meeting near Illinois Town, which was called together simply by sending notices through a district four or five miles square. My recollection is, that there was nothing done of any importance, as there were so many clashing interests that we could decide upon nothing which suited everybody concerned."

The Anglo-Saxon idea of compromise as the basis of all political action could not be more clearly shown than in the above statement. At a subsequent meeting, they doubtless settled upon some scheme that was the best that could be done under the circumstances; that, as far as possible, suited everybody. Americans were the only class of miners who recognized this principle as essential to any harmonious organization.

Our correspondent, in speaking of the mining-camps in which at various times he lived and labored, says that they "were mostly of limited size, say a small cañon and its tributary ravines, or a ridge between two cañons, or a river-bar." A mining-region of great extent, like Georgetown, Placerville, Coloma, or Nevada, "might contain numerous districts with entirely different laws. The work of mining, and its environment and conditions, were so different in different places, that the laws and customs of the miners had to vary even in adjoining districts." Nor were the laws of any district permanent: they had to be changed from time to time, as the district came to be "re-worked." This re-working of a district increased the size of a claim. With rich virgin soil, ten or twenty feet frontage was a large claim; but the same gulch when being worked over for perhaps the fifth time, for what predecessors had been unable to obtain, was divided up into claims of one or two hundred feet frontage. The ground worked at first by placer-miners with pick and pan, was again sifted and searched by rocker and long-tom process; then, perhaps, by ground-sluicing; and lastly, by various forms of the hydraulic process, the entire gulch, where dozens of small claims had once existed, passing under one ownership.

"Almost every mining-district," our correspondent writes, "kept written records from nearly the beginning, as claims had to be registered; but most of these records have been burned in the inevitable fires which have swept over almost every mining-town in California."

Some of the mining-counties of California, whose county-seats are towns that have grown from little mining-camps, are unable to show any historical records of earlier date than 1851. The lesser and migratory camps carried on most of their proceedings without any written records or documents of any sort whatever.

Notes sent by a California fruit-grower [1] describe his experiences in the mines. The only officer known in his camp was a recorder of claims, elected by the miners. His duties appear to have been clerical merely: the real business of the camp was transacted in open meeting by the assembled miners, who tried all criminal cases and disputes over claims, choosing a chairman, and voting *viva voce*. He never knew the miners of one camp to trespass upon the territory belonging to another camp. Difficulties of any sort were extremely rare. The camp being in a dry region, entirely dependent upon the water-ditches for working the claims, one of the district-laws was that all claims left idle a certain number of days after mining could be commenced, were considered to have been abandoned. Here we have

[1] B. D. T. Clough, of Alameda County, California.

hints of what was afterwards developed into a complete
and exact system of riparian regulations.

An account of the organization of Gold Hill Camp
has been secured through the kindness of a California
friend,[1] who interviewed an old miner named Morey,
and questioned him upon various features of interest.
The camp occupied a gulch and the adjoining hillsides, in the western part of Nevada County, and was
first prospected by several miners early in 1850, the
year that witnessed such surprising growth throughout
all that region. A few hours' labor convinced the discoverers that the royal metal was there in paying quantities, and they pitched their tent on the bank. Soon
the news spread; and within a week there were fifteen
or twenty men at work in the low, gravelly bed of the
creek. At first the camp had no organization or government, and every man's conduct conformed to his own
ideas of right and justice. Each miner had chosen a
spot to work in, and no question of encroachment could
possibly arise until their widening circle of operations
began to approach each other. About the close of the
first week after the establishment of the camp, the near
approach of two miners' operations caused a dispute
about the size of claims. One of the miners considered his rights infringed upon; and, a few days later,
after a good deal of talk, his friends circulated an informal verbal request through the camp, whose population had by that time increased to fifty or more, asking
for a miners' meeting in the evening. They all felt
that sooner or later definite laws must be adopted
for the government of the camp, or disorder would
prevail. The single question that had arisen could

[1] Rev. W. F. B. Lynch, of Centreville, Alameda County, Cal.; former
county superintendent of schools.

easily be settled by arbitration, but they must have
some general rules regarding claims.

When the miners of the new camp assembled, one
of their number called the meeting to order, and nominated a permanent chairman, who was at once elected.
The chairman then stated that there had been a little
trouble about claims, and might easily be more. They
could no longer let matters take their own course, but
must make a serious effort to get the camp into shape.
Its bounds were then established, making it about
three miles in length, and nearly two miles in width.
A few regulations were made about the size of claims;
some informal talk was indulged in regarding roughs
and thieves; and the meeting adjourned, to re-assem-
ble whenever called together by the chairman, who was
regarded as continued in office, and, in fact, as the head
of the camp, until such time as a new election took
place. At subsequent meetings, some further difficulties about claims were settled by vote; and the punishment of several thefts was fixed in the same way.

This camp never had a recorder or a jury, either of
six or of twelve. The whole meeting constituted the
jury; their decisions were final, and their punishments
immediate in execution. The chairman simply named
such miners as he thought sufficient to "carry out the
sentence of this meeting." Every man in the camp
was liable to be called upon to act as an executive
officer; and each law-abiding citizen of the camp was
a public prosecutor, unless he had been expressly appointed to defend the prisoner. Meetings assembled
whenever an offence had been committed, and disbanded
as soon as it had been punished. This crude but efficient law gave general satisfaction until the civil and
criminal law of the State stepped in to take its place,

and Gold Hill Cañon became a small and lessening village in one of the townships of the county.[1]

One of the Nevada-county pioneers writes of the beginnings of Rough and Ready Camp. The ravine was "located" in 1849 by a company of ten persons, who were followed by another similar company; and the two parties tried to maintain a monopoly of the gulch. One of the leaders went to the Atlantic States, and hired men to work for his company; but during his absence the influx of miners, who paid no regard whatever to the extensive claims of the first settlers, swept every thing before it. In September, 1850, there were five hundred miners at work in the gulch, and they had staked it out from end to end with claims of the ordinary size. Yet there was "no trouble, no shooting, or difficulty of any sort:" the monopoly scheme had failed, and that was the end of it all. Some of its members secured claims for themselves, and some were compelled to buy interests in claims already taken up. All the camps of this period rose and fell in population with a surprising rapidity. At Gold Flat there were two cabins in August, 1850; in July, 1851, over three hundred miners were at work there; in 1852 the place was abandoned. Washington Camp, settled in 1849, contained a thousand miners within one year; and during the winter of 1850–51, over three thousand men were at work in the immediate vicinity. Moore's Flat diggings, within a year from their discovery, grew into a camp of five hundred miners; Orleans Flat, into one of six hundred. Grass Valley had fifteen cabins in

[1] The township of California is not like the township of New England. It is much larger, often containing three hundred square miles. It only elects road-supervisors and constables, and these only on the county ticket, and has a proportionate vote in the county board of supervisors.

October, 1850, and a hundred and fifty by March, 1851 : four years later, its population was three thousand five hundred. In each of these camps, organization kept pace with the growth of population; and there was never any serious disorder.

A pioneer of 1849, who, after many wanderings among the camps new and old, has settled down as the editor of a Boise City newspaper,[1] lays great stress, in his reminiscences, upon the law and order maintained with little difficulty in the camps of California. In his experience, all persons who attended a meeting were allowed to take part in its deliberations, whether residents of that particular district or not. If it was a criminal case that the court had assembled to consider, the accused was granted counsel, both sides were heard, and a vote was taken. In some instances the amount of punishment awarded was excessive, but it usually inclined towards mercy's side. In one case, in the little Sierra camp in which he dwelt, a meeting was held to try an Irishman and a Dutchman on a charge of stealing an old shovel and pick from a claim where they had been left by the owner to hold possession for him ; the rule of the district being that all claims were forfeited so soon as the tools were removed. They were convicted on the evidence of witnesses who saw them carry the tools off. Their plea was, that the tools were so old and worthless that they supposed no one else wanted them. But the claim, it was answered, by that act, through no fault of its owners, had been thrown open to the next prospector ; and therein lay the guilt of the accused, since they were fully aware of the law of the camp. They were there-

---

[1] Mr. D. Bacon, editor Boise City (Idaho) Republican.

fore sentenced to be whipped, and expelled from the diggings. One of them received a portion of his lashes, but a motion was then made and carried to remit the remainder; and the two men were escorted to the border of the camp, and told to seek fresh pastures. The miners' meeting then gravely and earnestly advised the owners of the claim to be careful and leave better tools there another time, so that the object of so leaving them might be indisputable.

After giving various regulations about the size of a claim, similar in their leading features to those previously spoken of, this correspondent says that this method avoided endless litigation; and that the system of later years, adopted in the newer Territories such as Idaho and Montana, which allows a man to hold twenty acres of valuable mineral-ground, to the exclusion of all others, has produced bitter fruit. The smaller plots of the California miners were much better for the community. All were contented, and none were hopelessly poor. A group of California prospectors, in those early days of which we are writing, seldom attempted to determine the superficial extent of the placer, and then divide it up among themselves. When they did attempt it, the effort always came to grief, as in Rough and Ready Camp. They seemed rather to wish to ascertain how much surface-ground would give an operator a full season's work; they chose the richest spots they could find, marked out their small claims, and left to later comers the ascertaining of the limits of the auriferous deposits of the district. Very often, indeed, when a miner had worked out his claim, there was plenty of equally good and never-occupied ground close at hand.

But the lesser differences in all these early camps

were innumerable. An old miner writes me from Chili, where he owns a large *hacienda* on the borders of the Araucanian country, and states that a Yuba county camp he helped to organize in 1850 did not permit the transfer of claims, either by sale or by gift; and disputes were referred to the oldest man in camp, whose decision was final, but was in every case so in accordance with justice, that it was invariably accepted. An old miner whom the writer once met illustrated a similar method in vogue in one of his early camps: "When we come back to dinner, Bill an' I, two strange fellers was at work in our claim. We sat down on the bank, an' told them there was plenty of good gravel, jest as good, a mile down the river, an' that was our diggin's. They didn't stir, so one of us went an' asked Cap'n Bob Porter, the best an' quietest man in camp, to come up; an' we all had a drink outen the cap'n's flask, an' then we talked it over, he bein' spokesman. Pretty soon they said it warn't no use making a row, an' went off very friendly."

This very summer of 1884, the dwellers in a cottage on one of the fairest islands of Casco Bay interviewed a rugged old sea-captain, a pioneer of the gold period, and a kindly, white-haired giant of a type not unlike brave John Ridd in "Lorna Doone." He had toiled in many different camps, but chiefly in the noisy town of Spanish Bar, Placer County, where an elected alcalde ruled, and where "every one drinked as much whiskey as they wanted." The size of claims in his experience varied, but at Spanish Bar it was ten feet square in the dry diggings. Tools left on a claim held it for three days' absence, and a claim-notice protected it for seven days. Claims on the river were one hundred feet in length, as a rule; though sometimes, when a camp was crowded, and all the best claims taken up, a new company of miners would come along, and, calling a public meeting of the miners, persuade them to diminish the prescribed size of claims, so as to give all an equal chance. Sometimes the first-comers exceeded their rightful bounds, but readily yielded when other miners arrived.

This sort of evidence and illustration, afforded by letters from pioneers of California, might easily be extended beyond the limits of a single chapter; but we must turn to a more definite discussion of the laws of the camps, and the various systems under which they were controlled. The flexibility of the government known in the Sierra camps, and the freedom with which it assumed different forms, were quite as admirable traits as were its earnestness and efficiency. Even in the quotations already given, there are hints of different methods of governing camps; and these must now receive consideration.

CHAPTER XIV.

FORMS OF DISTRICT GOVERNMENT. — FOLK-MOOT, STAND-ING COMMITTEE, AND ALCALDE.

As we have seen, the forms of local organization under which laws, civil or criminal, were made for the governing of mining-districts, were varied and sugges-tive; but they are all reducible to three types, — that rule of the whole body of freemen, which we have here-tofore denominated the "folk-moot of the Sierra;" that rule of a select and permanent committee or council to whom supreme authority was sometimes delegated; and, lastly, that individual rule of the alcalde, or of the miners' justice of the peace, offices of nearly similar powers and duties in the eyes of the early gold-seekers. Behind the seldom-questioned supremacy of council and alcalde, preventing them from unjust, despotic, and arbitrary extremes, was the tacit acknowledgment of the right of the community to interfere in extreme cases. Society ever kept a watchful eye upon its au-thorized dispensers of justice. The "folk-moot" was the original and central institution.

This assemblage of the people, called together by any person or persons, after choosing a temporary offi-cer, proceeded to discuss subjects of interest, try cases, make laws, and enforce them. It was literally govern-ment by the miners of the district. Boys of fifteen and sixteen, broad-shouldered and self-reliant, often took part in the deliberations of the meeting. It was this miners' court, that our Norse and Saxon ancestors, could they have risen from burial-mounds like Beowulf's "on the steep, seen by sea-goers from afar," reared there by the "battle-brave hearth-companions" of the dead, would undoubtedly have recognized as akin to those folk-moots held of old in primeval German and Scandinavian forests. In both alike were the right of free speech for all freemen, the right of unhampered discussion, the visible earnestness, the solemn judgment, not only in the name of the people, but by the people themselves, assembled to right wrong, to try offenders, to smite even to death, or to justify and set free. Out of this meeting, containing such possibilities for good and for evil, other forms of government known to the miners developed, or in this meeting were of their own free will adopted. No alcalde, no council, no justice of the peace, was ever forced upon a district by an outside power. The district was the unit of political organization, in many regions, long after the creation of the State; and delegates from adjoining districts often met in consultation regarding boundaries, or matters of local government, and reported to their respective constituencies in open-air meeting, on hillside or riverbank.

In all cases of criminal trials, the miners' court assumed much of a judicial aspect. Whatever legal talent the miners possessed was brought into service. In 1849 hardly a camp existed on the great Sierra slope, that did not contain miners who were graduates of colleges and law-schools, or were lawyers of considerable experience. Many of these men, in after-years, became leaders in county and State affairs. Earnest, intelligent, and cultivated speakers stood ready to defend the accused. When acting as tribunals of life and death, all who appeared were entitled to a vote, and to be heard; but when deciding laws concerning claims and local government, members of other camps could not vote. The accused — camp-thief, sluice-robber, horse-stealer, or murderer — was guarded by men with revolvers, or was tied to a tree. The miners' court was in such cases assembled at once, not by formal notices, but by a cry running from claim to claim, from height to height, proclaiming, for instance, that "they've caught the fellow that robbed John Smiley's sluice-boxes last night." Nearly every one then came into camp, and the case was usually brought to trial within half an hour.

Short speeches were made for and against the prisoner; the presiding officer charged the jury " to do the fair thing accordin' to common-sense;" and after a brief deliberation they rendered a verdict, and the presiding officer decided the penalty. If there was no jury, the case was submitted to the decision of the miners present, who also fixed the punishment. In small camps, where only thirty or forty men assembled, this was perhaps the usual system; but in larger camps, the jury-system prevailed. In one case, a trial was had, and the prisoner hung within an hour; it being a cold-blooded murder, with a dozen witnesses to the act. In another case, the jury spent four days in taking testimony and listening to arguments. When it was decided to hang the prisoner, the crowd guarded the town and the building where he was confined, having reason to fear an attempted rescue; they gave him four days to prepare for death, and then, on the ninth day after his arrest, hung him to a bridge in the presence of more than two thousand men, with all the dignity and solemnity imaginable.

Capital punishment was not, in the miners' code, confined to murder: it was often inflicted upon those guilty of lesser crimes. Thus the roads were made safe, the cabins of the lonely miners secure; as in the days of good Duke Robert, "gold bracelets might hang untouched from an oak by the public highway." Horse-stealing was sometimes considered a capital offence; partly because of the great value and scarcity of horses in the mines, partly from the fact that a desperado once mounted was infinitely more dangerous than before to society. The entire absence of jails and prisons in which to confine criminals reduced available penalties to three, — banishment, whipping, and death. In practice the punishment awarded for theft was whipping for the first offence; but if repeated, it was at the peril of the offender's neck. The cases in which men were hung for theft were justified by the miners under the plea of necessity; the lawless classes being sometimes strong and defiant, only checked by the stern determination of Americans to protect their property from claim-jumpers and thieves.

Cases of whipping were very numerous. A man who stole a sack of flour, just after the Nevada City fire of 1851, was given twelve lashes. In 1850, in Grass Valley, a mule-thief received thirty lashes. In Trinity County, at Hay Fork, the first thief was whipped by the entire camp, each miner giving a blow. Hardly a camp existed in the mining-region, where, sooner or later, the assembled court did not decree this form of punishment to some offender. In one case, a man who entered the tent of a Chileno woman one night during her husband's absence, and attempted violence, was whipped so severely that he was hardly able to drag himself out of the camp he had disgraced. A store-

keeper was once whipped for swindling the miners out
of their gold-dust by false balances. In Calaveras
County, a man stole a small amount of dust, received
ten lashes; returned that night, and committed another
theft; was given twenty lashes, and sent out of camp.
He went to the next camp, and there stole a mule on
which to leave the country; but the miners of this
camp caught him, and the court sentenced him to fifty
lashes well laid on. When stripped, however, his condition from previous punishments appeared so dreadful
that a vote of forgiveness was passed; and the owner
of the mule took the culprit to his tent, and dressed the
bleeding wounds.

The miners' court was never wittingly cruel in its
judgments, but it was liable to be swayed by prejudice
or passion. The change to a committee or council form
of government, which occurred in quite a large number
of cases, was a decided improvement. The best example of this type occurred at Rough and Ready Camp,
Nevada County, early in 1850, after the State government had been organized, but while three-fourths of
the mining-region still depended upon miners' courts.
This camp, established late in 1849, had a population
of several hundred persons. They held a mass-meeting,
and elected a committee of three persons to administer
justice. The miners then went about their business,
and left the management of the affairs of this thriving
camp entirely in the hands of these three citizens.
There was no higher court; and their authority was
nearly absolute, and always well sustained.

Before this council, a man who was accused of stealing was tried with the forms of law, was found guilty,
and was given thirty-nine lashes, after which he was
banished, and warned never again to appear in that

camp. The three members of the council had equal powers, and all voted in such cases. Presumably a majority ruled. In quite a number of cases, the punishment given to offenders was "forty stripes save one."

The council had civil jurisdiction, as well as criminal. They settled quite a number of disputes about claims; they laid out the streets of the town, and apportioned the town-lots among its citizens; they even appointed a constable, issued writs as occasion demanded, and accepted bail-bonds for the appearance of accused persons. One of these bonds is still in existence, and shows that a person charged with horse-stealing offered bail to the amount of one thousand dollars, and afterwards came forward and stood his trial.

The nearest fully established court of justice was at Nye's Landing, afterwards Marysville, over thirty miles distant, where a justice of the peace had been elected under the State laws. Nevada City had an alcalde, but he exercised no jurisdiction outside of that district. The Grass-valley miners met in November, 1850, under a large oak-tree, and elected by ballot a justice of the peace, and constable. But Rough and Ready district was satisfied with its council, which accordingly decided all disputes, administered justice with an equitable hand, and in all respects made their management of camp affairs so satisfactory that it lasted until the jurisdiction of the county was fully established.[1]

This sort of government by a committee, or council, to whom all powers are intrusted, re-appears in Tuolumne, Placer, and Shasta counties. The influence of the idea is, perhaps, manifest in the adoption in many

[1] Rough and Ready was then in Yuba County's jurisdiction. H. Q. Roberts, James S. Dunleavy, and Emanuel Smith formed this Committee of Vigilance and Safety.

camps, almost simultaneously, of the principle of arbitration, according to which permanent officers were chosen, and given the duty of acting as arbitrators whenever called upon. In some camps, as late as 1854, all disputed claims were referred to a standing committee; and the laws of many districts, as will be shown hereafter, contain traces of this principle. No case of the miners' court interfering with, or revising the action of, such a committee, seems known to record or to tradition.

The third, and historically the most interesting form of camp-government, was by means of an alcalde, that Spanish-American official of time-honored authority and dignity. It seems to have given satisfaction wherever adopted; as the camps which in 1848 organized under that form made no change until their incorporation as towns under a city council, or their subjection to the general county system. The duties, powers, and many-sidedness of the office in its typical development have already been described.

Removal of the office from the immediate control of the military governors of California to places far in the interior, and difficult of access, had practically emancipated it from all superior authority. We have already seen what close supervision the alcaldes of the coast-towns received under Kearney and Mason, and what jurisdiction General Riley claimed and exercised; but over the alcaldes of the mining-region, there is no evidence that the control elsewhere exercised by the *de facto* governor of California was ever felt or acknowledged.[1] The miners were not in the habit of writing

---

[1] The California Documents containing the official correspondence of Kearney, Mason, and Riley, at various times during 1847, 1848, and 1849, to various officers, are crowded with letters to alcaldes in coast-

letters of inquiry when difficult cases were brought before them, or of waiting for weeks till, by slow and uncertain methods of communication, advice was received from Monterey. Even when the Constitutional Convention was called, it proved impossible for more than half the miners to vote; again, when the question of adopting the constitution was submitted to the people, the same difficulty occurred. Even a tax-gatherer could not keep the run of the new camps. Each little district in the Sierra was a body politic by itself, conscious of no outside control; its alcalde seldom paid any attention to the doings of his neighbor alcaldes, nor conformed his rulings to the strict letter of Mexican alcalde-law, nor, indeed, to the letter of any law whatever.

The typical plan by which a single officer was elected, and clothed with full alcalde powers, was often modified. It sometimes happened, that, at the very first miners' meeting of the district, a sheriff was chosen to aid the alcalde; and a recorder to register mining-claims, sometimes to act as clerk of the alcalde-court. A camp provided for in this lavish manner was considered to have given proof of its permanence to all the world. The chairman of the meeting administered an official oath to the newly elected officers, who were at once installed. The alcalde issued writs and summons according to forms copied from the nearest available law-book, or evolved from his own inner consciousness and sense of fitness, and often expressed in untechnical — even ungrammatical — language; the sheriff served

towns. But no letters were written to, or received from, any alcaldes east of the Sacramento and San Joaquin Rivers; nor were any removals, appointments, or changes made east of those rivers. Even when Mason and Riley visited, in 1848 and 1849, the camps, there were no appeals made to them: the miners had already organized.

these writs and summons, made arrests, preserved order, and saw that prescribed punishments were duly inflicted.

The compensation allowed to these officers varied. The alcalde usually received about sixteen dollars for trial of a cause. The sheriff had pay for serving writs, and mileage for all travel performed in the discharge of his duties. Jurors received six dollars apiece for each case tried, and witnesses were paid their actual expenses.

Funds for these and other necessary expenses were secured by the system of registering claims. The fees for this were from fifty cents to one dollar for each registry, of which the recorder received a percentage; and miners were so restless, so constantly taking up new claims and abandoning their old ones to others, that even small camps were kept in funds for all necessary judicial expenditures. There was no waste whatever. Every dollar, except the recorder's small percentage, was used for legitimate expenses. A camp that charged no fees for recording claims had two financial resources, — one, and the most frequent, by means of a collection; the other, by a direct assessment upon the claims. Thus we see that the miners had solved the problem of obtaining financial support to their courts of justice, and, in full accordance with the socialistic features of their system, had made taxation equal. The amount to be raised was small: no miner felt the payment of a dollar when he registered a new claim. No tax-collectors were needed, for the fact that unregistered claims were liable to be "jumped" in short metre was a sufficient incentive. The district thus provided for was a self-governed, independent, and self-supporting state in miniature.

The jury for civil cases was usually composed of six persons, perhaps from questions of economy; in criminal cases, it was always twelve.   The alcalde's decision, it need hardly be said, was final.

In many cases, a camp was long governed by occasional miners' courts, and did not adopt the alcalde system until nearly the full organization of State and county courts.   Thus, in March, 1850, "the need of more authority was felt at Caldwell's Upper Store;" and a man named Stamps was by ballot elected alcalde, two hundred and fifty votes being cast.   At the same miners' meeting, the name of the camp was changed to "Nevada City."   Only two months later the county officers at Marysville ordered an election for justice of the peace to supersede the alcalde, so his reign was a brief one.[1]   The evidence of Governor Riley, as noted in a previous extract from his report of a visit in 1849 to the Tuolumne camps; also the evidence of Mr. Bayard Taylor, who describes alcalde rule as "nearly universal in the Butte-county region," — is sufficient to show the extent to which the system was adopted.   It suited the demands of the mining-community; being simple, efficient, thoroughly representative, and always responsible to the people.

Stories of curious alcalde decisions are numerous in the mining-region, and some of them are extremely characteristic.

In Columbia district, Tuolumne County, the first case brought before the alcalde was an American miner's complaint against a Mexican for stealing a pair of old leather leggings.   That official, himself an American, remonstrated; but, justice being demanded, he fined the Mexican three ounces (about fifty dollars) for the theft, and the miner one ounce for making a complaint

[1] Thompson and West's History of Nevada County; chapters on Early Courts, and on Nevada City.

over such a trifle. The second case in this court was
a miner's suit against a neighbor, for a pick stolen from
his claim. Judgment for plaintiff, for value of pick, one
ounce; and costs, three ounces.

In 1849 an El Dorado alcalde had a case of trespass
on mining-ground brought before him, and settled it to
the satisfaction of both parties. The district treasury
was nearly empty. Turning to the astonished sheriff,
the alcalde ordered him to pay the costs, since the tres-
passing miner was poor, and had infringed unwittingly
upon his neighbor's rights, while the mulcted officer
owned the best claim on the gulch. "If you don't do
it, the boys will have to take up a collection." Protests
were ineffectual, and the sheriff paid the costs.

In one of the Calaveras camps of 1849, a sailor de-
serter, too lazy to work, stole several thousand dollars
in dust and coin from under a miner's pillow, was captured, left tied to a tree the rest of the night, and in
the morning given a jury-trial, and found guilty. The
alcalde sentenced him to one hundred lashes well laid
on, though the crowd wanted him hung as an example
and warning. All the miners favored stringent and
rigidly enforced laws against theft. A law permitting
capital punishment for theft remained for a few months
on the State statute-book.

One more story of early alcalde methods will suffice.
It was in one of the northern mines; and the alcalde
had a slow, oracular delivery, and a mild, gentle, persuasive manner. To him one day a well-dressed young
man who had stolen a purse, and tried to escape on
horseback, was brought for punishment; the evidence
being so clear, that after five minutes' listening to the
testimony, the alcalde said in his most seductive ac-
cents, —

"Would you like to have a jury-trial, my son?"

"No, judge: it isn't worth while to do that."

"All right, my son. Now you must return the dust you stole."

"Certainly, judge."

"And the court regrets the necessity, but really, my son, you ought to pay costs, — two ounces."

"Oh, I can stand that: here it is, and thank ye, judge."

"Now the court is fully satisfied, with the exception of one trifling formality. — Boys, take him out, and give him thirty-nine lashes well laid on."

We must remember that all the various forms of camp-government existed in one place or another, at the same time; that the older and more prosperous camps were assuming the appearance of towns, and perhaps had a town-council, sheriff, and recorder, besides the alcalde; while the newer camps were in the first stages of growth. Nevada camps of 1849 were in somewhat the condition of El Dorado camps of 1848; Trinity-county camps of 1851 were ruled as simply and directly as were those of Nevada in 1849. For months after the State judicial system was adopted and established at the various county-seats, the remote camps saw only the tax-collector, and continued to govern themselves by their favorite local methods. Long after Sonora Camp had organized a town government, and elected a council and mayor, though without State authority, there were hundreds of small camps where no officer except the chairman of the miners' court had ever been known. The primitive folk-moot reigned supreme in these temporary camps. A chronological study of the life of various camps is impossible. Some were blossoming, others decaying; some began under committee-rule, others with one-man power. But none, after electing an alcalde, chose to abandon the system and return to primitive methods; although in more cases than one they asserted the right of the camp to sit in judgment on the actions of their elected ruler.

Brief though the reign of the mining-camp alcaldes was, it left a deep impress upon mountain society; as an occurrence in northern California a few years ago will perhaps illustrate. There is a school-teacher there, a man of mighty frame and great energy, whose boyhood was spent in the placers of Siskiyou, and his young manhood on the cattle-ranges of eastern Oregon, and in adventurous wanderings along the frontiers of British Columbia. When the late war began, he went East, and joined a regiment; returning to his mountain wilderness in 1865, a crippled and battered veteran. He had always been a close reader and hard student: so, as a teacher, he soon won a reputation for success over three counties. Under these circumstances he was called to take charge of what, with undoubted justice, was called one of the worst schools in northern California. The mail-rider threw off the trustee's letter at the door of this man's summer cabin, perched on a pine-clad height of the Sierra; trout-stream within a stone's throw; grouse, deer, and bear in the woods; his gun and rod in the corner, his "Marcus Aurelius" and "Noctes Ambrosiana" on a rustic shelf. He saddled his horse the next morning, and reached the village, once a mining-camp, before nine o'clock. When school was called to order, he found that efficient work demanded a re-classification; because the previous teacher had tried to gain cheap favor by advancing grades without reason, and skipping the hard places. After a few weeks he had come to grief by trying to persuade a large boy

not to smoke a cigarette in school-hours; for the play-
ful innocents had ducked him in the adjacent stream,
sousing him up and down until he escaped, waded to
the farther bank, and sought other fields for his peda-
gogic prowess. But the new teacher possessed frontier freedom of resource, and military discipline of
character.

"I must turn you back in your grades," he said, after
several hours of examination. An ominous murmur
of rebellion followed. Several boys rose in their seats,
and announced that their parents "would see about
that."

The teacher then made his first and last speech to
the excited school. He took a book from the table, and
addressed the most noisy of the rebels.

"Do you know what this is?"

"Yes, sir, — the school-law."

"And it defines the grades; and you think that last
year you passed an examination, and that I cannot go
behind the law?"

"Yes, sir."

"Very well, you are quite mistaken. I am the alcalde of this school. I am sheriff, and register of
claims, and judge of the camp, and the whole jury. I
am absolute finality here!" With this comprehensive
statement, he threw the school-law out of the open win-
dow, and then, in the midst of an awe-struck throng,
proceeded to break up and consolidate class after class.

"Yes, an alcalde was what the district needed," was
the opinion of the old pioneers of the village when the
story was told; and a better school, for the rest of
the year, northern California never knew.

CHAPTER XV.

HOW AN ALCALDE WAS ONCE DEPOSED. *

WE have said that in the mines there always was a tacit recognition of the power vested in the people of the camp to depose an alcalde from his high office. One of the best known instances of the exercise of this power occurred in the southern Oregon mines, as late as the autumn of 1852; and its history throws more light upon the ideas of justice and law which underlie these frontier courts, than could be obtained by pages of barren generalization.[1]

It is not our purpose to describe the beginnings of local government in Oregon, the famous " Wolf Meeting " of the settlers of the beautiful Willamette Valley in 1843, and those earlier local organizations in that region in 1838 and 1839, which preceded and made possible that notable assembly. The Spanish-American and gold-seeker elements were entirely foreign to the struggle that organized Oregon under a legislative committee and supreme judge, while the ownership of her territory was as yet undetermined. That interesting struggle of Americans to gain control in the north-west must be studied elsewhere.[2]

[1] The points for this chapter are obtained from an article, "Pioneer Justice in Oregon," Overland Monthly, first series, vol. xii. p. 225, and from letters of correspondents.

[2] Oregon: Barrows; American Commonwealth Series, p. 265. Mrs. Victor's articles on Early Oregon, Overland Monthly, first series. Gray, W. H., History of Oregon. Overland Monthly, November, 1884, p. 555.

* In the volumes entitled *Popular Tribunals*, Bancroft describes this same episode. While Bancroft's account agrees with Shinn's in essentials, it differs in some details and offers additional information. Bancroft states that the affair took place in the autumn of 1852 at Jacksonville. He gives the name of the rascally partner as Sims, not Sim, and bestows upon the offending judge the title of justice of the peace, not alcalde. Bancroft, *Works*, XXXVI, 626–630.

But in south-western Oregon there were placer-mines; and to these narrow gulches, clad with spruce and fir, California miners went, bearing with them the organization perfected through fierce struggles and dire necessity in the camps of 1848 and 1849. They governed their Oregonian camps on the plans adopted in Siskiyou and Shasta, in Amador and Fresno, in Tuolumne and Nevada. North of the Calapooia Mountains, the pioneer Oregonians were, and always remained, totally unacquainted with that famous Spanish office, the alcaldeship: south of those mountains, there were several alcaldes chosen by the settlers, and given the extensive powers of the office as known in California camps. Before January, 1852, there were no county organizations in the south-western fourth of Oregon, and for a year later the alcaldes continued to rule supreme in that region. Returned Oregonians, who had determined to prospect nearer home after one or two seasons in California, were influential forces in all the earlier Oregon camps.

The miners of Jackson-creek Camp, Rogue-river Valley, had an alcalde named Rogers. He was not at all popular, but was thought to be honest and capable until events showed him in an unexpected light. His election had occurred before the camp had "boomed:" the few early miners on the creek had chosen him, and the crowds that came later had accepted his authority.

It happened that there were two mining-partners, named Sim and Sprenger, who worked a claim together, and were unnoticed and unknown in the mass of busy workers till a sudden difficulty brought them into prominence.

Sim took money from the funds of the concern, and went to Portland to lay in their winter's stock of pro-

visions. During his absence his partner, Sprenger, met
with an accident, and was crippled, helpless, and sick
in the cabin, nursed by a few sympathizing friends,
when Sim returned. The real nature of Sim revealed
itself: without any compunctions he at once ejected
Sprenger from their cabin and their claim. Of what
use was a sick and crippled partner?

The wronged and unfortunate miner secured the services of a young man named Kinney as his lawyer, and
took his complaint to Alcalde Rogers. But Sim, as
events proved, had forestalled him by arguments of another sort: putting little trust in his claim of a verbal
sale, and his extremely doubtful witnesses, he bribed
the unworthy alcalde, who, disregarding local custom,
mining-law, and the plain dictates of reason and justice,
rendered his verdict against Sprenger. The plaintiff,
in sad destitution and misery, and urged as a forlorn-
hope by some of his friends, begged the alcalde for a
re-hearing of the case, which was promptly refused: a
judge could not be expected to overrule his own decisions. Nor would he grant a jury-trial. Restitution,
and re-instatement in his possession of one undivided
half of cabin, tools, provisions, and claim, appeared un-
attainable for poor Sprenger.

The story was told throughout the camp, and it was
openly said that there had been bribery of the witnesses, perhaps of the alcalde; but the camp, though
populous, was a scattered settlement, and concerted
action was difficult. There was indignant talk, but the
men and the hour had not yet arrived. Sprenger found
shelter in a friendly cabin, and Sim began to look about
for an able-bodied partner who wanted to "buy in."
But no one desired the situation of partner to such a
man.

Matters were in this condition when Sprenger, still brooding over his wrongs, still urged by sympathizing friends, heard that a miner in the camp, named Prim, was a first-rate lawyer, a graduate of some law-school, and an attorney of considerable experience. Hoping against hope that some new mode of procedure might yet be devised, Sprenger hobbled to Prim's claim, and begged for his assistance. At first this was denied; and Prim even said he was no lawyer, and could not leave his work. But Sprenger's penniless and piteous condition became an appeal that could not be disregarded: the miner threw down his tools, hunted up Sprenger's former attorney Kinney, and they held a conference.

Further appeal to the alcalde was clearly useless. But Prim proposed to reach the territorial courts north of the Calapooia Mountains, — to go, in fact, to Portland itself, — and there obtain powers to organize a district court with appellate powers over the entire region. There was constant need, he argued, for a more complete scientific system. They could not continue the unbalanced, uncontrolled, irresponsible alcalde system without a higher court to check its abuses. The practical difficulty in the way was, that all this would take months, and their unfortunate client would probably starve long before the close of the approaching winter. Then, too, the value of the interest he owned in the claim from which he had been ousted was steadily diminishing, as Sim worked there from daylight to dark. And if Sim should succeed in finding a partner, a new element of difficulty would be added.

At last Kinney is reported to have exclaimed, "Who but the people made the damned scoundrel alcalde, anyhow? We can organize our own court of appeals."

Prim caught eagerly at the idea. They sent a man

up and down the gulches, and over the ridges, to the extreme limits of the district within Alcalde Rogers's jurisdiction. It took a day of hard travel to summon them all, but nearly every one heeded the appeal to his sense of justice. There was no attempt to pre-judge the case, or to bias men's opinions. Each miner was told that numbers of persons thought a great wrong had been done, and that it was desired to exam-ine the entire subject with all fairness and deliberation, sustaining or reversing the former judgment as the evi-dence should warrant.

So the eventful morning dawned; and over a thou-sand miners threw down their picks and shovels, left their rockers, long-toms, and sluices, and came hasten-ing to the main camp. Every man of them all suffered a loss, by his day's idleness, of whatever his work that day would have earned, — perhaps five dollars, perhaps fifty dollars; but the miners of Jackson Creek were willing to suffer loss if justice, as between man and man, could thereby be established.

The court met in the open air, and chose a presiding officer. They then elected a committee of three well-known miners to wait on Alcalde Rogers, and respect-fully request him, "in the name and by the authority of the citizens of Jackson-creek Camp," to re-open his court, and give the case of Sim *vs.* Sprenger a new trial: they asked also that a jury be allowed. Rogers refused point-blank, and retired grimly defiant to the intrenchments of his log-cabin. The committee re-turned, and made a report in open meeting. It was then discharged, and the first act of the drama had closed.

Only one course was left for the miners' meeting, — to organize their higher court, and invest it with full authority to review any and all proceedings of the court below. This seems to have been done by these bold reformers on the supposition that it might have to be a permanent thing: it was not merely an expedient by which to re-instate Sprenger in his rights, if such rights a fair trial proved him to possess. It had dawned upon the minds of those earnest men assembled in that winding Oregonian ravine, that the time had come for a higher judicial organization. With strong good sense and sturdy independence, they grappled with the problem.

First, a miner named Hayden, one of the most respected and intelligent men in the entire community, was nominated and elected to serve as chief judge of the district. He declined the responsible position, begging them to choose some one else; but the duties of the office were urged upon him until he was forced to accept.

Judge Hayden displayed the greatest promptitude, dignity, and good sense in his proceedings. He at once asked for a sheriff and a clerk, who were immediately elected, and reported themselves ready for duty. Within an hour after Hayden's acceptance, a writ of *certiorari* commanding Alcalde Rogers to appear in the new and duly established court, before Judge Hayden, and submit the records of his proceedings, was served upon that officer by the newly installed sheriff of Jackson Creek. To the surprise of all concerned, the stubborn alcalde refused to yield, and proceeded to impugn the motives of certain leaders, and deny the legal existence of the court. History has failed to keep an exact record of his language; but, beyond a doubt, it was profanely belligerent.

The crowd of miners were by this time tired and

angry. It was suggested to batter down Rogers's
cabin, take possession of his records, and lay them
before the newly chosen superior judge. But to this
Judge Hayden objected, as defeating the ends of justice. He called the sheriff, and issued new writs, ordering both parties in the original controversy to appear
before him at once for a trial: in other words, he ignored
all former proceedings, and asserted original as well as
appellate jurisdiction over the camp. The impressiveness of the scene had now become indescribable. Those
hundreds of brawny, bare-armed, red-shirted men,
grouped in the open air, under giant oaks, were moving
without noise or excitement to the full accomplishment
of their appointed task.

Plaintiff and defendant came before the new court,
and were assured of a full and fair trial. Witnesses
were summoned; a jury impanelled, sworn to do their
duty; and lawyers appointed for each side. Tradition
reports that Sim's lawyer was able and courageous, but
that his witnesses weakened under the severe cross-
questioning of his opponent. Both lawyers made appeals to the jury, and the case was submitted. No one
can doubt, from the dignity and earnestness which had
hitherto prevailed, that a verdict for the defendant,
though contrary to the general expectation, would have
been accepted by the assemblage. By the verdict of
that jury, those freemen who had left their claims lying
idle for miles were tacitly pledged to abide; and Prim,
Kinney, and Hayden would have been the first to ac-
quiesce, the last to propose any "new deal."

The court, in his charge to the jury, said that they
must strip the case of technicalities, regarding no law
but right and wrong, no test but common-sense. They
listened with approval, and at once proceeded to dis-

agree on a vital point: some wanted to hang Sim, who had been proved guilty of bribery; several wanted to hang Alcalde Rogers. This dangerous phase soon passed away; the jury found a verdict for the plaintiff, and left the sentence with the court, where it evidently belonged. Judge Hayden then, amid breathless silence, announced his decision: Sprenger was to be re-instated in all his former rights, as half owner of cabin, tools, provisions, and claim; Sim was also ordered to pay the costs of his partner's sickness. The court then adjourned.

But some of the evidence offered had revealed so much rascality and malfeasance on the part of Alcalde Rogers, that none of the miners were satisfied to let him longer hold the office he had so disgraced. Who could any more put confidence in so untrustworthy an official? How could a thousand men, some of them living five miles from the central camp, be expected to leave their claims, and administer justice by newly organized courts each time there was need thereof? The crowd proceeded to Rogers's cabin, growing angrier and more tumultuous each moment. A cry that he should be hung swelled like a mountain torrent in time of flood; but Hayden, Prim, Kinney, and Jacobs (who had been Sim's lawyer), made speeches, and reason again prevailed. One thing, however, was certain, — Alcalde Rogers must resign; and this he did without demur. Judge Hayden's court was then re-assembled, and it levied an instant execution upon some mining-property which ex-Alcalde Rogers had illegally and unjustly obtained; it being part of the Sim-Sprenger claim, given to him by Sim as a retainer at the time of the first trial.

The Hayden court lasted until county organization, a

few months later, but no other case of any importance was brought before it. The lesson taught by the sight of those assembled pioneers had proved sufficient.

The typical nature of this remarkable case is best shown by the facts that Sim's lawyer, Mr. Jacobs, has since become chief justice of Washington Territory; that Mr. Prim has been chief justice of Oregon; that Judge Hayden for many years has been one of the leading citizens of southern Oregon; that the full records of the case are on file in the archives of Jackson County, Oregon; and that variants of the story can be heard in mining-camps hundreds of miles from Jackson Creek. Years ago, in Douglas-city Camp, Trinity County, Cal., the writer first heard of "Judge Hayden's appellate court:" to-day, perhaps, the story is told in the Kootenay passes, and under the Uintah pines.

In points of interest and importance, this case is only surpassed by the equally famous Scotch Bar case of the Siskiyou mines. But at Scotch Bar the problem was of a different nature, and cannot be considered in this connection: we must first return to the California camps of the early gold-era, and discuss a curious institutional link between the alcalde of full and unlimited powers, and the ordinary justice of the peace of ten years later.

CHAPTER XVI.

THE MINERS' JUSTICE OF THE PEACE.

THE most important officer the miners had under the early State and county organization was a justice of the peace, on whom, in practice, partial alcalde powers were bestowed in a number of cases.

The State law of 1850 ordered the election of justices of the peace in every township, and abolished the office of alcalde. The length of term was fixed at one year; jurisdiction to extend over the township, often as large as the average county of an Atlantic seaboard State. The justice had cognizance of action to recover damages, or specific property of not more than two hundred dollars in value.

In 1851 the powers of this office were greatly enlarged. The justice of the peace was given authority to try all civil cases when the amount involved did not exceed five hundred dollars, all cases of forcible entry and detainer, and all disputes over mining-claims and cases involving mining-properties, whatever their value. It was this last clause which made the miners' justice of the peace a much more powerful potentate in 1850–52 than was his brother of the valley townships. His criminal jurisdiction included all cases punishable by a fine of not more than five hundred dollars, or not more than a year's imprisonment.

Hon. A. A. Sargent, in his valuable "Sketch of the Nevada-county Bar," says, —

"The jurisdiction of justices of the peace in 1850–51, who were then the only judicial officers known in these diggings, was a little shadowy, or very substantial, as the reader pleases."

Some examples are given by Mr. Sargent. In 1851, in Rough and Ready, just after the famous council retired to private life, a case which involved possession of a mining-claim on Lander's Bar — a claim worth fully one hundred thousand dollars — was tried before Justice Roberts. Among the counsel was Mr. Lorenzo Sawyer, now on the supreme bench of California. The trial lasted three days, and the jury disagreed. A new trial was commenced on the following day, which lasted ten days, and was one of the most closely contested legal struggles of the period. Able and brilliant lawyers fought the ground over, inch by inch, and exhausted every resource of the profession. This trial resulted in a verdict, and the losers paid a bill of costs amounting to nineteen hundred and ninety-two dollars in gold-dust.

In September, 1850, one of the "coyote-hole claims," near Nevada City, was owned by several Frenchmen, and is said to have paid as high as nine hundred and twelve dollars to the pan.[1] Several Americans coveted the mine, and so demanded to see the owners' foreign-tax receipts. The Frenchmen had none less than two months old, but were ready to pay whenever the collector appeared. The Americans drove them off, took possession, and began work. Suit to recover was brought before the justice of the peace. The case went to a jury, and the chief plea of the Americans was that "they wanted a slice." Of course the verdict was against them; a sheriff's posse at once re-instated the true

---

[1] "Coyote claims," small holes on the hillside to reach rich gravel, which is carried to the nearest stream, and washed out.

owners, and the claim-jumpers were warned against repeating such exploits.

Quite a number of cases are on record where a justice of the peace issued writs of injunction to restrain parties from working valuable mines until their true ownership could be decided. In one case, this injunction was made perpetual.

The justices were not always fit men to hold office. A miner near Placerville was once on trial before a justice for assaulting a claim-jumper. The story is admirably told in Parsons's Life of Marshall. The trial began at eleven P.M.; and the justice kindly adjourned the court every few minutes, so that prisoner, prosecutor, jury, witnesses, officers of the court, and spectators could fraternize at the bar of the neighboring saloon. When morning came, "a drunken lawyer addressed a drunken jury, on behalf of a drunken prosecutor, and, a drunken judge having delivered an inebriated charge, a fuddled verdict of acquittal was rendered."

At Nevada City, in 1852, a thief was sentenced by the justice, to receive twenty lashes: so he was tied to a pine-tree, and given his punishment before the court adjourned. Stories of equally summary judgment and execution are told of pioneer justices of the peace at "Piety-hill" Camp in Shasta, and at camps in Klamath and Butte.

In one very amusing case reported from Nevada County, two alleged horse-thieves were brought before an old justice of the peace whose fame for honest, original, and usually sensible decisions had gone abroad. The friends of the two lawyers who conducted the case had laid wagers as to which lawyer would make the best speech; but of this the justice was, of course, kept in ignorance. The lawyer for the prosecution made out an unusually clear case; but the defendants' attorney called up a man from a neighboring camp, and asked, "What was the prisoners' character at the East where you knew them?"

"It was good," replied the witness.

"Good character!" squealed the brusque and excited old justice. "Good character, when they have been proved to be damned thieves? That evidence won't do. They stand committed.—Sheriff, take them to jail." A shout went up from the assembled crowd, and all wagers were declared "off."

The early justices of the peace in Tuolumne County were endowed with the same miscellaneous assortment of judicial powers that we have noted in Nevada: in some respects the survival of alcalde powers was more complete in the southern mines, where those powers had always been more despotic.

Justice Barry of Sonora, successor of the last alcalde of that region, was a type of a large class. He had an advertisement inserted in the Sonora "Herald" of July 4, 1850 (the first issue of the first newspaper published in the mines of California), which read as follows:—

"All persons are forbid firing off pistols or guns within the limits of this town under penalty; and under no plea will it be hereafter submitted to; therefore a derogation from this notice will be dealt with according to the strictest rigor of the law so applying as a misdemeanor and disturbance of the peaceful citizens of Sonora."

In the foregoing, "the judicious printer" had evidently corrected the orthography; but no printer could destroy the expressiveness of "derogation" and "strictest rigor." The following decision is given *verbatim et literatim*, and in the annals of frontier-justice documents it certainly deserves a high place. The affair which drew out this paper was a case in which the

State was prosecutor, and a Mexican named Barretta
was defendant. The trial lasted nearly two days, lawyers being engaged on both sides. Justice Barry, after
several hours of study and reflection, returned his decision in the form of a written document, still in existence. It reads as follows: —

"Having investigated the case wherein —— Barretta has bean
charged by an old Mexican woman named Maria Toja with having
abstracted a box of money which was burried in the ground jointly
belonging to her self and daughter, and carrying it, or the contents away from her dwelling, and appropriating the same to his
own use and benifet, the supposed ammount being over too hundred dollars; but failing to prove posittively that it contained more
than twenty, and that proven by testimony of his owne witness,
and by his owne acknowledgment, the case being so at variance
with the common dictates of humanity, and having bean done
under very painful circumstaces, at the time when the young
woman was about to close her existance, the day before she died,
and her aged mother the same time lying upon a bead of sickness
unable to rise or to get a morsel of food for her self, and he at that
time presenting him self as an angel of releaf to the poor and
destitute sick, when twenty poor dollars might have releaved the
emediate necessitys of the poor, enfeabled, sick, and destitute old
woman, far from home and friends. Calls imperitively for a severe
rebuke and repremand for sutch inhuman and almost unprece-
dented conduct, as also for the necessity of binding him over to the
Court of Sessions in the sum of 500\frac{00}{000}$.

        "(Signed)   R. C. BARRY, J.P.
"SONORA, Nov. 10, 1851."

Amusing as is this summing-up, this special pleading,
this honest indignation, and characteristic of the mining-
camp justice as is the entire document, yet the reader
cannot but feel a sense of disappointment at the out-
come. One fully expects a sentence that shall fitly
punish the Barretta enormities. But Justice Barry
recognizes the rights of the newly established court
of sessions, — though evidently with a struggle, — and

he will keep strictly within his powers as defined by
State law.   The court of sessions consisted of the
county judge and two justices of the peace, and had
original jurisdiction in all criminal cases except murder,
manslaughter, and arson.   Justice Barry was a member
of this court.   Sonora was in 1851 the county-seat of
Tuolumne.   In 1863 the sessions courts of California
were abolished by a constitutional amendment.

From papers still in the Tuolumne-county records, it
appears that Justice Barry acted as town coroner, for
which his fees were ten dollars in each case.   Between
Oct. 20, 1850, and July 28, 1851, we have the following
record of violent deaths: William Doff, Michael Burk,
James Haden, and William A. Bowen, all murdered,
"no clue to the perpetrators;" George Williams, suicide; William Bowen, hung at Curtis Creek, for killing
A. Boggs; T. Newly, killed by an outlaw named Fuller,
who made his escape; Leven Davis, "killed by a rifle-
shot in a Jumping Claim Row;" two homicides decided
to have been justifiable.   Almost every document winds
up with, "Justice fees ten dollars," or "Coroner's fees
ten dollars."

One document (No. 997) in Justice Barry's court,
was a writ issued to the sheriff, ordering him to summon
parties charged with having jumped a town lot belonging to "one Donnalld," who "claims his rights as an
American cittizen by claiming a writ to disposess them,
and to have restitution according to law with appropi-
ate damages for the imposission now about to be carried
out against him by sutch high-handed and mercenary
arrowgance on the part of aforesaid accused." [1]

---

[1] These records of Justice Barry's courts are taken from a very rare
pamphlet, published at Columbia, Tuolumne County, in 1856, by Hecken-
dorf and Wilson, and entitled a Miner's and Business Directory.   It

Many other stories of the early courts of justices of the peace might be told, but enough has been said to give some idea of their methods and powers. Calaveras, Stanislaus, Amador, El Dorado, and Tuolumne appear to have contained a large number of camps where these officers had more extensive powers than elsewhere.

The men who were chosen justices of the peace in these mining-camps were often eccentric and illiterate, but as a rule their honesty and good judgment were unquestionable. They had the full confidence of the people, and were conscious of the responsibilities of their office. In many a town of the mining-region, the pioneers still remember their names with respect, and still smile over their eccentricities. One of them, when dying, left "all his money, after paying funeral expenses" (some five hundred dollars), to "the boys for a treat;" and it was duly spent in the saloons of the camp. Yet he is said to have dealt out justice with firmness and good sense: his official conduct was satisfactory.

The race of such "miners-justices" has disappeared; and the office has shrunk each year to lesser powers and narrower duties, until it is now only the smallest wheel in the complex judicial machinery of the Commonwealth. But there is no doubt of the fact, that socially the position held to-day by a justice of the peace in the old mining-region retains something of its former prestige and dignity: the justice is often "judge" or "squire," terms that one seldom hears thus applied in the valley counties.

was lent me by the kindness of Mr. William G. Dinsmore of Oakland, California.

CHAPTER XVII.

ORGANIZATION OF TOWN GOVERNMENTS BY THE MINERS.

THE nature of the town organizations adopted by the miners in a number of instances next claims our attention. As soon as a camp was thought to be "permanent," — that is, supported by rich mines, and by lesser and tributary districts, — there was always talk of town government; perhaps from those used to the town councils of the Eastern States, perhaps from ambitious politicians. Sometimes the compromise that was made consisted in the election of a "committee of management," a council of three or five to attend to town affairs. Of fully organized town government, however, the best examples that the mines afford are those of Sonora and of Nevada City.

Mention has already been made of the struggle to obtain control of Sonora Camp in the days of '48, when an American alcalde was first chosen. The border-land position of the camp makes all its history interesting. Few of the mining-camps offer material of equal value for our investigation. The Americans of Sonora and that vicinity were from the first outnumbered by the foreign population, and only united action saved them from being overwhelmed. There were but nineteen "white men," two of whom were Frenchmen, four Spaniards, and the rest English, Scotch, and Americans, in Sonora Camp in 1848: the rest of its population were Mexicans and Chilians. Before the close of 1849 the total population was five thousand, and the camp was ruled by Americans. The manner in which town organization then arose was entirely unforeseen and unpremeditated.

As soon as the rainy season of 1849–50 set in, multitudes of miners, many of them Mexicans, were attacked with scurvy, owing to their exclusive diet of salt meat, since vegetables could be obtained only in small quantities, and at enormous prices. The resources of charitable individuals were evidently inadequate to cope with the evil, and it was proposed to organize and establish a town hospital. Nov. 7, 1849, this idea took form in the creation of a town government, it being felt that every thing had best be kept under one management. Mr. C. F. Dodge was then the alcalde of Sonora, and he was asked to act as mayor of the town. A council of seven members, five Americans and two Frenchmen, were elected to serve until further notice. They at once established a hospital, which was successfully maintained for more than six months, or until the ravages of scurvy were checked.

Expenses were enormous. Lime-juice cost five dollars a bottle, potatoes one dollar and a half a pound; canned fruits and all anti-scorbutics were twenty-fold the usual prices. Wages of servants were eight dollars a day.

The alcalde dedicated his official fees to hospital uses, and the citizens contributed largely; but the chief financial resource was soon seen to consist of the vacant town lots. The council, shortly after its organization, ordered a survey of the town, and had quite a number of new streets laid out. Up to this time, any one who chose took possession of a vacant lot, with the understanding that no one was to occupy more than one such lot of a reasonable size. All the hillsides not claimed under the mining-laws of the camp were unfenced, and used as common pastures until thus taken up for building-purposes. The winding streets of the earlier portion of the town followed the base of the cañon, or the lines of old pack-mule trails on the hillside. Land had possessed no value, except as used; and no one had taken more than he needed, for that only involved the building of more brush or picket fence. But when the new council had streets laid out, and lots surveyed, it gave them a positive value. Seldom, if ever before, has an American town attained to a population of several thousand without a great deal of very lively land-speculation; but the miners of Sonora Camp had lived in blissful unconsciousness of that resource.

Just about the time the survey was completed, but before the town council had asserted any particular rights over outside lands, the first State Legislature met, divided the State into twenty-seven counties, — of which Tuolumne was one, — and selected Sonora as its county-seat. Before the latter fact was known outside of the committee-rooms, one of the legislators wrote to a member of the Sonora town council, informing him that the county-seat question had been settled in favor of Sonora, and asked him to "take some of the boys, and secure possession of just as many town lots as possible," expecting, of course, to share in the profits.

The councillor was thoroughly indignant. He walked into town meeting that very night, with the letter in his hand, read it to the mayor and council, and offered a resolution, which was unanimously passed, that no one should be permitted to take up vacant lots, "be-cause all such unoccupied lands do belong to this town in its corporate capacity." This action was promptly enforced. From time to time, the lots were sold to the highest bidder, and the proceeds devoted to the town hospital.

When the county of Tuolumne was fully organized, it was found that the town government could have no legal existence without a special charter from the Legis-lature. It was therefore disbanded; and, the office of alcalde having been abolished, the only officer to rule the town was the "miners' justice of the peace," the Justice Barry mentioned in the previous chapter. But a charter was procured; and under it, in 1851–52, a mayor, marshal, attorney, sheriff, treasurer, clerk, re-corder, assessor, and seven aldermen were elected. This proved too expensive; and in 1855 the town gov-ernment was simplified, under a new charter, to a board of five trustees, with merely municipal powers.

The early Sonora town-council experiment seems in-teresting chiefly because of its spontaneity of growth. Established to secure a town hospital, and relieve the alcalde of its extra duties, it at last took all the man-agement of town affairs upon its shoulders; while the mayor, still acting as alcalde, decided disputes and criminal cases brought before him. The councillors received no salaries, and most of them could devote only their evenings to their official duties.[1]

[1] As illustrating with clearness the "political atmosphere" of the mining-camps of 1850–51, the following instance deserves attention. Tuolumne County elected as one of its representatives a young man whose poverty was so great, that, after he was chosen, the citizens of his district assembled, regardless of party, and voted him a gift of sev-eral hundred dollars to buy clothes, pay stage-fare to the capital, and live comfortably till he could draw his salary. He made the best of records, afterwards practised law, and gained a competence.

Nevada City also had an experience of town government under the mining *régime*. The camp that in the spring of 1850 was only a collection of a few tents and brush huts, grew by August to a town of two thousand inhabitants; while within a radius of four miles a population of eight thousand men were at work, in a dozen or more lesser camps. On Dec. 22, the "Alta California" called Nevada "a frost-work city;" for hundreds of miners had abandoned the region, and the town seemed in the last stages of ruin. In the spring of 1851, all mining-interests revived, and the town soon recovered its former prosperity. Its enthusiastic citizens now procured a charter for a city government, and incorporated it on a liberal scale, providing for a mayor, marshal, clerk, recorder, and nine aldermen, including the "president of the council." They purchased a city-hall, built a jail, and established a hospital; for here, also, miners were dying of scurvy.

But Nevada City had no common lots to sell, no taxes, and few license fees were collected; and the financial resources of the organization were soon at an end. By September the town government had run itself eight thousand dollars in debt, and a public meeting was called to consider the problem. The aldermen agreed to discharge all the city officials, and suspend operations. Early the following spring, the State Legislature repealed the charter. Some of the scrip issued by the city was never redeemed, because the very disastrous fires which occurred late in the gold-era crippled its resources for some time. In 1853 the town was again incorporated, under a less expensive form of government.

Fifteen or twenty mining-towns received charters, and organized some sort of town government during the gold-era. Weaverville, Shasta, Oroville, Grass Valley, Nevada City, Jackson, Placerville, and some places that are now but waste and almost deserted villages, organized on a liberal plan, so soon as the day of tents and rough shanties had passed. It must be remembered that a great deal of capital went into permanent investments in these thriving and energetic towns. Brick blocks, three-story hotels, stores, banks, and fine residences embowered in blossoms and surrounded by lawns, were not infrequent long before 1856 in all the towns we have named. Population lessened as the mines decayed; and in many cases such investments proved unprofitable, or, indeed, nearly worthless. But the spirit of confidence that led miners to organize town governments so soon was eminently praiseworthy. Some of the schemes of the time were notable. A costly plank-road between Grass Valley and Marysville was discussed; plans for railroads were made public; the toll-road system developed rapidly, and was very important; local improvements, town-halls, theatres, costly bridges, met with hearty indorsement. Unity of action, and sympathy of interests, gift of early camp-life, are peculiarly characteristic of mountain towns of the gold-region, even at the present time. The towns are but overgrown and permanently settled camps. Nothing that is likely to happen will ever destroy this mining-camp atmosphere, that still pervades such peaceful and orchard-surrounded towns as El Dorado, Auburn, Grass Valley, with the loyalty and earnestness, the strength and freedom, of their tent and rocker period.

CHAPTER XVIII.

THE DIFFICULTIES WITH FOREIGNERS IN VARIOUS CAMPS.

THE heterogeneous population of the mining-region included a strange medley of races from the islands and shores of the Pacific, from the provinces of Mexico, and the countries of Southern Asia. Outlaws, desperadoes, men who had long before flung defiance in the face of law and society, were far too abundant in this conglomerate mass. Difficulties with such foreigners were inevitable, and they only served to weld the Americans into a closer union. Sometimes, however, the Americans were unjust and overbearing, or were at least careless and indifferent to the rights of others. It is an old story, still told in the mines, that idlers and gamblers have often been known to "raise a stake" by a double collection of the foreign-miners' tax from Chinese or Mexicans. The treatment of the early French miners, who, in 1849 and 1850, were forcibly driven from their claims in several camps, was simply outrageous; and the better class of miners did not always interfere to protect them against the bands of ruffians who desired their property. The filibustering expedition of Count Raousset* to Sonora, with its romantic features and tragic termination, would probably never have occurred, had it not been for the attacks which drove so many Frenchmen from the mines.

* Bancroft, in *Works*, XXIII, 585–592, tells the story of the ill-fated expeditions led in 1852–1854 by Count Gaston Raoux de Raousset-Boulbon, a French adventurer. Cf. *Grand Larousse Encyclopédique* (9 vols., Paris, 1960–   ), IX, 14.

As for the Chinese, there were large numbers of camps where none were allowed to work or hold claims at any time. They now find employment in many of the old and nearly exhausted gulches, working over the gravel, and often, it is thought, making quite valuable "finds." Their patience, perseverance, and industry are tireless. Even at the present time, however, there are camps within whose precincts no Chinaman is ever allowed to set foot. The local laws of Churn Creek District, Shasta County, as late as 1882, forbade any miner to sell a claim to a Chinaman, or to give employment to one. The feeling is, that, so long as white races find it pays to work the district, they shall be allowed to do so: when they desert the camp, the Chinamen may, of course, take possession. In many of the camps of the flush period, however, Chinamen were allowed to hold and work claims, by paying their foreign-tax. It was the experience of American miners, that many of the Chinamen were adept claim and sluice-box thieves; and to this fact the beginnings of the undoubted prejudice against them can be traced.

One of the cases* where indignation against foreigners had much justification was during 1850 and 1851, in the southern mines. In June of the former year, the collector appointed by the State to receive the "foreign-miners' tax," then thirty dollars a month,** arrived in Sonora. This sum had not been exorbitant in the newer camps, but in many cases men began to find it difficult to obtain so much. The foreigners, chiefly Mexicans, met, and denounced it, held public meetings, refused to pay a cent, and seemed so determined, that rumors went abroad to the effect that armed resistance could be expected. The miners of the surrounding camps armed themselves, and, to the number

* Bancroft, *Works*, XXIII, 405, dismisses this episode as having threatened serious trouble only briefly, but in the volumes entitled *Popular Tribunals* he gives a much more dramatic version that closely parallels Shinn's. Bancroft, *Works*, XXXVI, 152–155.

of several hundred, marched into the town, set a watch, organized patrols, and offered their services to the alcalde "for the preservation of peace and the suppression of crime." The Spanish-Americans in Sonora and in several Mexican camps adjoining, or not over four miles distant, seem to have far outnumbered the tax-supporters, and there was every reason to expect a collision.

About this time many of the Mexicans left their claims, and, retiring to the mountain fastnesses, became outlaws; so that, in a few weeks, robberies and murders were of almost daily occurrence. July 3 the citizens of Sonora met in public meeting to discuss "the public safety, and methods of self-protection." They resolved to organize a rifle company "of twenty-five men good and true;" they elected a captain, and ordered him to raise his company at once, and report to the new "court of sessions." They also chose a finance committee of three members, and began to take subscriptions from different individuals and camps.

July 10 four Mexicans were discovered piling brush upon and burning the bodies of two American miners. They were arrested, and hurried into Sonora. A crowd assembled; a jury was empanelled, and a judge chosen. The defence set up was, that the bodies had been lying there for several days, that the real murderers were unknown, and that it was the Mexican custom to cremate the bodies of the dead. But by this hasty and illegal trial, — illegal, because the court of sessions was fully organized, and the case came within its jurisdiction, — the prisoners were condemned. A *riata* was passed over the limb of an oak, and the trembling Mexicans brought forward to meet their doom. At this exciting moment Judge Tuttle, one of the bravest and

---

** The statute clearly specifies "the sum of twenty dollars per month." *The Statutes of California, Passed at the First Session of the Legislature* . . . (San Jose, 1850), p. 222 (Chapter 97, section 6, of the act passed April 13, 1850).

best of the pioneers of that region, accompanied by Judges Marvin, Radcliffe, and other gentlemen, arrived. Judge Tuttle made a thrillingly earnest appeal, saying that now the county had law, had courts, and could not afford to disgrace its record. The prisoners were given up, and taken to jail by the town officers.

The next week, district court and county court were both in session, and for the first time. Monday morning over eighty armed citizens of the town marched through the streets; and three hundred miners from " Green Flat Diggins," where the murdered Americans had been found, arrived to see the laws carried out in the punishment of the murderers. Every knife and revolver in every camp within a radius of a dozen miles was strapped to some stalwart miner's side, and either already in Sonora, or on its way to that place. The assembled miners were assured that speedy and reliable justice would be afforded, and they prepared to remain till the end of the trial.

Rumors of an uprising in a Mexican camp three miles distant were so numerous that the sheriff, with a posse of thirty American miners, went thither, arrested one hundred and ten Mexicans, marched them to Sonora, and confined them in a corral until the next day, when they were cross-examined by an interpreter, and, proving their innocence, were released.

Tuesday was the beginning of the famous trial. Fully two thousand armed and excited men were in the streets of the town. There was much talk; but the resolution to support the law, and abide by the decision of the court, was steadily increasing in strength. Part of Tuesday and all day Wednesday, the trial continued. " There did not appear a tittle of evidence against the prisoners, and the jury acquitted them." So, at least, runs the report of the newspapers of the time. And the crowd, ashamed, it may be, of their haste and eagerness for blood, signified their approval, and separated in silence.

Before the close of this eventful day, there were accounts of new outrages and murders. A public meeting was held, and Judge Tuttle was the speaker. He urged the necessity of active organization to arrest the progress of crime, and secure the safety of citizens. The chairman of the meeting appointed a committee of safety, which called a mass-meeting to assemble four days later, and strengthened the town-patrol.

Resolutions adopted at this mass-meeting were to the effect that —

" *Whereas*, The lives and property of Americans are in danger from lawless marauders of every clime, class, and creed under the canopy of heaven, and scarcely a day passes that we do not hear of the commission of murders and robberies:

" *Resolved*, That all foreigners in Tuolumne County, except persons of respectable character, be required to leave within fifteen days unless they obtain a permit from the authorities hereinafter named.

" *Resolved*, That the authorities referred to be a committee of three, to be chosen by the American citizens of each camp.

" *Resolved*, That all foreigners in this county (except such as have a permit) are notified to turn over their weapons to the committee, and take a receipt for the same."

The other resolutions provide for carrying this plan into effect. But the really dangerous men, the scattered Mexican outlaws, whose camps were in the mountain fastnesses, and hardly two nights in the same place, could not be reached by any such method; and it was not enforced except in a few camps where difficulties of an aggravated type had occurred.

The next year, an attempt having been to fire the

town, and an organized band of thieves having been discovered, a new vigilance-committee was established, which was in session several times a day for three or four weeks; which punished petty crimes by whipping, and banished a number of suspected persons. This committee seems to have refrained from all excesses, and it turned over to the civil authorities the only man that was brought before its tribunal charged with a capital offence. When order was restored, the vigilantes disbanded, and left the regularly constituted authorities in full authority.

The "southern mines" furnish some of the worst cases of mob-law, as well as some of the best examples of law-abiding, justice-seeking organization. The greatest number of difficulties with foreigners occurred there, and some of the worst quarrels over disputed claims were in those southern camps. It has been said by some observers, that men were readier to resort to the arbitrament of the revolver in the southern than in the northern mines. If such were the fact, it would not be surprising; for gold-seekers from the South-west and South predominated in those camps, as men from the North-west and North did in the camps north of Placer County. Organization in the southern camps was under greater difficulties, but it seems to have been fully as complete and successful as in the more northern camps. Some of the most orderly of the southern camps were controlled by New-England men, some by Georgians and Virginians. The steady evolution of society in these camps, out of the chaotic mixture of men of every race and characteristic, deserves our admiration; but a close study of the newspapers of the time, and the evidence of pioneers, convinces us that it is difficult for the American frontiersman to avoid treat-

ing the Mexican frontiersman with a sort of contempt-
ious defiance. Joaquin Murietta, and his outlaw reign
of years, was the natural result, not of deliberate injustice on the part of the American miners as a body, but
of blameworthy carelessness that too often permitted
the viler elements of the camp to enforce by actions
their rude race-hatred of the "Greasers." This tendency to despise, abuse, and override the Spanish-
American, may well be called one of the darkest threads
in the fabric of Anglo-Saxon frontier government.

CHAPTER XIX.

THE FAMOUS SCOTCH-BAR DECISION.*

THERE was a very remarkable example of the gold-seekers' methods of settling serious disputes, which once occurred in the northern part of California. It fairly deserves to be termed one of the most important and interesting of litigations in the early history of the mines. In many respects, it is even entitled to rank as the unique example of a higher type of organized effort to do the best thing possible under each and every circumstance, than is shown in the history of any other mining-camp of the period. The following brief account of the case rests upon the recollections of one of the most genial, generous, and intelligent of early Californians, — Mr. Anton Roman, first publisher of the "Overland Monthly," who spent sixteen months during 1850 and 1851 in several of the most successful mining-camps in Klamath and Siskiyou. Upon his stories and recollections some of Mr. Francis Bret Harte's best prose-work is founded; and they still afford a mine of invaluable material, literary and scientific.

Scotch Bar is rather indefinitely located by my informant as "in the Siskiyou-Klamath region." It was a highly prosperous camp, "booming" as the miners said; and the fame of its rich placers had already extended to Trinity, Shasta, and Butte, attracting traders, prospectors, and parasites of the camp. Exactly what local

* The name "Scotch Bar" was probably a misunderstanding, occurring in oral transmission, for Scott Bar, which was at the point where the Scott River joins the Klamath River, in the north-

219

laws and local officers the camp had, we do not know; but probably much the same that were known to districts in the central part of the State. It is likely that they had elected a justice of the peace, allowing him to settle their disputes over boundaries, and to keep a record of their claims. At least, so it appears, the camp had been peaceable, law-abiding, and contented; the miners had dwelt together in concord, much in the spirit of the Arcadian days of '48; and it was " a royally good camp to live in."

Some time early in 1851, a discovery of some very "rich gravel," or mining-ground, was made, and made in such a way, also, that two equally strong parties of prospectors laid claim to it at the same time. There were about a dozen men in each party, and both groups were entirely honest in their belief of the justice of their respective claims. Each clan at once began to increase its fighting numbers by enlistments from the rest of the camp, till twenty or thirty men were sworn to each hostile assembly. The ground in dispute was so situated that it was best worked in partnership, and thirty claims of the ordinary size allowed in the district would occupy all the desirable territory of the new find. So there were two rival companies ready to begin work, and no law whatever to prevent a pitched battle.

It began to look more and more like fighting. Men were asked to join, and bring their bowies, revolvers, and shotguns. Men were even forced to refuse the honor, against their wills, because, forsooth, there were no more weapons left in camp. The two opposing parties took up their stations on the banks of the gulch; there was further and excited talk; at last there were eight or ten shots interchanged, fortunately injuring

western quarter of Siskiyou County, just south of the Oregon boundary. See Bancroft, *Works*, XXIII, 399, footnote 53; and no one. But by this time the blood of the combatants was fairly roused; the interests at stake were very large; neither side proposed to yield: and the next minute there probably would have been a hand-to-hand conflict, except for an unlooked-for interference.

The camp, the commonwealth, the community at large, had taken the field the very moment the first shot was fired. Dozens and hundreds of men, five minutes before mere spectators of the difficulty, at once compelled a parley, negotiated a truce, and urged a resort to legal methods. The moment this compromise was suggested, the combatants laid aside their weapons. They knew there was no legal authority within twenty miles, and not even in the camp itself any force able to keep them from fighting; for persuasion was the only argument used, and it is not supposable that the rest of the miners would have actually fought to prevent fighting. It was a victory of common-sense, a triumph of the moral principles learned in boyhood in New-England villages and on Western prairies. "Men more thoroughly fearless never faced opposing weapons;" but the demand for a fair and full trial in open court found an answering chord in every bosom. Both parties willingly agreed to submit to arbitration; but not to the ordinary arbitration of the "miners' court," or of the "miners' committee," or of the "miners' alcalde," all of which we have heretofore described. They thought out a better plan, and adopted it after a few moments' discussion.

The rude and often biassed jury of the camp was repudiated by both contestants alike. None of the ordinary forms of tribunal known to the mining-region seemed to them entirely adequate to this momentous occasion. They chose a committee, and sent it to San

Doyce B. Nunis, ed., *The Golden Frontier: The Recollections of Herman Francis Reinhart, 1851–1869* (Austin, 1962), 28–36, 97.

Francisco. There they had three or four of the best lawyers to be found, engaged for each party ; and they also engaged a judge of much experience in mining-cases. It was a great day at Scotch Bar when all this legal talent arrived to decide the ownership of the most valuable group of claims on the river, — claims that had been lying absolutely idle, untouched by any one, guarded by camp-opinion and by the sacred pledges of honor, ever since the day of the compact between the rival companies.

Well, the case was tried with all possible formality, and as legally as if it had occurred within the civil jurisdiction of a district-court. It is not reported in any of the California law-books; but no mining-case ever commanded better talent, or elicited more exhaustive and brilliant arguments. The lawyers and judge were there to settle the case; the entire camp wanted it settled; both parties to the dispute were anxious to find out who the real owners were. In order to show the childlike sense of fairness the miners had, we should mention that before the trial began it was arranged by mutual consent that the winners should pay costs. To the losers, it was sufficient to have failed to prove title to such rich claims: they must not be made still poorer.

Now, in ordinary cases of camp-rule, there is often too much compromise : one claimant gets less than he deserves, while the other gets more. But in this justly famous Scotch-Bar case, there was in the end a verdict squarely for one side, and squarely against the other. The defeated party took it placidly, without a murmur; nor then, nor at any other time, were they ever heard to complain. The cheerfulness of their acceptance of the verdict was not the least gratifying episode of the famous trial.

" Ah! it was a great case," writes our informant, after an interview with Mr. Roman. "The whole camp was excited over it for days and weeks. At last, when the case was decided, the claim was opened by the successful party; and when they reached bed-rock, and were ready to 'clean up,' we all knocked off work, and came down and stood on the banks, till the ravine on both sides was lined with men. And I saw them take out gold with iron spoons, and fill pans with solid gold, thousands upon thousands of dollars. Ah! it was a famous claim, worth hundreds of thousands of dollars."

On the bank, along with these hundreds of spectators, stood the defeated contestants, cheerful and even smiling: it was not their gold, any more than if it had been in Africa. And the successful miners brought their gold out on the bank, divided it up among themselves, — so many pounds apiece, — and each went to his tent to thrust the treasure under his blankets till a good opportunity arrived for sending it to San Francisco.

The community capable of that Scotch-Bar case was a community which could be trusted to the uttermost. Put it down on a desert island, and it would organize a government, pick out its best men, punish its criminals, protect its higher interests, develop local institutions; and soon, unless its natural surroundings forbade, there would be a healthy, compact, energetic state, with capital city, seaports, commerce, navy, and army. Put it down on a new continent, and it would eventually possess, control, and develop all its resources and energies; doing the work that Rome did for Italy, that the Puritans did for New England, and through New England for the United States. And if the evidence of travellers, of the pioneers themselves, and of the institutions they organized, can be trusted, there were many such camps in California. The Siskiyou region did not monopolize that habit of self-control, of acceptance of the situation, of submitting questions to the best obtain-able courts, and of abiding by their decisions. From Klamath to Colusa, from Siskiyou to Fresno, from Lake Bowman to Trinity Peak, manhood and honesty ruled the camps of the miners. Some were ruled better than others, but all were ruled well.

CHAPTER XX.

THIS portion of our subject would not be complete without some allusion to irregular and sporadic forms of miner organization, to burlesque meetings, to later forms connected closely with the earlier assemblages of "all the miners of the district," and, lastly, to cases of mob-rule.

Rough and Ready Camp, in Nevada County, so interesting by reason of its simple and effective standing committee, or council, affords a valuable though eccentric example of independence. The township contains about a hundred and twenty-seven square miles, and was very prosperous in 1850, when a miner named Brundage conceived the idea of having a permanent and separate organization to be called the "State of Rough and Ready." He called a meeting, evidently in dead earnest, and proposed the scheme; urging that none of them had voted for the State Constitution, nor helped, through delegates, to make that instrument. About a hundred persons favored the plan, and for some time he continued to agitate its adoption; but the funny and absurd elements of the proposal so appealed to the miner's abundant sense of the ludicrous, that the entire scheme disappeared at last, in a fit of irrepressible and Homeric laughter. It became a topic of conversation in every cabin, and beside every long-tom,

for miles; but the State of California was good enough
for the light-hearted, keen-witted miners.

A curiously burlesque assembly gathered together in
Grass Valley in the winter of 1852–53, and is known
in local history as " The Hungry Convention." The
winter had been so severe that supplies were short:
bacon and flour had once again risen to the prices of
1849. Miners could not work their claims, and were
assembled in the town, spoiling for some enterprise or
excitement. So a meeting was called, in dignified earnest, to consider whether the scarcity of provisions could
in any manner be relieved. Every one soon saw, that,
in the condition of the roads, there was nothing for it
except patience: the merchants would secure supplies
at the earliest moment possible. The meeting immediately degenerated into a wild burlesque. Speeches of
the most desperate and communistic order were made,
and hailed with shouts of laughter and applause. A
duly elected committee reported, declaring war upon
San Francisco, and their resolve to have supplies thence
"peacably if we can, forcibly if we must."

The later history of the mining-camps affords innumerable examples of the keen pleasure that the average
American pioneer takes in public meetings, in resolutions, in committees, chairmen, and "big talks." He
does it in sober earnest most of the time, but now and
then he does it for the mere fun of the thing. The men
of the mining-region are even now, after all the changes
of the past thirty years, a race of men peculiarly ready
to assemble for free discussion, peculiarly apt to have
debates in the district-schoolhouse, to start arguments,
and listen to stump-speeches. The early training of
miners' courts and of camp-life has left its impress upon
the people of the mining-region. They differ from the

people of the valleys, as the mountaineers of Tennessee differ from the dwellers in the lowlands. But they have closer and better organization, a more abiding habit of seeking each other's counsel, of meeting in assemblies, and of discussing their affairs, than ordinary mountaineers have. The life of the gold-seeker brings men closer together in their camps and districts, and creates links of town-life, while the purely pastoral mountains still remain almost a wilderness.

Yet one must ask, in reviewing the subject of camp-government, Did the machinery of justice set in operation by the miners never degenerate into the weapon and excuse of a mob? Were the innocent never punished, the guilty allowed to go free? Did not feverish excitement and unreasoning violence too often rule? What, after all, was the miners' court, but an appeal to lynch-law, as that term is now understood? Were not council government and alcalde government, scarcely less than the miners' court itself, based on the will of the mob, and liable to strange outbursts, fluctuations, and monstrosities?

We find, throughout the mining-era, sporadic cases of true mob-law; of men being hung without judge or jury, without fair trial, and perhaps without justification. Considering the population, these cases were scarcely more numerous than in the Western States to-day. Regularly organized miners' courts proceeded with great care, and gave the prisoner the benefit of every doubt. Those men who were killed by mobs were usually caught red-handed in the act. In one notable case, a murderer was beaten to death before he was a hundred yards away, by pick-handles caught up hastily from a barrel in front of a store. In another instance, the murderer was stoned to death, with more than Hebrew energy, before he could climb the steep banks of the ravine where his victim lay.

The men who had led in organizing miners'-courts were the first to advocate their abandonment in criminal cases so soon as the county organization was possible, and were the first to oppose mob violence. In Nevada County, in 1850, a man named Studley was falsely accused of stealing a nugget worth three hundred and twelve dollars from a miner; and the crowd seized him, tied him to a tree, and proceeded to administer a flogging. Judge Roberts and several friends were passing; and they rushed into the crowd, released him, and soon proved his entire innocence of the theft. At Rough and Ready, in 1851, two miners, Stewart and Watson, rode into the town one afternoon, and saw a stranger being led by a mob who purposed to hang him. They drew their pistols, ran into the crowd, shouting, "You have the wrong man: let go of that man!" organized a committee, secured a fair trial; and in an hour the prisoner, who was accused of having stolen three hundred dollars, was set free. Cases like these were not the work of camp-organization, but of the roughs and hangers-on of the camp. And even the courts at that time awarded capital punishment for grand larceny.[1] " Law-abiding citizens from the first " is what Hon. A. A. Sargent calls the old "forty-niners." Nearly always, when passion and prejudice swayed the crowd, men of nerve and courage were at hand to check the tendency to mob-law. Sometimes it was the county or township officers who first interfered; as at

[1] For about a year, 1850–51,* a law which permitted a jury to bring in a verdict of death for grand larceny was on the statute-books. Under this law, one man was hung in Nevada County, one in Marysville, one in Sacramento, and one in Tuolumne County.

* The statute in question was not passed until April 22, 1851. *The Statutes of California, Passed at the Second Session of the Legislature* . . . (n.p., 1851), pp. 406–407 (Chapter 95, sections 1–3).

Beckman's Flat in 1852, when a miner was accused by his partner of theft, and was about to be hung by the crowd, when the county sheriff and the district attorney arrived on horseback, and rescued the prisoner, who was proved innocent. Perhaps the worst case of mob violence that ever occurred in the northern mines was at Newtown Camp, in March, 1852, where a jury of twenty-four, a presiding judge, and a clamorous crowd condemned on the merest suspicion of theft a negro, and hanged him immediately. As late as September, 1855, the Grass Valley community, roused to deep indignation against incendiaries, came near hanging a man who was found lighting his pipe near some unfinished buildings. In 1874 the mountain town of Truckee, infested by persons of bad character, was purified by a secret organization known as "601," which killed one person, and severely wounded another, besides banishing quite a number.

Cases of lynch-law occur from time to time in almost every frontier community, and too often in older communities also. But the difference between the true miner-courts of the gold-era, and such cases of mob-law, is fundamental and generic. Lynch-law, in the plain, every-day acceptance of the term, is the work of an association of men who have determined to violently expedite, or to suddenly change the course of, judicial procedure in one individual case. They announce no new laws, create no new system, add nothing whatever to the jurisprudence of the land. The moment the piece of work they were banded together to do is accomplished, they separate, and the association ceases to exist. They keep no records of their proceedings; the names of their leaders are sedulously concealed; and the regular officers of the law are often, in the discharge of their duty, brought into open collision with the lynchers. The utmost that may be said for them is that they often, though unintentionally, compel better administration of the laws; but, on the whole, lynch-law is manifestly selfish, cowardly, passionate, un-American.

In every important particular, the organizations of the typical mining-camps, which we have been considering, offer sharply outlined contrasts. Camp-law has never been the enemy of time-tried and age-honored judicial system, but its friend and forerunner. Axe of pioneer and pick of miner have levelled the forests, and broken down the ledges of rock, to clear a place for the stately structures of a later civilization. Rude mountain courts, rude justice of miner-camps, truth reached by short cuts, decisions unclouded by the verbiage of legal lexicons, a rough-hewn, sturdy system that protected property, suppressed crime, prevented anarchy, — such were the facts; and on these, frontier government rests its claims to recognition as other than mob-law, and better than passionate accident.

Later illustrations of vigilants-justice than those of California can readily be found. When, after a reign of terror almost unexampled in American frontier history, the tried and true miners and merchants of Montana organized during the winter of 1863–64, and in a few weeks hung twenty-four desperadoes and murderers, they performed a solemn duty laid upon them as American citizens. The present peace, order, and prosperity of that empire in the high Rockies, the "land of the silver bow," as its children love to call it, are the result of this acceptance of weighty responsibilities. Not until nearly a hundred persons had been waylaid, robbed, and slain, in various parts of the Territory, by members of a fully organized band of assassins, did society accept the challenge, and supply the absence of civil authority with the military firmness of the Vigilantes. It is a matter of history, that this organization, like that of San Francisco, never hung an innocent man, and that, when its work was done, it quietly disbanded.

In studying the nature of the mining-camps of California, we are irresistibly compelled to think of the whole race of American pioneers, from the days of Boone and Harrod to the days of Carson and Bridger; heroic forest chivalry, heroic conquerors of the prairies, heroic rulers of the mountain wilderness, ever forcing back the domains of savage and wild beast. Well did one of the most eloquent of American lecturers once exclaim, —

"Woe to the felon upon whose track is the American borderer! Woe to the assassin before a self-empanneled jury of American foresters! No lie will help him, no eloquence prevail; no false plea can confuse the clear conceptions or arrest the just judgment of a frontier court."[1]

When the pioneers of the newer West pushed into California, adding the leaven of such ideas to the mass of ancient Spanish civilization; when youth and energy from older communities of the Atlantic States, and adventurers from every land under the sun, joined in the famous gold-rush of 1849, — the marvel of marvels is, that mob-law and failure of justice were so infrequent, that society was so well and so swiftly organized.

[1] Dr. John C. Lord, lecture on "Land of Ophir;" delivered in Buffalo, February, 1849.

CHAPTER XXI.

LOCAL LAND LAWS AND LEGISLATION FROM 1848 TO 1884.

HERETOFORE we have considered only the appearance, general government, and criminal procedure of the early mining-camps; but there is a broad field of special mining-jurisprudence as yet comparatively untouched, and that, also, the field of most permanent value and greatest historical interest. The civil regulations of the miners were more varied and numerous than their criminal codes; and, reduced to their primary significance, they were "land-laws of the frontier."

It is difficult to express the supreme importance of laws which govern the ownership of land. The social, economic, and political history of the human race has turned upon the pivot of changes in systems of land-tenure; and here is a battle-ground of the future, as of the past. Nothing which serves to illustrate the workings of any land-system, or of any method by which lands were actually held in any community, can ever be called irrelevant or worthless; for the entire field of study is so broad, and broken into so many angles, that each ray of light is needed. Earnest students have explained the prominent features of the land-system of the ancient Germans, and have followed its history to the present time: they have told us how the primitive equality of the *Mark* system gave way in some remote past to the allodial system of village life, and how the holdings of lands in common yielded slowly to rights of separate ownership and inequality of estate, until thus the foundations of royal families and of feudal duties were laid. The ownership of land among the Saxons of the fifth century "was the outward expression, rather than the basis, of political freedom," so Mr. Stubbs tells us, "and in itself a usufruct rather than a possession." Landed property in England before the Norman conquest was of four distinct kinds, — the *folk-land*, belonging to the nation; the *common-land*, held by communities, as it is still held under the Russian *Mir* system, by the villagers of India, and in the pueblos of New Mexico; the *heir-land*, which had become partially alienated from the common-lands, and could pass by will, perhaps by purchase, with the consent of all the members of the community; lastly, the *book-land*, with its full and separate ownership, under a grant from king and witan. At last the hereditary freemen of the township became the tenants of the lords' manor, and the modern system of individual ownership of land was ultimately developed.

Now, the study of the mining-camps of the Far West reveals the presence of primitive Germanic ideas more clearly in their land-laws than in any other department of their jurisprudence. The rights of the individual over land were strictly subordinate to the rights of the camp, for use was made the proof of ownership. Then, also, the legislative enactments of the mining-camp clustered with peculiar force about the central question of land-tenure; and a large body of laws was thus created, setting forth with great exactness the size of a claim, the conditions under which it could be held, the circumstances which would work its forfeiture, and the methods of settling disputes in reference to its possession.

Moreover, the establishing of district land-laws led inevitably to meetings of the miners of many districts, who harmonized their diverse district codes into one which should be binding upon all the miners within the county, — a still further step in institutional progress.

The claims of each district were numbered and recorded, and their size was according to local regulation. The miners' meeting, when sitting to decide upon questions of this sort, was in fact like a local legislature, or a committee of the whole. It decided how many claims a person could hold; how much work he had to do upon each one to retain possession; what forms of conveyance were requisite; what relative rights and duties the owners of adjoining claims had; what constituted abandonment of a claim; in what manner riparian rights could be secured and maintained; lesser regulations about water-supply; rights of, or restrictions upon, aliens in the camp; and hundreds of cognate subjects. It could levy assessments for general or particular expenses of the camp as a body corporate, and could at any time adopt such new regulations as seemed desirable for preserving and protecting private rights. And these powers of the miners' meeting, or of committees, or officers appointed by them, lasted long after the State was organized.

In each new district, the framing of local mining-laws became the most important legislative duty of the miners. The laws of the hundreds and thousands of camps that grew and decayed in the Pacific-coast region, differing though they did in many particulars, all agree in recognizing discovery and appropriation of mineral property as the source of title; and development by use and working, as the condition of continued possession. This acceptance of the law of equal ownership in the gifts of nature deserves more than a passing notice. Probably every man in the gold-region had been educated in the doctrine of individual ownership of land : yet this instinctive return to first principles, this adoption of the ancient idea of "free mining-lands," common to all as once the woods and fields and pastures of England were common, will ever prove an attractive theme for students of historical and social topics.[1]

That mining-claims should become a subject of speculation, of sale and purchase, of transfer from owner to owner, seems to have been foreign to the views of the earliest placer-miners of California; and in some camps a man who sold his claim could not take up another. But it was not long before claims were everywhere acknowledged as real-estate property, held by "miners' title;" and the process of perfecting minor regulations went on with great rapidity. For all this, the miners' sole and all-sufficient plea was "imperious necessity;" and so thoroughly did they accomplish the work of creating a land-law, that until a comparatively recent

[1] Mr. Henry George, in his Progress and Poverty, writes:—

"For the first time in the history of the Anglo-Saxon race, these men were brought into contact with land from which gold could be obtained by the simple operation of washing it out. . . . The novelty of the case broke through habitual ideas, and threw men back upon first principles; and it was by common consent declared that this gold-bearing land should remain common property, of which no one might take more than he could reasonably use, or hold for a longer time than he continued to use it. This perception of natural justice was acquiesced in by the general government and the courts; and while placer-mining remained of importance, no attempt was made to overrule this reversion to primitive ideas. . . . Thus no one was allowed to forestall or to lock up natural resources. Labor was acknowledged as the creator of wealth, was given a free field, and secured in its reward. The device would not have assured complete equality of rights under the conditions that in most countries prevail; but under the conditions that there and then existed, — a sparse population, an unexplored country, and an occupation in its nature a lottery, — it secured substantial justice."

date the titles to all the mining-property of the newer
States and Territories has rested upon these local laws
and miners' enactments.

We therefore proceed to a minute analysis and comparison of the land-laws and consequent regulations by
which mining-camps were and are governed. We have
taken the laws actually enforced for a period of years
in many of the leading camps of various States and
Territories; sometimes abbreviating their enactments,
but omitting nothing essential to a full understanding
of the subject. The laws in their complete form are
usually concise, well-worded, and clear in meaning. In
some cases they were evidently drawn up by lawyers;
in other cases, by persons of good general education,
but as evidently ignorant of law. The period to which
they refer ranges from the summer of 1848 to the close
of 1884.

As regards the important question of the number of
mining-districts which have been governed by local
laws of their own devising, the United-States Reports
on Mineral Resources state that in 1866 there were
over five hundred organized districts in California, two
hundred in Nevada, and one hundred each in Arizona,
Idaho, and Oregon. There were, perhaps, fifty each in
Montana, New Mexico, and Colorado. Here is a total
of more than eleven hundred camps in the Far West,
as late as 1866. Since then the number of districts has
diminished in the older mining-regions, and increased
in the newer ones; but State and National legislation
has in a great degree restricted the field for local enactments. The number of actual placer-camps in California during its " flush period " is not recorded; but it
could not have fallen below five hundred, and probably
exceeded that figure. Mining was carried on vigorously

in twelve large counties, and to some extent in three others.

The first camp to which we shall invite the attention of our readers was situated five miles from Sonora, the county-seat of Tuolumne County, Cal., and was in one of the richest ravines known to the early miners. It bore the homely appellation of "Jackass Gulch" from the days of its first organization in 1848, but its earliest laws were not committed to writing. A square of ten feet of ground " often yielded ten thousand dollars from the surface dirt," and ten feet square was the maximum size of the claim allowed. After 1851 the laws, as adopted and enforced by the camp, were as follows : —

" *First*, That each person can hold one claim by virtue of occupation, but it must not exceed one hundred feet square.

" *Second*, That a claim or claims, if held by purchase, must be under a bill of sale, and certified to by two disinterested persons as to the genuineness of signature and of the consideration given.

" *Third*, That a jury of five persons shall decide any question arising under the previous article.

" *Fourth*, That notices of claims must be renewed every ten days until water to work the said claims is to be had.

" *Fifth*, That, as soon as there is sufficiency of water for working a claim, five days' absence from said claim, except in case of sickness, accident, or reasonable excuse, shall forfeit the property.

" *Sixth*, That these rules shall extend over Jackass and Soldier Gulches, and their tributaries."

The greatly lessened value of the mining-ground is shown by the size of the claim being increased from ten feet square to one hundred feet square. Requirement of claim-notice renewals during the idle season was common in most of the camps, unless a miner lived upon his claim. Thriving though the camp was in 1851, still crowded with miners by the hundred, it was rapidly exhausted; and in 1856, according to the Tuo-

lumne Directory of that year, had only twenty-two
voters.

Springfield District, whose leaders were men of New
England, trained in town-meetings and local self-government, was able to create an organic law far superior
to that of the preceding camp. Its laws were adopted
in written form at a mass-meeting of the miners, April
13, 1852; were revised Aug. 11, and again Dec. 22, 1854.
After describing the boundaries with great minuteness,
the preamble (of 1852) declares —

"That California, is and shall be, governed by American principles; and as Congress has made no rules and regulations for the
government of the mining-districts of the same, and as the State
legislature of California has provided by statute, and accorded to
the miners of the United States, the right of making all laws, rules,
and regulations that do not conflict with the constitution and laws
of California, in all actions respecting mining-claims; therefore
we, the miners of Springfield District, do ordain and establish the
following rules and regulations."

There are sixteen articles. The size of the claim is
fixed at one hundred feet square, no person under any
circumstances to hold more than one; work must be
performed upon it at least one day out of three during
the season for mining. Claims must have substantial
stakes at each corner, and must be " registered and described in the book of the precinct registry," to which
the owner or owners shall sign their names. Several
persons, each owning a single claim, may concentrate
their labor upon one of those claims.

Disputes are to be referred to a standing committee
of five miners, or to any member or members of this
committee, as arbitrators; or a miners' jury may be
summoned. Each member of the standing committee
shall in each case be paid two dollars for his service.

It is easy to see that a single arbitrator was in many cases entirely satisfactory for both disputants. The laws proceed to further define the process of arbitration. The head of the committee is to be sworn by a justice of the peace, provided such an officer be appointed in this mining-district, and is to administer the oath to his associates and to the witnesses. In some of the early camps, the alcalde administered this oath "to honestly arbitrate," to his deputies. The decision arrived at in either jury-trial or arbitration must be received as conclusive and binding upon the parties thereto, and be deemed and considered final in all such cases. Either party may compel the other to come to trial, by giving three days' notice of time and place. Costs shall be paid in the same way as in magistrate's courts. Disputes over water-privileges are especially named for arbitration.

Thirty days' desertion of a claim during the working-season results in forfeiture without remedy.

Article thirteen reads as follows : —

"No person not an American citizen, or where there is a reasonable doubt of his being entitled to the privileges of an American citizen, shall be competent to act on any arbitration, or trial by jury."

The next article provides that "companies which go to great expense running tunnels" are allowed "two claims for each member of the company." The first code of "tunnel-claim laws" adopted in this region was several years later, — Jan. 20, 1855; and it defined a legal tunnel-claim as "one hundred feet along the base, and running from base to base through the mountain."

Article fifteen provides for the election of a district recorder, who is to have fifty cents for recording the title of each mining-claim.

The last article provides that "all claims held by foreigners who have failed to secure their State license" shall be forfeited. This was to aid in the enforcement of the State Act of April 13, 1850, passed at San José. A list of the unnaturalized foreigners was to be kept in each county. The recorders of the different districts usually aided in its preparation.

These laws of Springfield District show plainly how much dependence was placed upon the arbitration — or, as the Spanish termed it, the *conciliacion* — plan. We shall find equal care in this regard in many other districts. Springfield is said to have been the first district in the Sierra Nevada that built a church before it built a gambling-house. It has remained an orderly, flourishing, and energetic community, since the days of its first organization.

Jamestown District, settled in August, 1848, by Southern and Western men, was regulated by miners' meetings assembled every six months, and sometimes holding special meetings to consider particular cases. In 1853, several persons having attempted to pass unpopular laws, the miners held a rousing assembly, repealed "all previous laws, of every sort whatever," enlarged the boundaries of the district, adopted the usual standard size for claims, — one hundred feet square, — and declared that all claims secured under former laws were publicly acknowledged as legal.

In this district, within three days from the time of location, a claim must have a ditch one foot wide and one foot deep cut about it: notices must also be posted, and stakes driven at the corners. Failure to work a claim within six days after the mining-season begins, causes its forfeiture. A miner can hold other claims only upon proof of purchase. Miners shall have the use of water from the ditches according to the date and situation of the location of their claims.

An important clause is to the effect that miners may dig up any farm, or enter within any enclosure, by giving the owner security that they will pay all damages inflicted. In no case, however, shall they dig within twelve feet of a building, or obstruct the entrance. Payment of damages meant only compensation for growing crops and improvements.

Shaw's Flat District required the claim to be "in one lot, and square in form." A notice would hold a claim for ten days after the season began. Part of a company could not "hold the claims of a whole company during the absence of a part of its members." Claims in "deep-diggings," where pay-dirt is twenty-five feet or more below the surface, may be laid over without work from Dec. 1 to May 1, if they are well defined by marks and notices, and recorded in the district register, which shall always be open to inspection. For some years there was an annual meeting to revise the district law, besides several meetings called by the chairman when it seemed desirable.

The laws of Sawmill Flat, Brown's Flat, Mormon Gulch, and Tuttletown districts present many points of resemblance. Two of them begin by saying, —

"*Whereas,* This district is deficient in mining laws and regulations, and disputes have arisen : therefore we, the miners of ——— district, in convention assembled, do pledge ourselves to abide by the following laws."

In three of the districts named, the laws provide that the discoverer of new diggings shall be allowed to hold twice the usual amount of mining-ground.

The laws of Sawmill Flat provided for a committee of three persons, elected by the miners, to call meetings of all the miners of the precinct, either to enforce the laws, or whenever, for any reason, they deem such meeting necessary. The arrangement for arbitration is as follows: —

"Whenever any dispute shall arise respecting claims or water-privileges, each party shall choose two disinterested persons; the four thus selected shall choose a fifth; and the five thus selected shall hear evidence according to the laws of this precinct."

The law of Brown's Flat provided that "all arbitrators shall be appointed by the committee" of three which then governed the camp. They were to be five in number; and were to "examine all disputed territory, hear testimony, and decide accordingly." This governing committee of Brown's Flat was elected "to hold office until superseded." It was the court of appeals in cases where the arbitrators failed to satisfy the parties. Its members were paid "wages for summoning the arbitrators, and for other duties;" but the amount is not named.

The Tuttletown laws say, "No person shall hold more than two claims, either by purchase or otherwise." They also provide that any one who destroys a notice or claim-stake shall be fined not less than five dollars nor more than fifty dollars. Notices of discontinuance of work on deep claims during winter are to be posted in some convenient and public place in the district. Tuttletown was so named because Mr. Tuttle, afterwards first county judge of Tuolumne, built and occupied the first cabin there. The miners of the district organized a water-ditch company in June, 1851, and carried their enterprise to a successful termination. Mormon's Gulch and Brown's Flat were first mined in 1848. Sawmill Flat became a great resort of Mexicans, Chilenos, and Peruvians, in 1850-51. Joaquin Murietta, the notorious outlaw, was a monte-dealer there in 1852.

Yorktown, Poverty Hill, and Chili camps had similar laws; and these pioneer camps were organized early in 1849. The first and last were settled by Mexicans and Chilenos, but Americans soon ruled all three. At Yorktown, within a month after its discovery, the Americans and other miners met, " and elected P. Cutrell for alcalde, and Mr. Rochette (better known as ' *Frenchy* ') for sheriff," under whose administration the district was governed well and quietly. The alcalde system was retained in its main features until superseded by county organization. In these districts, the miners assembled to pass legislative enactments; but they only referred to size of claims, and possession thereof, not in any case to "arbitration," because that was one of the alcalde's most important duties. The camp-laws limited " deep-diggings " to claims " of thirty feet square on unworked ground, and to fifty feet square on previously worked ground." A claim of sixty feet square was set apart for the discoverer of a placer. A claim must be worked within three days after staking it out, and placing a claim-notice upon it. Ten days' absence in the working season subjects it to forfeiture, and throws it open to re-location as an abandoned claim.

Chinese Camp also had an alcalde system ; and its laws, passed at a miners' meeting Sept. 17, 1850, were in operation for many years, without change. The alcalde elected at this meeting had "power to decide upon all disputed claims ; " his fees were fixed at three dollars for his decision, and a dollar a mile for traveling expenses from the central point of the camp to the disputed claims, and return. The legislative enactments of the district confirmed all claims " as made by the present settlers;" confined all future claims to "twenty feet square;" and required a ditch two feet wide and one foot deep to be dug about each claim, "unless prevented by rock or clay," in which case the removal of the surface-soil and the erection of corner-stones was considered sufficient. In this district, Isaac Caps was the first alcalde, and S. E. Chamberlain the first sheriff.

The laws of Gold Spring Camp presented some features differing materially from those of other districts in the region. Claims must be worked one day in every seven. Arbitrators were "earnestly recommended," but not made essential. Miners were compelled to make a new road if they destroyed the old one in their operations. This is often a bone of much contention in mining-districts. Gold Spring Camp had a population of about eight hundred, and was ruled in 1850 by an alcalde; in 1854 the population was five hundred. The gold of this district minted more than that of any other of the early diggings.[1]

Columbia District was always a large and important one, including several lesser camps, such as Yankee Hill, where many fine nuggets, one weighing twenty-three pounds, were found in the early days. The history of this camp was highly characteristic of the mining-era. March 27, 1850, five prospectors — all New-Englanders, and three, at least, from the woods of Maine — camped beside a gulch, and tested the gravel. To their delight it was found that they could make eight or ten ounces a day to the man, though water was

[1] Gold-dust, which at first passed at uniform rates in the mines, and in San Francisco, at one time falling to seven dollars per ounce, was carefully tested by the express companies; and they found that it ranged in value in different localities, from $14.50 to $19.50 per ounce.

very scarce. They named the place Kennebec Hill, and proceeded to wash gravel with their utmost energy, knowing that others would soon find the gulch. Within a week, another prospector joined them, and succeeded in taking out two pounds and a half of gold-dust during his first day's work. Within thirteen days from the time the five original prospectors camped on Kennebec Hill, there were eight thousand miners in the new town. Many gamblers came with the crowd; and at one time there were not less than a hundred and forty-three monte and faro banks in operation, the funds of which were nearly half a million dollars. Men were often seen to turn a card for three or four thousand dollars, sometimes for several times as much. It was one of the most rapid developments of a great and prosperous mining-camp ever known in California.

Within a fortnight, the need for some system of government was manifest. A public meeting was called to talk up the subject; but nothing in particular was done except to give the camp a name, — Columbia. Two or three days later, at another and much better attended mass-meeting, Major Sullivan was chosen alcalde, and allowed fees collected from registry of mining-claims. June 1 the new State tax on foreigners was enforced, and the population decreased greatly. In 1852, 1,229 votes were polled in the district.

The points in the mining-law in Columbia, which differed from those previously noted, were as follows: Full regulations respecting "dry-diggings," and gold-bearing earth thrown up in heaps to remain till winter rains, such heaps being held to be private property; full regulations to prevent persons from diverting water flowing naturally through gold-bearing ravines, from its course, without the consent of all parties interested; the presence on a claim of tools, sluice-boxes in condition for use, or other mining-machines, accepted as *prima-facie* evidence of occupation.

There are no regulations for arbitration, that being one of the alcalde duties in this camp. The alcalde appointed jurors in civil cases when asked for. The other officers were sheriff and recorder; and the sheriff chose his own assistant, or selected a posse whenever thought necessary. Recorder-fees were at first a dollar, but afterwards fifty cents.

But far the most important sections of the Columbia-District law were as follows: " Neither Asiatics nor South-Sea Islanders shall be allowed to mine in this district, either for themselves or for others." " Any person who shall sell a claim to an Asiatic or South-Sea Islander shall not be allowed to hold another claim in this district for the space of six months." " None but Americans, or Europeans who intend to become citizens, shall be allowed to mine in this district, either for themselves or others." These laws were in full operation in 1856, when Columbia had more than five thousand inhabitants.[1]

Montezuma Camp, Tuolumne, allowed " three squares, of a hundred feet each," to constitute a surface claim; a hundred and fifty feet in width was a " tunnelling-claim; " a hundred feet wide by three hundred feet long was a deep-sinking claim. All shaft-claims must be recorded within one week after location, and must receive three full days' labor each week. The recorder was

---

[1] In 1854 the town was incorporated. In 1855 the miners were anxious to aid the progress of a water-company's ditch; and three hundred or more of them took their picks, and gave several weeks' work to the enterprise. This company, in ten months, constructed forty-four miles of canal and fluming, and supplied twenty-five square miles of mining-ground.

elected "for one year, and until his successor is chosen, unless dissatisfaction occurs:" then the miners of the district "may call a special meeting, and by a two-thirds vote declare said office vacant, and proceed to elect his successor." Arrangements are made for an annual meeting, called by the recorder. His fees are a dollar for recording each claim, and a dollar for each arbitration. He presides over the arbitration court, which consists of two miners chosen by each of the disputants. If either party refuses to choose arbitrators, the two others and the recorder shall decide; and their decision is final.

Jacksonville Camp allowed for a claim fifty feet in width on the river, and extending from the centre of the stream to the adjacent mountain; in the small ravines, three hundred feet constituted a claim, one hundred and fifty feet on the flat, and sixty feet in certain deep-diggings. Fifteen days' idleness in the working-season destroyed claim-rights. In Garote District, fifty yards up and down the creek were allowed, and seventy-five yards on neighboring gulches.

In 1856 the mining-laws of French Camp, Stanislaus County, — then called La Grange, — contained the following, after providing for arbitrators: "In the event of any of the disputing parties not acknowledging the decision, then the miners of this district will assemble, and compel said party to recognize the umpire's decision."

The Sweetland mining-district, Nevada County, was organized in 1850, claims then being thirty feet square. Two years later the privilege was increased, and claims of eighty by a hundred and eighty feet allowed. In 1853 the miners met, and subdivided the district into three; and different regulations were adopted in each. North San Juan, one of these districts, and long the great hydraulic-mining centre of California, provided, in its earlier code, for "one claim by location, and an unlimited number by purchase. The claim-notice must be renewed every thirty days, unless obviated by the daily presence of the owners or their representatives." An expenditure of five hundred dollars in prospecting or opening up a claim secures it for two years. A recorder was to be elected annually by the miners, with the usual fees; and each sale or transfer was to be placed on record within a week.

Pilot Hill, Calaveras County, passed laws about 1855, to the effect that each "gulch-claim" should be a hundred and fifty feet long, and fifty feet wide; each "surface-claim," two hundred feet by a hundred feet; and each "tunnel or shaft claim" should be a hundred feet in width, and extending through the hill. On the last class of claim, work to the value of twenty-five dollars per week is required from each company. "Occupation and use" is required of the owners of the other species of claims.

New Kanaka Camp, Tuolumne County, allowed, in 1858, "creek-claims" of two hundred feet in width, and from bank to bank; also "gulch-claims," of one-fourth that size; and "bar or flat" claims, of twenty feet in width and fifty feet in length. Work must be done "one full day in three, unless the owner is sick or on a jury." On this point, the law of a little Trinity-county camp in 1854 said with grim humor, "and a physician's certificate is needed;" there being at that time but one or two medical men in the county, and none at all in that particular camp. New Kanaka furthermore ordained that each miner might hold one claim by preemption, and one by purchase, but no more. The Chinaman was shut out; "not allowed to own, either by purchase or pre-emption." All disputes were left to three arbitrators, who "must be paid at the rate of three dollars per day for their time." One curious item was, that the elected recorder should number each claim registered, and himself attach to a claim-stake, in the presence of witnesses, a piece of tin bearing that number. The laws of Copper-Cañon District, Calaveras County, were similarly exact on this point; requiring the recorder to visit each claim, and examine its bounds.

One of the most remarkable instances of definite regulation of the "legal representation" of miners at all meetings was that afforded by Brown's Valley Camp, Yuba County. The miners of this place appear to have been sufficiently energetic; for we find them, early in 1853, assembling, and repealing a "previous arbitrary and oppressive set of laws to-day revoked by common consent." They met again Aug. 8, and resolved, —

"That each claim shall be entitled to a vote in the miners' meetings of this district by the proper owner, or may be represented by a power-of-attorney from the proper owner, specifying the object of that power, and its limitation."

These meetings were semi-annual, and claims not represented were declared to be forfeited. This code was in full force until 1864, and many of its provisions lasted until a few years ago.

Examples of kindred regulations might easily be quoted from the laws of placer-camps in California. We have before us notes from pioneers upon the codes of Cherokee, Nimshew, Bangor, and Forbestown camps, in Butte County; of La Porte, Hungarian Hill, and Grizzly Creek, in Plumas County; of Port Wine, Forest City, Monte Cristo, and Downieville, in Sierra; of Slabtown, Tiddletown, and Volcano, in Amador; of Mount Ophir, Blue Gulch, Peñon Blanco, and Horseshoe Bend, in Mariposa; and of many other camps once famous, but now lost in oblivion. None of them present important variations from those already described. The laws of Mud Springs, El Dorado County, as late as 1863 provided for the use of arbitrators; and Georgetown Camp in 1866 clung to many of the primitive forms. In 1868 each district in Placer County had its own rules, and little uniformity was manifest.

A claim-notice posted in San Andreas District, Calaveras County, in 1862, was as follows: —

NOTICE. — The Undersigned claims this ground for mining-purposes, known as the Robert McCall Claim, being a deep or shaft claim, and bounded on the northwest by the Gilchrist & Cornwell Claim, & on the southeast by the Plug-Ugly Claim, and he intends to work it according to the laws of the San Andreas Mining District.

(Signed)   WILLIAM IRVINE.

JOHN SKOWALTER, *Recorder*, Aug. 18.

Another notice found by the writer over a deserted claim in Shasta County, a few years ago, was of a much more primitive type, and read after this fashion: —

NOTIS: To all and everybody. This is my claim, fifty feet on the gulch, cordin' to Clear Creek District Law, backed up by shotgun amendments.

(Signed)   THOMAS HALL.

A few quotations from other " claim-notices " that were in their time accepted as " good and sufficient " may perhaps be pardoned. One man wrote: " TAKEN. — This is my Honest Claim of Ten feet each way." Another: " TO MINERS. — Look further. Respect my claim stakes driven by the rules of Douglas Bar." Still another grew combative with his " CLAME NOTISE. — Jim Brown of Missoury takes this ground; jumpers will be shot." Some camps prescribed the proper size for

the "notice," and that it "should be written in ink,"
others required it to be "painted or cut on wood;" and
it was often boxed, or otherwise protected from the
weather. One camp described the legal claim-stake as
four feet high and five inches square. There was evidently a great deal of honest attention paid to details
of this sort.

All the laws we have hitherto described are those of
placer-districts where mines were worked at comparatively little cost, except when tunnelling was required.
But the first quartz-mining began in 1850–51, near
Oroville; and the necessity of having laws by which to
regulate the size of quartz-claims, and their tenure, was
at once manifest. The miners soon took steps to enlarge
their code, and extend it to county jurisdiction. Late
in 1852 the miners of the various districts of Nevada
County held a meeting at which there was a full discussion of the subject, and a free interchange of opinion.
A committee was appointed to report at another meeting,
called for Dec. 20, at which time a convention of the
quartz-miners from all the districts of the county was
held at Nevada City. The laws they adopted at this
meeting were still in force in 1881, and have served as
the regulations of all the quartz-mining of that region.
They carry the force of law, and have sustained various
judicial decisions. The jurisdiction of these laws was
declared to be "over all quartz mines and claims in
Nevada County." The extent allowed to a claim was
"one hundred feet on the ledge," including "all dips,
angles, and variations," or, as later laws read, "all dips,
spurs, and angles." The discoverer was entitled to two
hundred feet. The marking and staking of a claim
must be done within three days, and the recording
within ten days; and within thirty days, work to the

cost of one hundred dollars, or twenty full days' labor, must be done, and the same repeated each year to hold the claim, until a company is fully organized, and has a mill worth five thousand dollars "contracted for in good faith." The recorder may then give the company a title-deed to the mining-property, guaranteeing possession and proprietorship forever. Failure to comply with this provision about the quartz-mill, ultimately works forfeiture. Any citizen of the United States can take up one quartz-claim, and may also hold "all that he purchases in good faith." The regular county recorder of Nevada County was to serve as mining-recorder in the matter of quartz-claims. His deputy was to be elected by the district.

The Sacramento-County miners assembled in 1857, and passed laws that were in force until after 1868. They required twenty days of work per year on each quartz-claim; the work when done "to be examined by the recorder of the local district," and a certificate given. Whenever a quartz-mill worth five thousand dollars has been contracted for in good faith, the company is entitled to receive a permanent title-deed to the lands from the county recorder. Only citizens, or "those who have declared their intentions of becoming so," are entitled to hold claims. About 1855 the miners of Sierra County formed a code, requiring work to the value of a hundred dollars per year, allowing "foreigners who pay their miners' tax" to hold claims, and limiting the size to two hundred feet on the lode, by a total width of five hundred feet. In 1858 the miners of Tuolumne County assembled, and made uniform laws for the quartz interests.

At the present time most of the counties in the State have held "miners' meetings," at one time or another, to regulate the interests of the owners of quartz-lodes. There was a plan suggested, some time before 1860, for a State convention of delegates from all the mining-districts of California, to formulate a general mining-code; but the need was not sufficiently felt at that time, and Congressional action a few years later rendered such a convention useless. No student of the life of the camps, however, can deny that the full possibility of a State-wide organization existed.

Enough has been said to show how exact and definite were the California camp-laws which regulated property rights. They dealt in a practical manner with river and placer mine-rights, with cement and deep-gravel rights, with tunnel and water-ditch rights, and with leads, ledges, and lodes of every description. These laws thus created became the common heritage of the entire body of American miners, and were in a few years adopted by camps in far-distant regions.

In the Territory (now the State) of Nevada, Virginia-city District adopted its first code Sept. 14, 1859. Quartz-claims were to be two hundred feet on the lead, including "dips, spurs, and angles." Three days of work were required each month. Each quartz-claim was to receive a name, and to be recorded within ten days. "Hill and surface" claims might be a hundred feet square. "Ravine and gulch" claims were to be a hnndred feet wide, and extend "from bank to bank." Claims of every sort were forfeited if not worked. The recorder, elected for one year, should hold his book "subject to inspection," and should post copies of the district-laws in two conspicuous places within the camp. Reese-river District in 1864 extended twenty miles north and south. Its laws were numerous and definite. A written notice signed by fifty claim-owners could at any time be called to depose the recorder. That officer's fees were one dollar; and he could appoint deputies, since the district was so large. The written application of twenty miners would at any time call a special district-meeting.

The regulations of the famous Alder Gulch in Montana, the richest for its size that has ever been found, were adopted in miners' meeting, Sept. 16, 1864, and consisted of two articles in thirty-one sections. They were draughted by a select committee chosen by the miners in open "folk-moot;" and were approved in like manner, clause by clause, after free discussion. The officers of the district were president and secretary. We have now passed beyond the utmost limits of the alcalde and the "government by committee" systems. A written application of five claim-owners was sufficient to call a special meeting. Much space is devoted to riparian rights, laws of trespass, and flume ownership. Tailings must not be permitted to accumulate on another miner's land. Bar-claims, creek-claims, hill-claims, and other classifications are mentioned. Three days per week is the work-requirement. All in all, it is a highly organized and definite code, and shows the influence of experienced miners from Idaho, Colorado, and California. The growth of Montana was marvellous. Before 1867 twenty-five hundred mineral-lodes were prospected and recorded in the Territory. In Confederate Gulch, in 1866, three miners are said to have taken out four hundred and forty-one thousand dollars from a claim three rods square. Montana miners in 1865–70 founded dozens of new camps, even as far north as the Saskatchawan.

We must turn to the later manifestations of law in single mountain camps, organized by Americans. In

the autumn of 1883, away up in the northern corner of
Idaho, the Cœur d'Alêne placers were discovered, south
of Lake Pend d'Oreille, in fastnesses of the North
Rockies that romance and tragedy have made their
own.   The mining excitement that followed was enough
to revive the most vivid memories of 1849.   From New
Mexico, Arizona, Colorado, California, hardy prospectors by the hundred started for Spokane and Rathrum,
the gateways of the region.   They surged in from
Minnesota, from Puget Sound, from Winnipeg and the
Assiniboine, from British Columbia, and the wheat-
plains of Dakota.   Mining-papers devoted columns to
the new mineral belt.   Some doubted, some warned,
some condemned; but still the gold-rush continued.

On Pritchard and Eagle Creeks, Shoshone County,
Idaho, the first local laws of the new mines were
adopted.   It was early in March, 1884, in Cœur d'Alêne
mining-district; and the "by-laws," as the code is
termed, show clearly how the ideas of the earliest camp-
laws have since been modified.

The greatest of changes is in regard to size.   All
locations on lodes of quartz, conforming with the
United-States mining-laws of 1872, are to be fifteen
hundred feet in length by six hundred feet in width.
Placer-mine claimants are allowed twenty acres, so located that neither length nor breadth shall exceed eighty
rods.

Section three of the thirteen sections of this code
introduces a new factor.   It provides that authorized
agents for capitalists may locate and record claims for
them.   Such a thing was seldom or never heard of in
old California days; but, as all the world knows, the
professional prospector and locator for others is one of
the most prominent figures in Western camps.   "Give

me a grub-stake, an' I'll locate ye a dozen good mines,"
is the appeal made to each "tenderfoot," as a greenhorn
is affectionately termed.

Section four allows persons to locate one claim on
each gulch where mineral is found, and also to hold
other claims by purchase. This also marks the growth
of the interests of capital, and large moneyed enterprises.

Section five regards assessments and claim-work.
The first year after location, one hundred dollars of
work must be done; and twenty dollars each month between June and November of subsequent years. Necessary work, such as making roads or trails, building
cabins or other improvements, is allowed to count on
the assessment at the rate of five dollars per day. Between November and May, — the winter-season in that
trying climate, — all claims are "laid over;" that is, no
work is needed to retain their ownership.

The section relating to claims being recorded allows
fifteen days from the date of location, evidently because
the district is so large, and the mountain trails so steep
and difficult to travel over, that a shorter time would
inconvenience prospectors who wish to make long tours
before returning to camp.

Riparian rights, as always, receive careful attention.
The oldest locations have first privilege of water; but
cannot control the surplus, nor waste the water, which
is in every case to be returned to the channel of the
stream for the use and benefit of those below.

The regulation regarding company organization permits miners to unite their claims for purposes of working them better, and to perform "all their assessments
on one claim." This is extremely similar to the usage
in the early California mines.

The principle of arbitràtion is still preserved in almost its pristine exactitude. All difficulties are to be settled thus : " Each disputant to be allowed an equal number of arbitrators ; and, in case of a tie on the decision, said arbitrators shall have power to call in an assistant."

Claims located prior to the adoption of these laws are indorsed. Changes in the district-laws require the written application of at least twelve miners, and ten days' notice of a meeting posted in three or more conspicuous places in the district. Changes between the 1st of November and the 1st of June are illegal and void. Previous unwritten laws are repealed. The officers are a claim-recorder, and a chairman, who has power to call miners' meetings.

Now, these rules made for the government of the Idaho camp of 1884 have many resemblances to the laws of the California camps of 1848. The thirty-six years between have only caused those inevitable changes that come from the increased capital invested in the business, and from the more definite State and National legislation upon the subject. The generic relationship of the earlier and the later codes is manifest. American frontiersmen are ruling in Idaho, as once they ruled in California.

In October, 1884, a New-York gentleman who had been present at a miners' meeting, Eagle-creek Camp, in the Cœur d'Alêne, only a few months before, told the writer that the impression he received from it was that it was the true descendant of the New-England town meeting, and illustrated local self-government of the highest order. Another gentleman recently returned from a journey to the head-waters of the Peace River, the Frazer, and the Saskatchawan, about the gigantic precipices of Mount Hooker, says that the prospectors there were forming camps, and adopting their local codes concerning "claims," their primitive land-law. The process is going on at this hour in the narrowing realm of the pioneer, to the north and to the south, along the ridge of the continent; and the close of this century will not see its completion.

CHAPTER XXII.

THE student of mining-camps and their local customs
and enactments soon becomes interested in a class of
problems peculiar to those districts of the West that are
situated upon government-lands. He finds that class-
difficulties have arisen between farmer and miner; and
that not merely camp-law, but the decisions of the State
courts, have taken abundant cognizance of this fact.
These interests, naturally helpers, he finds at times
opposed to each other; and he can trace the sources of
many recent law-suits to early local legislation.[1]

Several of the district-laws quoted in the preceding
chapter recognize the duty of "restoring roads destroyed
in mining operations," and protect a few feet about
a building so that it shall not fall, nor slide into the

[1] Among the important decisions of early State courts, which deal
with the relations of miner and agriculturist, are the following : Hicks
vs. Bell, 3 Cal., 227; Irwin vs. Philips, 5 Cal., 145; Stoakes vs. Barrett,
5 Cal., 39; McClintock vs. Bryden, 5 Cal., 97; Tartar vs. Spring Creek
Mining Company, 5 Cal., 398; Conger vs. Weaver, 6 Cal., 556; Burdge vs.
Underwood, 6 Cal., 45; Nims vs. Johnson, 7 Cal., 110; Martin vs. Brown,
11 Cal., 12; Burdge vs. Smith, 14 Cal., 380; Henshaw vs. Clark, 14 Cal.,
460; Smith vs. Doe, 15 Cal., 100; Gillam vs. Hutchinson, 16 Cal., 153;
Coryell vs. Cain, 16 Cal., 573; Lentz vs. Victor, 17 Cal., 271; Fremont
vs. Seals, 18 Cal., 433; Rogers vs. Soggs, 22 Cal., 444; Ripley vs. Welch, 23
Cal., 452. For mining-*débris* cases, Woodruff vs. North Bloomfield
Mining Company, opinions of Judges Sawyer and Deady, printed in
San Francisco journals of second week in January, 1884.

gulch. At this point these local rules stop: arbitrators must decide the amount of loss in each individual case.

As a matter of fact, the mining-interests were in those days held to be altogether predominant in importance to the agricultural interests, over the entire gold-bearing area. Law was made by the miners, for the miners; and this meant in practice a disregard of agricultural interests that seems unjust and short-sighted, until we have analyzed its causes, and comprehended its reasons. Nominally, we may remark, the district-rule in early days, and the decision of State courts afterwards, was, that full damages must be paid: in practice the obtaining of a fair compensation was often difficult.

At an early date the State courts of California decided that "agricultural lands, though in possession of others, may be worked for gold;" that "the right belongs to the miner to enter on public mineral lands, although used for agricultural purposes by others, and whether enclosed, or taken up and entered under the Possessory Act." "All persons," it is held, "who settle for agricultural purposes upon any mining-lands in California, so settle at their own risk;" they do it "subject to the rights of the miner, who may at any time proceed to extract any valuable metals which he finds in such lands." At a later date, some cases of great hardship and loss having occurred, it was decided that "the enclosure about the house and outbuildings of a farmer is protected against entry." The burden of proof was thrown upon the miner, who was required to justify his right to enter upon and work a farmer's land by showing that the land was public land, that it contained mineral, and that he proposed to occupy

it for the *bonâ-fide* purpose of mining; and he must pay
for the growing crops destroyed by his operations.

The State passed an Act, April 20, 1852, providing
that persons using public lands for pasturage or agriculture might bring action for damages against miners
who enter upon said lands, but must not interfere with
their operations. An Act of April 25, 1855, protected
"growing crops, buildings, and other improvements,"
in the mining-districts; but closes with, "Nothing in
this Act shall prevent miners from working any mineral
lands in the State after the growing crops on the same
are harvested." Decisions under these Acts were numerous. In every case, the right of the agriculturist
to use and enjoy public lands was considered inferior to
the right of the miner when gold was discovered in the
land. The Government would issue no patent to a
pre-emption claimant upon mineral lands who claimed
it for agricultural purposes. Mere entry and possession
gave no right to the exclusive enjoyment of public
mineral lands. "The mines of gold and silver are as
much the property of the State, by virtue of her sovereignty, as are similar mines in the hands of private proprietors;" and the State has, therefore, the "sole right
to regulate and govern these mines." Growing wood
and timber on public lands "belong to the prior appro-
priator." No person, under pretence of holding land
as a town-lot, can take up and enclose a tract of mineral land in a mining-district, as against persons who
afterwards enter on the land in good faith to dig gold,
and who do no injury to the use of the premises as a
residence or for business purposes. Decisions like
these, and many of a similar nature, help us to understand the completeness of the early mining-rights.

The license granted by the State to each and every

miner, allowing entry upon land for mining-purposes, as we have amply shown, was restricted to the public lands. No person could enter upon agricultural lands held by a United-States patent, and most of the farms in the mining-counties of California are at present so held.[1] In cases where the land has never been "withdrawn as mineral land," but, on the contrary, has been classed by the Surveyor-General as "agricultural public lands," the burden of proof rests on the mineral claimant. Within the last year, the Secretary of the Interior has rendered a number of decisions upon controversies of this character, in some cases overruling the decision of the commissioner of the Land Office. He has decided, in regard to placer-mining on small, unnavigable streams, that it is well settled that such places "may be appropriated; and that, as to the water, the locator obtains only a usufruct in it;" and granted a patent to a claim in the bed of Bear River, California. Local laws are allowed great weight in such decisions in the Territories.

The foregoing illustrations only serve to emphasize the predominance of the mining-interests during the gold-era, when all the lands of the Sierra region were unsurveyed; when there was no farm in the mining-counties, that miners could not condemn and mine out, paying for only the actual damages done. The fairest of gardens, the thriftiest of vineyards, the most fruitful of orchards, one and all were liable to be destroyed without remedy, by the early placer-miners. The gold-seekers could, and often did, sluice away roads, or cut them across by channels impassable for years, undermine houses, wash away fertile land, move towns to new sites,

[1] See the famous case of Boggs vs. Merced Mining Company, 14 Cal. Rep., 279, in which Chief Justice Fields gave the decision.

and tear the old location down to bed-rock with torrents of water.   There are towns in the mining-region
that have been twice or thrice thus removed; there
are others that have been "tunnelled," and "coyoted,"
and "drifted," until "caves" and "breaks" are of not
infrequent occurrence in the midst of streets or town-
lots.

But it has not been destructive always, this endless
onslaught of the miners upon rock and hillside, vale
and cliff.   Lands have as often been created as others
have been ruined; barren beds of rock have often been
filled up to the very brim with rich hillside soil, the
alluvial deposit of ages, and so turned into gardens of
magnificent beauty and exhaustless fertility.   Farmers
on mountain streams in the early days have more than
once found that the mud-laden waters from mines above
them brought added fruitfulness to their soil.   Many
persons have occupied adjoining tracts for mining and
for agriculture, and have used water first for gold-
washing and then for irrigation.   Though the pre-
eminent rights of the miner over all public lands
sometimes worked hardship, yet the full recognition of
these rights was the only logical conclusion of early
California society; and the only wonder is, that so few
serious difficulties occurred in the gold-period, over this
difficult problem.

The earliest authenticated case of forcible entry upon
fenced-in property used for agricultural purposes, of
which we have an account, occurred in Grass Valley, in
the spring of 1850.   There was in all the mountain
land no more lovely and fertile a spot than this valley,
when the placer-miners began work there, and stripped
its soil to the bed-rock along the wonderfully rich
ravines: there is no lovelier spot to-day, when the re-

storing hand of time, and the labor of loyal home-builders, have embowered it in gardens of unsurpassed beauty; it is one of the fairest and most prosperous of the long array of mining-towns, once mining-camps, that nestle in the Sierra foot-hills, or rest in its pine-clad cañons.

But in 1850, when Grass Valley was the "camp," two men fenced in a natural meadow. Here they could annually cut two heavy crops of hay, which was worth eighty dollars per ton; they counted upon receiving at least four hundred dollars per acre that year. However, before a month had elapsed, a prospector climbed the brush fence, sunk a shaft through the soil, struck "pay gravel," and in less than twenty-four hours the whole hay-ranch was staked out in claims of fifty feet square; and, as tradition reports, the ravaged proprietors, through neglect or inability, did not obtain a single claim. The tract was not property, in the miners' definition. The possessors had fenced it, subject to the risk that there might be mineral there. They ought to have prospected it for themselves first, and whispered the secret thereof to their intimate friends: so the sturdy, red-shirted, blue-overalled miners said.

In 1851, it is said that two miners began to sink an exploration shaft in Main Street, Nevada City, nearly in front of the office of the South Yuba Canal Company, and in the business centre of the town. A sturdy merchant came out, and expostulated with them; but was promptly told that nobody had made any law against digging down to bed-rock, and drifting out the streets, and they proposed to try it. "Then, I'll make a law to suit the case," said the irate and energetic citizen, himself an ex-miner. Walking into his store, he came out with an army-revolver, and by its persuasive presence established the precedent that Main Street, at least, was not mining-ground. Of course, this was an extreme case. A jury, or a miners' court, would probably have decided to exempt Main Street from exploration, as more valuable for business uses. But in the lesser towns of the mining-region, permanence did not exist. Nothing was sacred : all rights were subject to the claims of the miner. Many a case occurred, where the entire town was moved to an adjacent spot, and every inch of the soil on which it stood was sluiced away from grass-roots to bed-rock. In many other cases, the miners thought it better to tunnel underneath, and work out the layers of rich gravel as best they could ; though this sometimes caused disasters, and buildings slid from their foundations with the crumbling soil during winter rains.

As regards the destroying of roads by miners, an instance which came under the writer's observation may serve to illustrate the custom. Nine miles of well-built mountain road connected a village of two hundred inhabitants with the county-seat. Though there was no district organization remaining (in 1878), its influence was still strong. Along the river-bed, filled twenty feet deep with the wash and *débris* of the mines of 1850, were rich spots, neglected by those careless, hasty pioneers. About a dozen men spent their illy-paid days in making experiments here and there, trying to find one of these unspoiled, unrifled bits of a placer. Two of these prospectors sank a shaft at the edge of the gravel, five or ten feet from the county-road, and "struck it rich." They worked a few days, and found the pay-streak extended into the hill ; they cut a rough and barely passable wagon-road through the dense thicket, a hundred feet higher up the slope, and in a week had torn out fifty feet of the road, leaving a chasm twenty feet deep. Farmers, merchants, county officials, passed by, swore at the climb, told them to hurry with their work, and asked how much they meant to clean up, but never hinted that the proceeding was illegal or unjustifiable. A few weeks passed, and the small, irregular piece of virgin ground overlooked by the early miners was swept clean, yielding enough, it is said, to pay for a well-stocked farm in the Sacramento Valley. The two miners tapped a ditch that passed by on the hillside, far above them, hired the use of the water, and sluiced earth, rock, and bushes down into the chasm until it was full to the brim, ready, when fairly settled down, to form a good foundation for the county-road again.

Countless stories might be told to exemplify the supreme position of the miner in early California. But there was little abuse of that supremacy. Once admit that the highest use of the soil was to yield gold, and the rest follows as a matter of course. The great majority of the early farms and orchards were planted on soil that was guiltless of containing gold in paying quantities, and so remained undisturbed. In one case a miners' court decided, when a small orchard of four-year-old apple-trees had been mined out, that the land was worthless; but that the trees, which had been brought overland from Oregon, were worth fifty dollars apiece, fruit being then excessively high-priced in the mines. They had not yet borne fruit, but the owner received twenty-five hundred dollars for them. We have heard of several instances where men who paid high prices for possessory claims to agricultural lands made extensive improvements; and, the lands being entered upon for mining-purposes, no equivalent damages could ever be obtained. In Placerville we were shown a bit of meadow, which in 1881 had been mined out five or six times, as it receives the rich wash from mines above, and the soil from the hillsides. Pieces of waste and worthless bed-rock, swept clean by the pioneers, have often been restored, and made into beautiful and profitable vegetable-gardens, clover-fields, and fruit-orchards, simply by the process of washing the rich surface-soil of the hillside down into the hollows, by using the hydraulic method.

As a rule, in the mines, agriculturists and miners lived together in harmony in those early days. The profits of vegetable-growing, hay-raising, etc., were so great, that the man who tilled the soil often made more than did the man who washed out gravel ; and their unity of interests has been so well recognized, that in the long struggle between the valley-farmers and the miners, over the *débris*-question, which has now passed into history, the farmers of the mining-region often helped to support the miners through their thoroughly-welded-together organizations.

Of that great struggle, which has been to all intents and purposes a suit between valley-counties and mining-counties, it is yet too soon to speak ; for a generation must pass away before its results are manifest. But it will always rank as one of the most important judicial decisions ever made in an American State. The calculations of engineers were, that, since 1876, a hundred million cubic yards of gravel, sand, and clay had been washed into the Yuba and its tributaries ; that in 1880 some 15,220 acres had been seriously injured by these "slickens" deposits; and that six hundred million cubic yards yet remained to be removed. The steady shoaling of navigable rivers and bays was also charged to the mining-detritus. It was testified, that, prior to 1862, at least thirty thousand miners worked the Yuba and its branches. The citizens of the valleys brought many suits of a representative character; and between 1877 and 1884 the issue was fought with the best legal weapons, and funds were raised on both sides by means of associations. The question was *sui generis:* the agricultural interests of the lowlands were pitted against the hydraulic-mining interests. The State Supreme-court decision of Jan. 7, 1884, was, that private rights could not be encroached upon under guise of "miners' customs," even in districts where the statutes recognize the validity of such local laws. The maxims of the common law in reference to water-rights were fully sustained, and a perpetual injunction granted against the miners "unless they can so mine as not to injure the valleys." The rights of miners to use places of deposit for "tailings" and other mining-*débris*, substantially supported by earlier decisions, were thus subordinated to agricultural interests; and only the alternatives of "drifting" out the rich gravel, or of impounding, satisfactorily to the courts, the hydraulic *débris*, have been left the miners. The hidden wealth of the pliocene river-channels is so great, that many portions of them will pay for working, even by these more expensive methods; but the early predominance of mining over agricultural interests, granted by local law, is now a thing of the past.

The time is not far off when the varied agricultural possibilities of the old mining-region will be recognized as second to that of no territory of equal size on the Pacific Coast; and when the population supported by agricultural and horticultural pursuits within those famous mining-districts whose laws we have studied, and whose early organizations we have described in the previous chapters, will be greater then that of those camps in their "flush times." The land, every acre of it, will pass under full private ownership, held by government-patent; and the mineral in the land will belong to the dweller thereon. Indeed, the railroads and various large corporations now hold a great part of the lands in this mineral belt once entirely public lands. The timber is being removed, the iron is being smelted, the valuable stone-quarries worked; in some places, colonies of settlers are planting orchards and vineyards, orange-groves and olivariums, using for irrigation the water of mining-ditches cut by the labor of the energetic pioneers of '49, enlarged and extended by the vast associated capital of later years. The future of the mining-region used to be a favorite subject of conversation with the late Mr. B. B. Redding, one of the foremost nature-students on the Pacific Coast, one of the noblest and most generous of men, the friend and associate, all his life, of the pioneers, founders, and leaders of the State. He used to say that Italy, Spain, and southern France, all combined, would some day seem poor in comparison with eight or ten counties of the mineral belt of California, whose resources in horticultural directions were simply incalculable. The work done in that region during the past five years has gone far towards justifying Mr. Redding's bold prediction.

CHAPTER XXIII.

THE miners' local land-laws, as we have heretofore seen, rested on the proposition that the soil was all government property, and that the nation allowed them the use thereof, under a possessory title, even though they should never wish to purchase it. Digging gold was early declared to be "a franchise from the government, and free to all." In this faith, American miners developed the system we have been studying in notes from the laws of different camps. But the hundreds of important mining-litigations that occurred during the gold-era of California preserve in their dreary wastes some precious bits of local history, like diamonds in the sea-sands. Law is the great shrine-builder, after all. The wrecks of old systems, the superstitions of forgotten races, the customs of perished kingdoms, are frozen in this iceberg of law, sealed forever in its translucent prison-walls, as mammoths in the ice of the Siberian tundras; or, if we choose, we may use a gentler simile, and call law the amber of the Baltic, making precious each bit of ancient life intrusted to its care.[1]

---

[1] Among the important cases in the California Reports referring to "local laws and customs," are the following, besides many others: People vs. Naglee, 1, 238; Hicks vs. Bell, 3, 219; Mitchell vs. Hagood, 6, 148; Davis vs. Butler, 6, 511; Fairbank vs. Woodhouse, 6, 433; Sims vs. Smith, 7, 148; McKeon vs. Bisbee, 9, 137; Packer vs. Heaton, 9, 568;

We find that because the early miners of California, in their plain, effective, and untechnical system, had made use the only basis of ownership, they also ordained that the same piece of ground could be occupied and owned by different persons at the same time, providing it was required and held for different purposes. If one man held a placer-claim for placer-uses, and another miner discovered a quartz-ledge on the same tract, it could be recorded and held without any interference from the placer-miner. If there was also an unclaimed spring or stream of water on the same tract, it could be taken up, or claimed, for mining-purposes, by still a third prospector; and these three men might long continue to use and enjoy the profits of their separate interests in the same small tract. Ground taken up for mining could be again taken up for fluming purposes. Riparian rights were possessory, and subject to much the same rules that governed the holdings of mineral lands; neither party claiming absolute ownership.[1]

The State courts recognized as legal mining-claims those held by local law and customs, and also those held by actual occupancy of government-lands. But

Jones *vs.* Jackson, 9, 237; O'Keiffe *vs.* Cunningham, 9, 589; Clark *vs.* McElvy, 11, 154; Waring *vs.* Crow, 11, 366; California *vs.* Moore, 12, 56; McGarrity *vs.* Byington, 12, 426; Jackson *vs.* F. R. & G. W. Co., 14, 22; Merritt *vs.* Judd, 14, 64; Brown *vs.* '49 and '56 M. Co., 15, 160 and 20, 198; Clark *vs.* Duval, 15, 85; Edmond *vs.* Chew, 15, 142; Roach *vs.* Gray, 16, 387; English *vs.* Johnson, 17, 107; Atwood *vs.* Fricot, 17, 37; Prosser *vs.* Parks, 18, 47; Gore *vs.* McBrayer, 18, 582; Logan *vs.* Driscoll, 19, 623; Table M. T. Co. *vs.* Stranchan, 20, 198; Copper Hill M. Co. *vs.* Spencer, 25, 18; Martin *vs.* Solambo, 26, 527; St. John *vs.* Kidd, 26, 263; Hess *vs.* Winder, 30, 349; Stone *vs.* Bumper, 46, 318; Shay *vs.* Ryan, 46, 33. Also California Legislature, Act of April 14, 1860; Act of May 17, 1861; and Act of April 4, 1864.

[1] "Surveys, notices, stakes, and blazing of trees, followed by work, . . . give title to unclaimed water." Kimball *vs.* Gearheart, 12 Cal., 27.

the size of claims must not be unreasonable: even where no local law exists to limit them, it must conform to the general usages of miners. The customs of miners in the definition of quartz-ledges are entitled to great if not controlling weight. Proof of similar customs in other districts besides that in which a claim is located is not improper. Subsequent mining-rules of a district have been accepted as valuable evidence to aid in determining prior rights. The entire mining-code of a district must be considered, not merely a portion of it. The State courts waived the right of inquiry into the "regularity of the modes in which these local legislatures or primary assemblages act. They must be the judges of their own proceedings. It is sufficient that the miners agree, whether in public meeting, or after due notice, upon their local laws, and that these are recognized as the rules of the vicinage." [1] Consonant with this is the decision that the authority of "mining-customs" is to be allowed to take precedence of written district-laws which have been disregarded or long neglected. What gives district-laws their authority is not their mere enactment, but the obedience and acquiescence of the miners following upon that enactment; and a custom in itself reasonable and generally observed ought certainly to take precedence over a generally ignored district written law. The moment a district-law falls into disuse, it is void. This question has been held "one of mere fact, for the jury to determine;" and similar in nature, recognizing the will and intention of the miners' assembly, is a decision, that, "although mining-laws were passed on a different day from that mentioned in the notice calling the meeting, they are not

[1] Gore *vs.* McBrayer, 18 Cal., 582.

invalidated. It is sufficient that the miners agreed when they did meet. The regularity of their local meetings is not to be questioned."

Controversies must be settled by the customs and usages of the "bar" or "diggings" embracing the claim in question, whether such customs be written or unwritten. Miners have the right to prescribe rules governing acquisition and divesture of title to claims, and their extent, subject only to State laws. But mining-rules must not limit the number of claims that a person may acquire by purchase, nor prevent prospectors from locating mines for others.

No acts are required of the miner other than use of his property in accordance with local laws. He need not live on his claim (though government-land could not be held for agricultural purposes unless used as a homestead by the claimant), nor need he build upon it, nor cultivate it, nor enclose it. His title is fundamentally different from that of the agricultural settler. And it has also been decided, that the right the miner has possessed since 1848 to enter and mine upon government-land carries with it the right to whatever else is needful, such as use of water and of wood. It includes the right to build, to make a home, to plant orchards and gardens. But fences are not necessary for the miner: the defining of his boundaries by district monuments is sufficient. He still keeps his homestead, not by agricultural pre-emption, but by a miner's possessory title, and as a privilege attached to the ownership of his claim.

It was decided by the Colorado courts, that not until compliance with district rules had been attacked, was any proof of such compliance required; that if the district, for instance, made "notices" and "prospect-stakes" sufficient without registry, it is taken for granted, without proof to the contrary, that the local law is obeyed.[1]

In Montana, as in California, it was decided that the rights of ownership vested in a person, under the rules of a given mining-district, are not affected by a change in the district boundaries: the old rules still govern as regards size, but not as regards method of working.[2]

In the old California camps, as we have seen, the verbal conveyance of a claim was sufficient. Until 1860 the validity of such verbal sales was fully sustained by the State courts, which had previously held that writing was not necessary to vest or to divest the title; which title is in the government, and the right to mine is in the local custom. A transfer may as well be by simple possession as by deed. All miners' claims, under local law, to public mineral lands, are to be regarded as titles; but the right passed by a bill of sale, without seal and without warranty, is only a possession, and is subject to a superior right.

The penalty of forfeiture fixed by camp-laws, if a certain amount of work was not performed, has been amply sustained by the courts. A person who had abandoned his claim was not allowed to re-assert his former interest to the prejudice of others. In questions of "abandonment," the intention governs. The rule, custom, and usage of the district must be open, plain, notorious, so that the miner leaving his claim knows that his action is tantamount to an intention of abandonment. If a miner attempts to hold more than local custom permits, any other miner can take possession of and work the surplus portion, and the injured party

[1] Sears *vs.* Taylor, 4 Colorado Rep.
[2] King *vs.* Edwards, 1 Montana, 236.

cannot recover damages.   The term "forfeiture of rights," as used in mining-customs, has been decided to mean "the loss of a right previously acquired to mine a particular piece of ground, by reason of neglect or failure to comply with local rules and customs." Forfeiture re-opens a claim to immediate location by a new owner.   But in the absence of any custom or local regulation of the given district on the point, the right of property in a claim is not nullified by lack of diligence in working it.   According to recent decisions of the Secretary of the Interior, it is not necessary to require miners re-locating a lode to furnish positive and complete proof of its abandonment by a former locator.   The fact that such abandonment was alleged in the notice of location, and published in the manner and for the time required by law, is thought sufficient, provided that no adverse claim is presented.   Full recognition of the force and authority of local laws is nowhere more evident than in the State-court decisions regarding abandonment of claims.

Those special rights granted to discoverers of, and first locators upon, new placers, receive encouragement from State decisions, which ruled that "the owner of the oldest location on a stream or cañon-bed may dam up the cañon to work his claim, even though it floods other claims the owners of which are *damnum absque injuria*."   Ordinarily each person mining in the same stream is "entitled to use, in a proper and reasonable manner," both the channel of the stream, and the water flowing therein.   According to good law and reason, miners were forbidden to deposit the waste gravel, or "tailings," on other men's claims.

As regards actual work done upon a claim, the local laws have been sustained and liberally interpreted by State courts. Work on adjoining land to construct roads; drains and improvements necessary to development of the mines; efforts made to procure machinery, as the hauling of the same; starting a tunnel, though at a considerable distance, to run into the lead or deep gravel-bed, — these and similar labors are termed "work" in the eyes of the law; such acceptance being in fullest accord with miners' local legislation.

Mining-claims having been recognized as property, and the course of local enactments being to give their ownership the permanence of real estate held under United-States laws, we find that in 1861 those provisions of the law exempting mines from taxation were repealed. "The interest of the occupant of a mining-claim is property liable to taxation, and to being taken and sold under execution."

We have previously seen how great a monthly tax was levied upon foreigners in the early mining-days. By 1861 the tax, once thirty dollars per month, had been reduced by successive State enactments to four dollars. The tax-collector of the county was then authorized to sell at public auction, on one hour's notice by proclamation, the mining-property of any person refusing to pay such tax. Americans connected in any way with foreigners in working mining-ground were held liable for the amount of license of each such foreigner. This tax upon foreigners was held to be only a license-fee, and its imposition not contradictory to the powers of Congress. And "the State alone can enforce the law which prohibits foreigners from working mines without a license:" other miners could not take the law into their own hands, and trespass on such claims.

The mass of printed material relating to the decisions

of district, county, Territorial, or State courts, upon
mining-subjects, is so extensive that the illustrations
already given form but a small part of the whole. Volume after volume of Western law-reports deal with
mining-cases, and contain laborious researches into
Spanish archives, and Californian provincial history,
and the masterly deductions of unsurpassed judicial
intellects. A book written by a lawyer, for lawyers,
upon some of the great mining-cases of California, from
those of the early fifties in Tuolumne, Placer, and
Butte, to the famous group of "mining-*débris*" cases
of the last few years, would be a notable work, and
one well worth the while of some fully-equipped jurist.

From a lawyer's stand-point, the worst thing about
the local laws of the early camps was their lack of
uniformity; but from an institutional stand-point, this
irregular and spontaneous element is their strongest
claim to a place in Western history. A great need
called them into existence: they grew in accordance
with the nature of things, as simply and surely as pines
grow in a forest. Yet we have previously shown many
points of resemblance; and a still closer analysis of the
hundreds of codes of old camps now obtainable — of
camps from every mining-county of California, Nevada,
Oregon, and some of the Territories — proves that the
local laws and usages over this great region are based
upon five principles: to have each claim of definite
size; to enforce the law of use; to maintain "inclined locations" (*gestreckfeld*) in case of quartz; to record all claims; and to insist on this record as final in
case of dispute. All these appear to be Germanic ideas,
now a part of our race-equipment for the world's battle,
but none the less a heritage from Teutonic ancestors.
German, English, American laws, adopt the "inclined-

location" idea, — that a man takes up a piece of mineral
land for the lode alone, and shall have the right to
follow it downward indefinitely, including all dips, spurs,
and angles. Spanish law insists upon "square locations," simply the surface, and all beneath it in a per-
pendicular direction. Some high authorities, such as
Professor Raymond, prefer the latter system, as greatly
lessening litigation. Commissioners, among whom were
Clarence King, J. W. Powell, and Thomas Donaldson,
recommended, in 1880, the abandonment of the "in-
clined-location" system. It is a question that should,
of course, be decided upon practical grounds; but it is
not likely that our present system will soon be dis-
carded.

CHAPTER XXIV.

THE EXTENSION AND PERMANENT INFLUENCE OF
MINING–CAMP LAW.

THE varied methods by which camps were governed, and district-law enforced, and the acceptance of their enactments by the early State courts, have probably received sufficient illustration; but the way in which these enactments spread over the surrounding territory, and ultimately aided to form a national system of mining-law, deserves our attention, as added proof of its creative force.

Recognition by State legislatures began with California, in 1851, when senators and representatives, acknowledging the fact that the miners had perfected a practical working-system, provided that in all actions respecting such claims the proceedings of the miners' meetings should be regarded by the courts, "so far as they are not inconsistent with the laws and constitution of the State." It was this Legislature that conferred jurisdiction in all cases of mining-claims, whatever their value, upon the local justices of the peace.

A little before this time, the very existence of the mining-code had been in great danger. When John C. Fremont was United-States senator from California, he introduced a bill to establish police-regulations throughout the mining-region, and levy a small tax upon the miners. At that time — the winter of 1850–51 — such

a measure would have destroyed the institutions so rapidly developing in the camps of energetic gold-seekers.
The discussion in the Senate was a tedious one. Many
of the senators favored sale of all mineral lands to the
highest bidders. But it is to those great but widely
different leaders, Seward and Benton, that the full
acceptance by the nation of the policy of free mining
on government-land was finally due. They vainly
urged it, and at last insisted upon delay in legislation.
A year later the local regulations of the mining-camps
were so satisfactory, that Congress hesitated to change
the system. Meanwhile, the miners accepted this delay as a tacit recognition of their demands, a tacit
promise to legalize their possessory rights. So they
pushed forward their explorations of gravel-beds and
rock-ledges, of ravines and mountains; they increased
their investments in machinery, water-ditches, costly
tunnels, flumes, embankments, and other requisites of
their gigantic undertakings.

By 1861 the miners' customs, usages, laws, and regulations had spread outward from California, whose
court-decisions were almost universally followed, and
were recognized in other States and Territories of the
West. In Colorado the miners made local laws long
before the Territorial legislature attempted to regulate
such things. Illinois District, Gilpin County, allowed
claims to be two hundred feet long by fifty feet wide,
and prospectors were allowed to locate claims for others.
In November, 1861, the Legislature of Colorado decided
that valid mineral locations could only be made in full
accordance with the local laws of the district in which
the location was made.[1]

---

[1] Sullivan *vs.* Hense, Colorado Rep., vol. 2, p. 425.

The laws of Nevada Territory, passed in November, 1861, declare that, —

"In actions respecting mining-claims, proof shall be admitted of the customs, usages, or regulations established and in force in the mining-district embracing such claim; and . . . [they] shall govern the decision of the action in regard to all questions of location, possession, and abandonment."

The laws of Nevada, in 1862, provided that, —

" All conveyances of mining-claims . . . shall be construed in accordance with the lawful local rules, regulations, and customs of the miners."

The "location and transfers of mining-claims . . . shall be established and proved before courts by the local rules, regulations, or customs of the miners in the several mining-districts." [1]

The Nevada statute of Feb. 27, 1866, provided that, —

" The extraction of gold or other metals from alluvial or diluvial deposits, generally called placer-mining, shall be subject to such regulations as the miners in the several mining-districts shall adopt."

Idaho, Feb. 4, 1864, ordained that, —

" The conveyance of quartz-claims shall be construed in accordance with the local mining rules, regulations, and customs in the several districts."

---

[1] The local laws of Reese-river mining-district, passed in 1862, and amended in 1864, provided for a mining-recorder, whose fees were one dollar for every location registered. The term of office of said recorder was one year, "unless sooner removed by an election called by fifty or more claim-holders." The size of a claim is fixed at two hundred feet on a ledge, "with all the dips, spurs, angles, offshoots, outcrops, depths, widths, and variations." An application of twenty-five miners is sufficient to call a miners' meeting.

Arizona provided that the size of the mining-claims, or *pertenencias*, should be regulated within given areas by the miners; and, further, that the records of mining-districts " shall not be rejected for any defects in their form when their contents may be understood." Twelve or more persons were allowed to form a new district, " make laws therefor, and elect a recorder." Montana passed a Territorial Act allowing thirty or more miners to hold district-meetings, and " make all laws not conflicting with vested rights." Oregon, in a statute of 1867, ordained that " any person may hold one claim by location, and as many by purchase as the local laws of the district allow;" also, that the miners " shall be empowered to make local laws " in relation to the possession of water-rights, the possession and working of placers, and the survey and sale of town-lots in mining-camps, " subject to the laws of the United States."

Thus the local law of the miners had won recognition in State courts, and had extended to other States and Territories. It also gained a hearing in the Supreme Court of the United States. In 1865 Chief Justice Chase, in one of his decisions, said, —

" A special kind of law, a sort of common law of the miners, the offspring of a nation's irrepressible march, — lawless in some senses, yet clothed with dignity by a conception of the immense social results mingled with the fortunes of these bold investigators, — has sprung up on the Pacific Coast, and presents in the value of a 'mining-right' a novel and peculiar question of jurisdiction for this court." [1]

Senator Stewart of Nevada, himself a miner of 1849, and one who helped to govern some of the early camps

[1] In Supreme Court U. S., Dec., 1865, case of Sparrow *vs.* Strong; appeal from Story Co., Nev. : 3 Wallace, U. S. Sup. Ct., p. 100.

of northern California, speaks eloquently of the legislative work done by the pioneers. In a letter to Senator Ramsay, and in a speech delivered in the Senate in June, 1866, he exclaims that the Argonauts "found no laws governing the possession and occupation of mines but the common laws of right which Americans alone are educated to administer. They were forced to make laws for themselves. The reason and justice of the laws they formed challenge the admiration of all who investigate them. Each mining-district in an area extending over not less than fifty thousand square miles formed its own rules, and adopted its own customs. The similarity of these rules and customs throughout the entire mining-region was so great as to attain all the beneficial results of well-digested general laws. These regulations were thoroughly democratic in their character, guarding against every form of monopoly, and requiring continued work and occupation in good faith to constitute a valid possession." [1] About the same time the Conness Committee Report to the Senate of the United States said, —

"The miners' rules and regulations are not only well understood, but have been construed and adjudicated for now nearly a quarter of a century. . . . By this great system established by the people in their primary capacities, and evidencing by the highest possible testimony the peculiar genius of the American people for founding empire and order, popular sovereignty is displayed in one of its grandest aspects, and simply invites us, not to destroy, but to put upon it the stamp of national power and unquestioned authority."

In another place the same report says, —

"The rules and regulations of the miners . . . form the basis of the present admirable system arising out of necessity; they

---

[1] Speech, reported in Cong. Globe, June 19, 1866.

become the means adopted by the people themselves for establishing just protection to all. . . . The local courts, beginning with California, recognize those rules, the central idea of which was *priority of possession.*" [1]

Congress passed an Act July 26, 1866, which recognized the "force of local mining-customs, or rules of miners wherever not conflicting with the laws of the United States." Subsequent Acts, principally the Act of 1872, have defined the entire subject of mining-law; and decisions of the courts and of the heads of the departments have followed in the lines laid down by the Acts of 1866 and 1872. The manner in which a United-States land-patent may be obtained for any land claimed and located for valuable mineral deposits is now fully set forth. The payment of five dollars per acre is required, and the smallest legal subdivision is ten acres. After a notice of "intention to purchase" a described tract of mineral land, sixty days are allowed for other parties to file their adverse claims, if any such exist; after the expiration of this time, no objection from third parties shall be heard except it be shown that the applicant has failed to comply with the law. Congress has required that placer-locations upon surveyed lands shall conform to public surveys in all cases except when this is made impossible by the previous appropriation of a portion of the ten or more acres desired (that is, by claims held under local law), or where it "is impracticable to so locate the claim." [2] It is the evident intention of the mining-laws to allow persons to take a certain quantity of land fit for mining. Where the entire placer-deposit in a cañon within certain limits is claimed, and where the adjoining lands are

---

[1] Report to Senate, May 28, 1866.
[2] Act of July 9, 1870; modified by Act of May 10, 1872.

unfit for any use whatever, the claimant need not conform to the survey-lines." [1]

The Revised Statutes of the United States, relating to mineral lands and mining-resources, supersede and repeal many provisions of the Acts of 1866, 1870, and 1872; but mineral lands are still "free and open to exploration and purchase . . . under regulations prescribed by law, and according to the local customs or rules of miners in the several mining-districts, so far as the same are applicable, and not inconsistent with the laws of the United States." The sections referring to locators and their exclusive right of possession and enjoyment of their mining-claims, to tunnel-rights, to miners' regulations and improvements, to existing rights, to vested rights in the use of water, to rights of way for canals, and to titles of town-lots as subject to mineral rights, are all of them distinct recognitions of early local law, and afford plain evidence of its wide-spread influence.

This liberal policy has filled the ravines of the Rockies with prospectors and miners. It has fostered freedom, and aided the beginnings of law. Men still form mining-camps, still govern them under local forms: but as soon as the district proves of permanent value, they usually abandon this form of organization, for township, county, and territorial forms; for they are not only miners, but also citizens of the Republic, and they look forward to State life and national relationship.

In the course of the development we have endeavored to trace, the most prominent fact appears to be the wide-spread effect of these informal laws of frontiersmen. The best talent in the State of California was

---

[1] Recent decision of Secretary Teller, February, 1884.

engaged at last in the task of codifying the scattered camp-laws, eliminating their manifold contradictions, and remedying their shortcomings. Slowly, through a long series of years, a multitude of wise judicial decisions moulded scattered customs, fragmentary camp-laws, relics of the folk-moot era, survivals of the alcalde period, usages of the time of the later hydraulic mining, into an apt, terse, strong, useful, and comprehensive system of common law, regulating not only the rights of miners over mineral ground, but also their riparian rights. Then the nation recognized its responsibility, and the work of creating a general system was begun. There is much yet to do; a National School of Mines must be established, and stricter legislation is required to prevent wasteful mining: but the great features of the present law are thoroughly consonant with the spirit of republican institutions. This we owe to the men of the mining-camp.

CHAPTER XXV.

EFFECTS, SOCIAL AND INTELLECTUAL, UPON WESTERN DEVELOPMENT.

CONSERVATION of energy is an axiom of science. Though every mining-camp perished to-morrow, the impulse that gave them birth would still survive. The local life, strength, and energy of the early camps has already passed as a powerful force, not as a name, into the warp and woof of society. So far-reaching and powerful have been the influences of camp-life and camp-law upon the growing communities of the Far West, that one might almost be justified in the belief that a new social order would thus be produced. Everywhere, over the great region we have been studying, the spirit of the past abides in multitudinous forms.

It matters not that the elder camps have decayed; nor that the elder pioneers have departed, as the "poet of the Sierras" expressed it, "to prospect the stars;" nor that county officials sit where alcaldes sat, and schoolhouses stand where folk-moots met of old. The men and women whose childhood was passed in these camps are beginning to control the State. Each community, once welded together in camp-life, possesses a unity of feeling that bids fair to be permanent. This is true of California, and may reasonably be expected to prove true of the later-settled mining-regions. We observe, in the newest camps of the British-Columbia border, the same spirit of swift, healthy camp-life, the same return to primitive forms of jurisprudence, the same American determination that crime shall be punished, property and life made safe: therefore we may have faith that the same results will follow there as in California, that stable communities will be established, and higher forms of society evolved.

The nature of the forces long ago set at work in new Western communities by the institutions of the typical camp can best be illustrated by a case which was but one of a thousand. It occurred in 1858, in California; and some of those concerned in the enterprise are still alive. The "surface diggins" of the camp were exhausted, but rich gravel was thought to lie beneath the mountain, to be reached only by a tunnel of great cost; and the men who owned the possessory right to tunnel were all poor. They met, and talked it over, counted their funds, and began work; blasted a hole forty feet in the rock — no more money in the treasury. They borrowed quite an amount in small sums, paying no interest, and drove the tunnel deeper. They appointed a number of men to continue the work, while the rest of the company hired themselves out at daily wages to support them, and buy the necessary tools and blasting-powder. Economy was the order of the day, and fraternal co-operation was its watchword. At last they won: a company of poor and uneducated men, by reason of perfect faith in each other, and grim, tireless persistence, carried a load that capitalists would have refused, and walked at last into Nature's treasure-house, finding a bed of gravel rich enough to amply repay them all. It was not thought a remarkable thing in those days. All over California, groups of comparatively poor men were standing by each other in the same manly way. Now, that, in the last analysis, was and is the feeling fostered in true mining-camp life. In camps, too, we have something of the guild idea. The weavers and the goldsmiths of the Middle Ages had the fraternity feeling, and so have the miners of America. Sturdy self-reliance, mingled and tempered with a high appreciation of one's dependence upon others; the power to stand alone; the power to organize, if need be, with sudden energy and startling swiftness, — these were traits fostered by the patient toil of the miners of America; and because of qualities such as these, the fame of the pioneers of California and the Rockies has gone wherever winds blow or waters run.

The physical spread of the mining-camp influence, through wandering prospectors and miners from deserted camps, assumes in this connection a greater importance than before. We have studied the growth of the miners' code from the rude regulations of the few camps of 1848. We have alluded to the nature of the frequent mining excitements that inevitably extended this code; but some of the features of this movement deserve especial prominence. In 1859, for instance, several thousand California miners went to Cariboo, British Columbia; in 1860 the first mining was done in Idaho, on the Clearwater and Salmon; and hundreds of Californians hastened thither. The same year, also, the Washoe rush began; and within two years the sage-brush deserts and treeless mountains of Nevada were explored, the treasures of Coso, Pioche, Tuscarora, Esmeralda, Potosi, Humboldt, Reese, and other districts had been unveiled; while Bodie in California was also discovered. The year 1862 also witnessed the rush to Boise, and to the John Day region in Oregon, in which State the Powder and Burnt River placers had been found the previous year. The Owyhee mines drew prospectors in 1863, the quartz of Alturas in 1864, the placers of the Big Bend of the Columbia in 1865, White Pine in 1866. California sent out thirty thousand or forty thousand stalwart and well-trained miners in these three or four years.

The reasons for such an exodus are not hard to find. When the surface-wealth of California became so nearly exhausted that men could no longer make the wages to which they had been accustomed, they became restless; when surface miners could no longer make living wages, their occupation was clearly gone. The game was "played out;" so was the camp. There were then a few, more fortunate or more frugal than the majority, who were able to unite in companies to purchase machinery, build forty-mile flumes, explore the deeper auriferous channels of blue gravel, tunnel solid rock and walls of lava, turn the course of rivers, sink deep shafts, — to hold their own, in brief, throughout the new era of capital and monopoly. The weak men sank into laborers for the new companies, or became searchers for precarious finds in the gravel-heaps of the past. Hundreds of energetic men of small means were still able to hold and work mining-property on a moderate scale, but the one resource of the strong was to find a new camp. The great majority of those to whom the mines were no longer liberal swarmed out of the busy hive, as has ever been the custom of the pioneers of our race. When the smallest coin used for change in California sank from a twenty-five-cent piece to ten cents, the emigration began; when it sank still farther to five cents, the disgust and despair of the genuine forty-niner can hardly be described. He felt the earth slipping away from under his feet. Even as late as 1878, in Trinity County, five-cent pieces were very rarely seen, and were sometimes refused. The smallest coin expected for a service was a quarter. Nickels were particularly obnoxious to the miners. Every thing smaller than half a dollar was rather disrespect-fully denominated " chicken-feed."

Under these conditions, hundreds of miners became tillers of the soil; but other hundreds swarmed out into the unexplored spaces, searching the ranges that loom higher and higher northward into British Colum-bia and Alaska, crowned with eternal snows, and dread-ful with arctic dangers. Perhaps some of them sailed up the Yukon, the "Amazon of the North," long before Carl Ritter had heard its name or knew its vastness. Indeed, in 1874, a San Luis Obispo (California) miner told the writer that he spent a summer prospecting in Alaska for gold, long before 1856. Miners once of California, but now of the world at large, prospected the chief districts of the new South-west and of the new North-west, becoming leading citizens in Arizona, New Mexico, Utah, Montana, Idaho, Wyoming; names familiar as household words to old Californians appear and re-appear in the records of Tombstone, Candelaria, Leadville, San Carlos, the Black Hills. They followed the Rockies across the lines, northward, southward. American prospectors drifted into the French-Canadian settlements on the Saskatchawan, bringing lumps of silver and nuggets of gold from the then unexplored regions which the Canadian-Pacific Railroad is entering from east and west with giant strides. American pros-pectors drifted into Mexico; adopted sombreros and tortillas; creviced for gold with Spanish *machetes*, in-stead of with Tuolumne-county butcher-knives; built rockers, long-toms, and sluice-boxes, of Mexic cedar, instead of California sugar-pine; affiliated with the people, fought Indians for them, taught them better methods of mining, and prepared the way for closer international relations.

But the migratory impulse circling outward from Sutter's ruined mill had a meaning for lands outside of North America. It ultimately became of world-wide influence. E. H. Hargreaves, for a time a California miner, returned to his home in Australia, leaving good diggings. He went to the government, received an appointment to search for gold, and in a short time discovered the placers of that mighty island-continent. Many Californians followed his footsteps, leaving a strong impress upon the local mining-legislation and "miners' councils" of Australia, particularly of Victoria. In 1860 thousands of miners went to Barbacoas, New Granada; but the mines proved a failure. Large companies were, however, organized at times in the placer-camps of California, and went to Central America, to Peru, Chili, Equador, Brazil, and Patagonia. They spent vast sums of money, endured extreme hardships, and surmounted enormous difficulties. Some of them acquired fortunes: others lost all their gains of toilsome years in California. Even within the past year (1884), many old and experienced miners have gone to the Transvaal Republic, to Australia, to Chili, to the United States of Colombia, and to Venezuela; some in the employ of capitalists, others on prospecting tours of their own, but all of them spreading abroad the spirit of American mining-law. Wherever, since the brave days of '49, these miners went, they "stood by each other;" they had "pards," and local government; they could not forget the hard but sweet discipline of their loved and lost camps once nestling beneath the Sierra snow-peaks; they clung fast to the ethics of that stormy world whose stern code, it was once said, " is the creation of the American miner; and he loves, trusts, and obeys it." As, of old, Greece was wherever Greeks dwelt; so the spirit of the typical camp is with all American miners, wherever they wander. Some have toiled in Tibet and Assam, in Siberia and South Africa, in the mountains of Abyssinia, and in the rivers of Guinea. The rich mines rumored to exist in Corea and in Madagascar have long attracted the hungry gaze of these bronzed and audacious prospectors. A party of them built a steamboat, and explored the Yukon two summers ago; another party has visited southern Arabia; more than one expedition of miners has gone gold-hunting in the South Seas, among the isles of the Indian Ocean. Last summer a number of California prospectors, after explorations in Alaska, met with a fearful storm; and their schooner went down with all on board. Everywhere it is the same type, — unconquerable kindliness, persistence, and simplicity, unwavering enthusiasm, unblenching courage.

The writer met a prospector in 1876, in Shasta County, California; age forty-five, health perfect, great fund of humor, keen observation, grammar-school education supplemented by much study. He rode a mule, total *impedimenta* was less than thirty pounds; had journeyed from northern Montana, was on his way to Mexico, staked his mule out by the roadside, and the total cost of the entire trip was expected to fall within twenty dollars. In 1881 we again met the same prospector near Calico Camp, San Bernardino County. He was riding a pinto horse, but otherwise appeared unchanged for better or for worse. When asked to give an account of himself, he replied that he had been in Lower California, had crossed northern Mexico, spent some months in Sonora, then in New Mexico; sold several good "prospects," and made money. He then went to Western Colorado to take a hand in the expected invasion of the Indian country; hunted for silver in "the Mormon country," for nitrates in southern Nevada; tried his fortune in one of the old mining-camps of Mono; and had gone on steadily in a similar round, seldom staying more than a few weeks at a place. But he had helped to start Calico, and it was a "pretty good camp," well-organized and prosperous: so he should probably stay there. Such a man is the individual prospector, a person who, though often solitary for days and weeks, can readily join others, and create a society, found a camp, establish a town.

Out of the camps of old, powerful currents have flowed into the remotest valley of the western third of the American continent. A central fact of early New England is the town-meeting; of early Virginia, the plantation; of the Pacific-coast and Rocky-mountain region, the mining-camp. It has taken hold of popular fancy, has become enshrined in tradition, and looms up across the gateways of the history of new States. We walk the streets of San Francisco: leaders in business here, who once were citizens of a camp, and swingers of picks in the beds of mountain torrents. We enter the political field: giants of debate and caucus here, whose first efforts to control their fellow-men were under the Mariposa oaks, or beneath the dome of Shasta. We traverse the pastoral regions of the West, prairies dotted for miles with cattle, herds upon a thousand hills: sun-browned patriarchal princes here, a hundred herdsmen at their command, five hundred horses in their *manadas;* and under the starlight, as we ride homeward, our host will tell stories of "how we druv' the Sydney Ducks outen Pine Flat," and "the hanging of the man what killed Steve Truegood's pard." We visit the prosperous and beautiful colonies of southern California, fair as a garden of the Lord, — realms of cherry and apple, olive and orange, grape and pomegranate, fig and guava, loquat and passiflora, fruits and flowers of two broad zones, mingled in rapturous profusion underneath azure skies as of Capri and Sicily; and here also, in the midst of colonists from all parts of the world, is some man of pre-eminent force and dignity of character, trained in the school of the early mines, transmuting by earth's subtle alchemy his golden nuggets of '49 to yet more golden apples of Hesperides, and planting golden-banded lilies of Osaka in the place of golden leaves from Proserpine's subterranean gardens. We may even seek the great cities, whither all currents flow, — New York, London, Paris, Berlin, St. Petersburg, — the marts of commerce, the counting-houses of Barings and Rothschilds, the courts of tsár and emperor, the wonderful Broadways of many a metropolis, flowing like Amazonian rivers day and night without pause: and we shall find men long-trained in the lessons of the mining-camps walking as calm conquerors through the midst of this world of tumult, action, and desperate struggle, ruling railroad systems, laying ocean cables, planning for isthmus canals, aiding in a thousand enterprises that require energy, capital, knowledge of men, and prestige of former success; yet faithful in heart, cosmopolites though they are, to the memories of their young manhood, the companions of their Argonautic quest, the "pards" of their pick-and-

shovel days in Sierra or Rocky. Upon facts like these
rest the social results of the mining-camp training.

But what of things intellectual? What new forces,
strong to shape the future, passed into the life of the
nation because of the mining-era? Again we must
turn to California as the first of the mining commonwealths. Here the era of the camps is already ancient,
and forever of the past. Its influence extends uncon-
sciously along the channels of daily existence, and
colors the opinions of thousands who never heard of a
mining-camp; but its fundamental importance consists
in its place as a classical and heroic background for
modern life. To all intents and purposes, the true
mining-era now lies a century or two behind the California of to-day. The system of compulsory arbitration,
and the ruling committee of seven elders, adopted in
1640 by the pioneers of Portsmouth, marked no greater
difference from the Rhode-Island Commonwealth of to-
day, than did the arbitrators and alcaldes of the mining-
camps represent a different California from that of the
present time. Institutionally, the mining-camp under-
lies these Western commonwealths, but intellectually it
represents a colonial era; while the Spanish period lies
behind it, a realm of romance and mystery. Some day
all this must pass into literature, not from the stand-
point of outside observation, but from the wiser stand-
point of men and women of home-training.

Of California's hoped-for poet, it has been said by one
of her younger writers:

> " He could not be among those mighty men,
>   The Argonauts, — their poem was the State;
>   Their hands were wed to pick and pan, and fate
>   Gave not to them to wield the slender pen.

.   .   .   .

" But from her children one shall rise ere long
To give her mystic legends fitting lays,
To make her birds and flowers known to fame,
And match her mountains with his lofty song." [1]

There is a faith held by many, that the mingling of civilizations, the crossing and tangling of varied eras, in California, affords an increasing opportunity for art and literature; that the best thoughts of the dwellers in this sunny land will some day be equal to the best the green earth affords. The same sort of influences are at work throughout the mineral region, from the ancient pueblo realm of New Mexico, to the shining " land of the silver bow," as the Indians called Montana. Laws change, systems decay; but the test of all that is highest and best in the life of a community is its literary expression, its poetry, its novels, its world-philosophies. The greatest value to the States of the Far West, of an environment so different from that of merely agricultural communities, and of institutional beginnings of such diverse origins, is in the precious materials thus being accumulated for art and song and tale, for literature in its world-wide illumination, and for the patient use of coming genius.

[1] Charles S. Greene, in Overland for January, 1883.

AUTHORITIES CONSULTED.

[*A complete bibliography of works relating to the subject-matter of this book, if extended to pamphlets and periodicals, would probably be quite sufficient to fill another volume. We must refer to the lists of books and manuscripts relating to Mexico and California in Mr. H. H. Bancroft's "History of the Pacific States of North America," and in the "Catalogue of the Mercantile Library of San Francisco;" also, to notes and references throughout the foregoing pages.*]

MINING IN ASIA AND EUROPE.

ASIA : Compendium of Geography and Travel. Stanford. London, 1882.

BOECKH : Public Economy of Athens. 2 vols.

BURTON (R. H.) : Gold Mines of Midian ; also his Explorations of the Highlands of Brazil (1868), chapter on Mining Systems.

CAMDEN : Britannia. ("Old Authors," 1870 edition.)

CHEVALIER : Remarks on Production of Precious Metals. Tr. London, 1851.

COMSTOCK : History of the Precious Metals. New York, 1849.

CORNWALL : Its Mines and Miners. London, 1857. Also Hunt's Romances of Cornwall.

ENGLISH MINING CASES, in King's Bench Reports : especially Rowe *vs.* Brenton, Concannen's Special Report ; Smirke's Report ; Rogers *vs.* Brenton ; Ivimey *vs.* Stocker ; Arkwright *vs.* Cantrell.

GMELIN: Reisen durch Sibirien. 4 vols. Göttingen, 1751.

HEEREN: Historical Researches into the Politics and Trade
of Africa and Asia. 4 vols. London, tr., 1860. Also
his Ancient History (published in 1833, translated by
Mr. George Bancroft in 1842).

HERODOTUS: Sayce's edition. Vol. i. and appendices. London, 1883.

HODGSON: History of Northumberland. 6 vols. 1857.

HUNT (Robert): Mineral Statistics of the United Kingdom.
1865. (Notes on Local Customs.)

JACOBS: Historical Inquiry into the Production of Metals,
etc. London, 1851.

LALOR: Cyclopædia of Political Science; article "Mining."
Professor R. W. Raymond. (Also, Professor Raymond's historical article, on "Relation of Government
to Mining," in the United-States Report for 1879 on
Mineral Resources.)

LODGE (Henry Cabot): The Anglo-Saxon Land Law.

MINING CUSTOMS and Mineral Courts Act (High Peak District), English Parliament. 1851.

POLLOCK (Frederick): The Land Laws. English Citizen
series, 1883.

REITEMEIER (Dr. J. F.): Geschichte des Bergbaues und
Huttenwesens bei den alten Völkern. Göttingen, 1785.
(Received prize of Royal Society of Sciences; contains
fragments of ancient literature on mines and mining-
organization.)

SCHÖMAN: Antiquities of Greece. London, 1826.

SEEBOHM: English Village Communities.

SPRENGER: Alte Geographie.

TRAVELS IN ASIA : Atkinson (Siberia) ; Curzon (Armenia, 1855) ; Haxthausen (Transcaucasia) ; Mouhot (Indo-China) ; Palmer (Desert of the Exodus) ; Pumpelly (Across America and Asia) ; Travels of Porter, Palgrave, Rawlinson, Richthofen, and Stanley; Yule's Marco Polo ; Gill's River of Golden Sand (Tibet, etc.) ; Colquhoun's Across Chryse (Chinese borderlands).

WILSON (Erasmus) : Egypt of the Past. London, 1882.

WYLD : Notes on the Discovery of Gold. London, 1851.

MINING IN AMERICA.

ACOSTA (Father Joseph) : Naturall and Morall History of the Indies (Hakluyt Society Publications).

ALCEDO (Antonio de) : Diccionario Geographico Historico de las Indias Occidentales. Edition of 1812.

ALSOPP (Robert) ; California and its Gold-mines. London, 1853.

ANDERSON : Silver and Gold of the South-west. St. Louis, 1877.

ARIZONA : Territorial Laws and Reports.

AUBERTIN (J. J.) : Flight to Mexico. London, 1882.

AVERY (B. P.) : California Pictures. New York, 1878.

BANCROFT (H. H.) : History of the Pacific States of North America. 13 vols. (Particularly Mexico, vol. vi., and California, vol. i. ; 1542–1800).

BATES (Mrs. D. B.) : Four Years on the Pacific Coast. Boston, 1860.

BARRY (and PATTEN) : Men and Memories of San Francisco. 1873.

BARTLETT : Personal Narrative. 1854.

BAUSMAN (William) : Early California. San Francisco, 1872.

BENTON (J. A.) : California Pilgrim. 1853.

BERRY : Gold of California. London, 1849.

BONWICK (J.) : Mormons and the Silver-mines of the West. 1872.

BORTHWICK (J. D.) : Three Years in California. Edinburgh, 1857.

BOWIE (August J.) : Hydraulic Mining in California. San Francisco, 1878.

BROCKLEHURST : Mexico to-day. London, 1883.

BROOKS (B. S.) : Alcalde-grants in San Francisco. Pioneer Monthly, vol. i.

BROOKS (J. T.) : Four Months among the Gold-seekers. London, 1849.

BRYANT : What I saw in California.

BUFFUM (E. G.) : Six Months in the Gold-mines. Philadelphia, 1850.

BURNETT (Gov. Peter H.) : Recollections of an Old Pioneer. New York, 1880.

BURTON : Across the Rocky Mountains. 1862.

CALIFORNIA DOCUMENTS : 1850. (Correspondence with alcaldes, and reports to the successive military governors.)

CALIFORNIA : Journals of the Senate and Assembly, 1849–1855 ; Debates in Convention of 1849, J. R. Browne ; Law Reports and Digest (40 vols.) ; Statutes of, 1854–56 ; Speeches of Gwin, Latham, and Rhodes ; Professor Trask's Senate Report (Sacramento, 1853–54).

CALIFORNIA: County Histories and Directories; Amador (1881); Alameda (1878); Calaveras (1880); Tuolumne (1856); Nevada (1867 and 1878); also Shasta and Trinity (1879).

CALIFORNIA PIONEERS (Society of): Addresses of Messrs. Van Voorhies, Dwinelle, Clark, Clay, Freelon, Kewen, Randolph, Holmes, Browne, and others.

CALIFORNIA: Works of Travel and Observation not separately noted; Writings of Bowles, Bushnell, Evans, Loviat, Linen, M'Clellan, Nordhoff, Ord, Parke, Parry, Prime, Rae, Revere, Roberts, Saxon, Seemann, Simpson, Soares, Todd, Vassar, Warren, Wilkes, Wilkinson, Winthrop, Wise, Wogan.

CALIFORNIA: Its Gold and Inhabitants. London, 1856. 2 vols.

CALDERON (Madame de la Barca): Life in Mexico. London, 1852.

CARSON: Early Recollections of the Mines. Stockton, 1852.

CASTANARES: Discovery of Gold in 1844.

CHAMISSO: Californien (1816).

CHEVALIER: Le Mexique, Ancien et Moderne; 2 vols. 1864.

CLAVIGERO: Historia Mexico. 1787.

COKE: Ride over the Rocky Mountains. London, 1851.

COLLIER: Pictorial Dictionary. London, 1721.

COLORADO Territorial Enactments; also, Law Reports. Also Fossett's descriptive work on early Colorado. New York, 1879.

COLTON: Three Years in California. 1856.

CONGDON: Mining Laws and Forms. San Francisco, 1864.

COULTER: Adventures in California.

DANA (R. H.) : Two Years Before the Mast.

DELANO : Life among the Diggings. New York, 1854.

EMORY : Military Reconnoissance. 1846.

ENGINEERING AND MINING JOURNAL. New York. 38 vols.

ENGINEERING AND MINING MAGAZINE. New York, 1869–74.

FARNHAM (E. W.) : California In Doors and Out. New York, 1856.

FITZGERALD (Rev. O. P.) : California Sketches. Nashville, Tenn., 1879.

FISHER (Walter M.) : The Californians. San Francisco, 1876.

FORBES : History of Upper and Lower California. London, 1839.

FOSTER (G. G.) : Gold Regions of California. New York, 1848–49.

FREMONT (and EMORY) : California Guide-book. New York, 1849.

FROEBEL : Seven Years' View in Northern Mexico. London, 1859.

GERSTACKER : Kalifornien Gold. Leipsic, 1856.

GLEASON : History of Catholic Church in California. Also, for missions, Reports of Padres Piccola (1702) and Serra (1773) ; Governor Figuero's Manifesto to Mexican Government ; Report of Father-Serra Centennial at Monterey, Cal., Aug. 28, 1884, in San Francisco dailies.

GRAY (William) : Pioneer Times in California. San Francisco, 1881.

HALL : History of San José (California). 1871.

HAWES (Horace) : Missions in California (pamphlet). 1856. Also, his arguments in Mexican land-cases.

HELPER (H. R.) : Land of Gold. Baltimore, 1856.

HELPS (Sir Arthur) : Spanish Conquest. 4 vols. London, 1861.

HITTELL (John S.) : Resources of California. San Francisco, 1874. Also, his History of San Francisco.

HUGHES (Elizabeth) : The California of the Padres. San Francisco, 1871.

HUMBOLDT (Alexander Von) : Essai Politique sur la Nouvelle Espagne.

JONES (William C.) : Report on Land-titles in California. Washington, 1850. Also, Pueblo Question solved. San Francisco, 1860.

KING (Clarence) : Mountaineering in the Sierra. Boston, 1872.

KING (Thomas B.) : California, Wonder of the Age. New York, 1850.

LETTS (J. M.) : California Illustrated. New York, 1853.

MARRYAT (Frank) : Mountains and Molehills. London, 1855.

MAYER (Brantz) : Mexico, Aztec, Spanish, Republican; also Mexico, New Mexico, and California. Baltimore, 1850.

MEXICAN LAW : Gamboa's Commentaries of 1761; Ordenanzas de Mineria of 1783 ; Recopilacion de las Leyes de las Indias, 1781 ; Constituciones de Mejico y de las Estados Mejicanos. Chapters in H. H. Bancroft, vol. vi., and Woolsey's Political Science, vol. ii., chap. vii. Decisions in California Courts relating to Mexican land-grants and mineral claims.

MINING AND SCIENTIFIC PRESS : San Francisco (49 vols.).

MINING RECORD (The) : New York (16 vols.).

NEVADA : Territorial Acts and State Reports.

NICOLAY : The Oregon Territory.   London, 1846.

OBER : Travels in Mexico.   Boston, 1884.

OVERLAND MONTHLY (The) : First and second series.   Articles on Indians, Missions, Spanish Period, Mexico, Pueblos, Mining-camps, Pioneer Days, Early Government, etc.   San Francisco, 1868–84.   The interregnum between the two series was occupied by "The Californian."

PALMER : New and Old California.   New York, 1852.

PATTERSON : Twelve Years in the Mines of California. Cambridge (Mass.), 1862.

PARRY : Mineral Products of the South-west.

PERIODICALS, etc. : Articles in New Englander, 1850 ; British Quarterly, 1850 ; Edinburgh Review, 1858 ; Blackwood, 1857 ; Quarterly Review, 1850 ; Macmillan's, 1867 ; Blackwood, 1851 ; Scribner's Monthly, 1878 ; Hesperian Magazine, San Francisco, 1856–64 ; Hutchings's Magazine, San Francisco.

PLUMMER : Vigilantes of Montana.   Helena, M. T., 1866.

PHILIPS (and DARLINGTON) : Records of Mining.   1862.

PRINCE : History of New Mexico.   1882.

RAYMOND (R. W.) : Statistics of Mines.   1869–73.

RÉMOND : Report on Northern Mexico, in Proceedings of California Academy of Sciences, vol. iii.

ROCKWELL : Compilation of Spanish and Mexican Laws relating to Mines.   New York, 1851.

RYAN : Personal Adventures in California.   2 vols.   London, 1851.

SHUCK : Representative Men of the Pacific.   San Francisco, 1876.

SOULÉ : Annals of San Francisco.

TAYLOR (Bayard): Eldorado. New York, 1850.

TYSON : Geology and Industrial Resources of California (including official reports). Baltimore, 1851.

TUTHILL : History of California. Also, works of Frost, Norman, Capron, Greenhow, Thornton, and others.

UNITED-STATES MINING-LAWS, 1866–1872 ; also Revised Codes now in force.

UNITED STATES (Mining before Californian Discoveries) : Bainbridge (Law of Mines) ; Law Reports of Louisiana, Missouri, Georgia, North Carolina ; scattered articles in periodicals and journals elsewhere referred to; also the United-States Mineral Reports.

VENEGAS: Natural and Civil History of California ; also Noticia de la Californie (1757).

VIGNOTTI (A.) : Coup d'œil sur les Richesses Métallurgiques du Mexique. 1868.

WEEKS : Laws of Mines, Minerals, and Water-rights. San Francisco, 1877.

WESTGARTH : Victoria, late Australia Felix. Edinburgh, 1851. (Notes on Organization of Early Australian Miners as compared with those of California.)

WILSON (Hon. R. A.) : Alcalde System of California. California Reports, vol. i., Appendix.

WHITNEY (Professor) : Mineral Wealth of the United States. Philadelphia, 1851. Also, California Geological Reports.

YALE (Gregory) : Legal Titles to Mining-claims and Water-rights in California. San Francisco, 1867.

INDEX.

Abandonment of claims, State decision, 275.

Accadians, their libraries and mines, 10; their *mana* becomes the Lydian *mina*, 13.

Alcalde, in Cuba, 47; Indian rights before an, 61; Indian alcaldes, 62; of towns, 75; land-granting privileges, 78, 80; history of the office, 83; alcalde in Mexico, 81, 85, 88; alcalde *de mesta* and *jueces del campo*, 51, 86; alcaldes in colonial California, 89–92; under American rule, 94; in San Francisco, 98; duties and powers, 103; in the mines, 109, 151, 182, 184, 185, 188, 190, 243.

Alcalde books, the, 92.

Alder Gulch, Montana, laws of, 254.

Athens, the mines a permanent tenantcy, 14; directors and management, 15; island tribute to Delphos, 16.

Arbitrators, in Dubuque lead-mines, 44; among Mexican miners, 54, 55; in Mexican villages, 85; derived from Roman law, 86; arbitration laws of Springfield district, 238; of Sawmill and Brown's Flats, 242; alcalde arbitration, 243, 246; fees of arbitrators, 247, 249; Idaho arbitrators, 257; the seven elders of Portsmouth, R.I., 296.

Argonauts of '49, the, 133; extravagance and energy, 139, 140; the realms they conquered, 142–144; elements of their society, 148; the "mining-camp atmosphere," 211; the Argonaut abroad, 294, 295.

Arizona, mining-laws of, 282.

Asiatics not allowed to mine, 213, 246, 248.

Assemblies, of Sonoma, Sacramento, and San Francisco, 100, 130.

Assession court, for mine-bounds, 34.

Associations, of miners, 112; of men going to mines, 113, 114; of tunnel-claim owners, 288.

Australia, California miners in, 292.

Avery, Benjamin P., his mining experiences, 161.

Bacon, D., on miners' generosity, 156; on law and order in camps, 172.

Bar-mote court, duties of, 34.

"Bear Flag Battalion," the, 91.

Blackwood's Magazine, views of gold-era, 154.

Blake, C. T., his experiences in the mines, 166.

Blast-furnace, first in New England, 38.

Borthwick, J. D., on organizing instincts of Americans, 155.

Revised June, 1965

harper ⚜ torchbooks

HUMANITIES AND SOCIAL SCIENCES

American Studies: General

THOMAS C. COCHRAN: The Inner Revolution: *Essays on the Social Sciences in History*   TB/1140

EDWARD S. CORWIN: American Constitutional History. *Essays edited by Alpheus T. Mason and Gerald Garvey*   TB/1136

A. HUNTER DUPREE: Science in the Federal Government: *A History of Policies and Activities to 1940*   TB/573

OSCAR HANDLIN, Ed.: This Was America: *As Recorded by European Travelers in the Eighteenth, Nineteenth and Twentieth Centuries. Illus.*   TB/1119

MARCUS LEE HANSEN: The Atlantic Migration: 1607-1860. *Edited by Arthur M. Schlesinger; Introduction by Oscar Handlin*   TB/1052

MARCUS LEE HANSEN: The Immigrant in American History. *Edited with a Foreword by Arthur M. Schlesinger*   TB/1120

JOHN HIGHAM, Ed.: The Reconstruction of American History   TB/1068

ROBERT H. JACKSON: The Supreme Court in the American System of Government   TB/1106

JOHN F. KENNEDY: A Nation of Immigrants. *Illus. Revised and Enlarged. Introduction by Robert F. Kennedy*   TB/1118

RALPH BARTON PERRY: Puritanism and Democracy   TB/1138

ARNOLD ROSE: The Negro in America: *The Condensed Version of Gunnar Myrdal's An American Dilemma*   TB/3048

MAURICE R. STEIN: The Eclipse of Community: *An Interpretation of American Studies*   TB/1128

W. LLOYD WARNER and Associates: Democracy in Jonesville: *A Study in Quality and Inequality* ‖   TB/1129

W. LLOYD WARNER: Social Class in America: *The Evaluation of Status*   TB/1013

American Studies: Colonial

BERNARD BAILYN: The New England Merchants in the Seventeenth Century   TB/1149

JOSEPH CHARLES: The Origins of the American Party System   TB/1049

LAWRENCE HENRY GIPSON: The Coming of the Revolution: 1763-1775. † *Illus.*   TB/3007

LEONARD W. LEVY: Freedom of Speech and Press in Early American History: *Legacy of Suppression*   TB/1109

PERRY MILLER: Errand Into the Wilderness   TB/1139

PERRY MILLER & T. H. JOHNSON, Eds.: The Puritans: *A Sourcebook of Their Writings*
Vol. I TB/1093; Vol. II TB/1094

KENNETH B. MURDOCK: Literature and Theology in Colonial New England   TB/99

WALLACE NOTESTEIN: The English People on the Eve of Colonization: 1603-1630. † *Illus.*   TB/3006

LOUIS B. WRIGHT: The Cultural Life of the American Colonies: 1607-1763. † *Illus.*   TB/3005

American Studies: From the Revolution to the Civil War

JOHN R. ALDEN: The American Revolution: 1775-1783. † *Illus.*   TB/3011

RAY A. BILLINGTON: The Far Western Frontier: 1830-1860. † *Illus.*   TB/3012

GEORGE DANGERFIELD: The Awakening of American Nationalism: 1815-1828. † *Illus.*   TB/3061

CLEMENT EATON: The Freedom-of-Thought Struggle in the Old South. *Revised and Enlarged. Illus.*   TB/1150

CLEMENT EATON: The Growth of Southern Civilization: 1790-1860. † *Illus.*   TB/3040

LOUIS FILLER: The Crusade Against Slavery: 1830-1860. † *Illus.*   TB/3029

DIXON RYAN FOX: The Decline of Aristocracy in the Politics of New York: 1801-1840. ‡ *Edited by Robert V. Remini*   TB/3064

FRANCIS J. GRUND: Aristocracy in America: *Social Class in the Formative Years of the New Nation*   TB/1001

ALEXANDER HAMILTON: The Reports of Alexander Hamilton. ‡ *Edited by Jacob E. Cooke*   TB/3060

DANIEL R. HUNDLEY: Social Relations in Our Southern States. ‡ *Edited by William R. Taylor*   TB/3058

THOMAS JEFFERSON: Notes on the State of Virginia. ‡ *Edited by Thomas P. Abernethy*   TB/3052

BERNARD MAYO: Myths and Men: *Patrick Henry, George Washington, Thomas Jefferson*   TB/1108

JOHN C. MILLER: Alexander Hamilton and the Growth of the New Nation   TB/3057

RICHARD B. MORRIS, Ed.: The Era of the American Revolution   TB/1180

R. B. NYE: The Cultural Life of the New Nation: 1776-1801. † *Illus.*   TB/3026

GEORGE E. PROBST, Ed.: The Happy Republic: *A Reader in Tocqueville's America*   TB/1060

---

† The New American Nation Series, edited by Henry Steele Commager and Richard B. Morris.

‡ American Perspectives series, edited by Bernard Wishy and William E. Leuchtenburg.

* The Rise of Modern Europe series, edited by William L. Langer.

‖ Researches in the Social, Cultural, and Behavioral Sciences, edited by Benjamin Nelson.

§ The Library of Religion and Culture, edited by Benjamin Nelson.

Σ Harper Modern Science Series, edited by James R. Newman.

º Not for sale in Canada.

ROBERT DAHL & CHARLES E. LINDBLOM: Politics, Economics, and Welfare: *Planning and Politico-Economic Systems Resolved into Basic Social Processes*
TB/3037

PETER F. DRUCKER: The New Society: *The Anatomy of Industrial Order*
TB/1082

EDITORS OF FORTUNE: America in the Sixties: *The Economy and the Society*
TB/1015

ROBERT L. HEILBRONER: The Great Ascent: *The Struggle for Economic Development in Our Time*
TB/3030

ABBA P. LERNER: Everybody's Business: *Current Assumptions in Economics and Public Policy*
TB/3051

ROBERT GREEN MCCLOSKEY: American Conservatism in the Age of Enterprise, 1865-1910
TB/1137

PAUL MANTOUX: The Industrial Revolution in the Eighteenth Century: *The Beginnings of the Modern Factory System in England* °
TB/1079

WILLIAM MILLER, Ed.: Men in Business: *Essays on the Historical Role of the Entrepreneur*
TB/1081

PERRIN STRYKER: The Character of the Executive: *Eleven Studies in Managerial Qualities*
TB/1041

PIERRE URI: Partnership for Progress: *A Program for Transatlantic Action*
TB/3036

Contemporary Culture

JACQUES BARZUN: The House of Intellect
TB/1051

JOHN U. NEF: Cultural Foundations of Industrial Civilization
TB/1024

NATHAN M. PUSEY: The Age of the Scholar: *Observations on Education in a Troubled Decade*
TB/1157

PAUL VALÉRY: The Outlook for Intelligence
TB/2016

History: General

L. CARRINGTON GOODRICH: A Short History of the Chinese People. *Illus.*
TB/3015

DAN N. JACOBS & HANS H. BAERWALD: Chinese Communism: *Selected Documents*
TB/3031

BERNARD LEWIS: The Arabs in History
TB/1029

SIR PERCY SYKES: A History of Exploration. ° *Introduction by John K. Wright*
TB/1046

History: Ancient and Medieval

A. ANDREWES: The Greek Tyrants
TB/1103

P. BOISSONNADE: Life and Work in Medieval Europe: *The Evolution of the Medieval Economy, the Fifth to the Fifteenth Centuries.* ° *Preface by Lynn White, Jr.*
TB/1141

HELEN CAM: England before Elizabeth
TB/1026

NORMAN COHN: The Pursuit of the Millennium: *Revolutionary Messianism in Medieval and Reformation Europe and its Bearing on Modern Leftist and Rightist Totalitarian Movements*
TB/1037

G. G. COULTON: Medieval Village, Manor, and Monastery
TB/1022

HEINRICH FICHTENAU: The Carolingian Empire: *The Age of Charlemagne*
TB/1142

F. L. GANSHOF: Feudalism
TB/1058

EDWARD GIBBON: The Triumph of Christendom in the Roman Empire *(Chaps. XV-XX of "Decline and Fall," J. B. Bury edition).* § *Illus.*
TB/46

MICHAEL GRANT: Ancient History °
TB/1190

DENYS HAY: The Medieval Centuries °
TB/1192

J. M. HUSSEY: The Byzantine World
TB/1057

SAMUEL NOAH KRAMER: Sumerian Mythology
TB/1055

FERDINAND LOT: The End of the Ancient World and the Beginnings of the Middle Ages. *Introduction by Glanville Downey*
TB/1044

G. MOLLATT: The Popes at Avignon: 1305-1378
TB/308

CHARLES PETIT-DUTAILLIS: The Feudal Monarchy in France and England: *From the Tenth to the Thirteenth Century* °
TB/1165

HENRI PIERENNE: Early Democracies in the Low Countries: *Urban Society and Political Conflict in the Middle Ages and the Renaissance. Introduction by John H. Mundy*
TB/1110

STEVEN RUNCIMAN: A History of the Crusades. Volume I: *The First Crusade and the Foundation of the Kingdom of Jerusalem. Illus.*
TB/1143

FERDINAND SCHEVILL: Siena: *The History of a Medieval Commune. Introduction by William M. Bowsky*
TB/1164

HENRY OSBORN TAYLOR: The Classical Heritage of the Middle Ages. *Foreword and Biblio. by Kenneth M. Setton*
TB/1117

F. VAN DER MEER: Augustine The Bishop: *Church and Society at the Dawn of the Middle Ages*
TB/304

J. M. WALLACE-HADRILL: The Barbarian West: *The Early Middle Ages, A.D. 400-1000*
TB/1061

History: Renaissance & Reformation

JACOB BURCKHARDT: The Civilization of the Renaissance in Italy. *Introduction by Benjamin Nelson and Charles Trinkaus. Illus.*
Vol. I TB/40; Vol. II TB/41

ERNST CASSIRER: The Individual and the Cosmos in Renaissance Philosophy. *Translated with an Introduction by Mario Domandi*
TB/1097

FEDERICO CHABOD: Machiavelli and the Renaissance
TB/1193

EDWARD P. CHEYNEY: The Dawn of a New Era, 1250-1453. * *Illus.*
TB/3002

R. TREVOR DAVIES: The Golden Century of Spain, 1501-1621 °
TB/1194

DESIDERIUS ERASMUS: Christian Humanism and the Reformation: *Selected Writings. Edited and translated by John C. Olin*
TB/1166

WALLACE K. FERGUSON et al.: Facets of the Renaissance
TB/1098

WALLACE K. FERGUSON et al.: The Renaissance: *Six Essays. Illus.*
TB/1084

JOHN NEVILLE FIGGIS: The Divine Right of Kings. *Introduction by G. R. Elton*
TB/1191

JOHN NEVILLE FIGGIS: Political Thought from Gerson to Grotius: *1414-1625: Seven Studies. Introduction by Garrett Mattingly*
TB/1032

MYRON P. GILMORE: The World of Humanism, 1453-1517.* *Illus.*
TB/3003

FRANCESCO GUICCIARDINI: Maxims and Reflections of a Renaissance Statesman *(Ricordi). Trans. by Mario Domandi. Intro. by Nicolai Rubinstein*
TB/1160

J. H. HEXTER: More's Utopia: *The Biography of an Idea*
TB/1195

JOHAN HUIZINGA: Erasmus and the Age of Reformation. *Illus.*
TB/19

ULRICH VON HUTTEN et al.: On the Eve of the Reformation: *"Letters of Obscure Men." Introduction by Hajo Holborn*
TB/1124

PAUL O. KRISTELLER: Renaissance Thought: *The Classic, Scholastic, and Humanist Strains*
TB/1048

PAUL O. KRISTELLER: Renaissance Thought II: *Papers on Humanism and the Arts*
TB/1163

NICCOLÒ MACHIAVELLI: History of Florence and of the Affairs of Italy: *from the earliest times to the death of Lorenzo the Magnificent. Introduction by Felix Gilbert* TB/1027

ALFRED VON MARTIN: Sociology of the Renaissance. *Introduction by Wallace K. Ferguson* TB/1099

GARRETT MATTINGLY et al.: Renaissance Profiles. *Edited by J. H. Plumb* TB/1162

MILLARD MEISS: Painting in Florence and Siena after the Black Death: *The Arts, Religion and Society in the Mid-Fourteenth Century. 169 illus.* TB/1148

J. E. NEALE: The Age of Catherine de Medici ° TB/1085

ERWIN PANOFSKY: Studies in Iconology: *Humanistic Themes in the Art of the Renaissance. 180 illustrations* TB/1077

J. H. PARRY: The Establishment of the European Hegemony: 1415-1715: *Trade and Exploration in the Age of the Renaissance* TB/1045

J. H. PLUMB: The Italian Renaissance: *A Concise Survey of Its History and Culture* TB/1161

GORDON RUPP: Luther's Progress to the Diet of Worms ° TB/120

FERDINAND SCHEVILL: The Medici. *Illus.* TB/1010

FERDINAND SCHEVILL: Medieval and Renaissance Florence. *Illus.* Volume I: *Medieval Florence* TB/1090 Volume II: *The Coming of Humanism and the Age of the Medici* TB/1091

G. M. TREVELYAN: England in the Age of Wycliffe, 1368-1520 ° TB/1112

VESPASIANO: Renaissance Princes, Popes, and Prelates: *The Vespasiano Memoirs: Lives of Illustrious Men of the XVth Century. Introduction by Myron P. Gilmore* TB/1111

History: Modern European

FREDERICK B. ARTZ: Reaction and Revolution, 1815-1832. * *Illus.* TB/3034

MAX BELOFF: The Age of Absolutism, 1660-1815 TB/1062

ROBERT C. BINKLEY: Realism and Nationalism, 1852-1871. * *Illus.* TB/3038

CRANE BRINTON: A Decade of Revolution, 1789-1799. * *Illus.* TB/3018

J. BRONOWSKI & BRUCE MAZLISH: The Western Intellectual Tradition: *From Leonardo to Hegel* TB/3001

GEOFFREY BRUUN: Europe and the French Imperium, 1799-1814. * *Illus.* TB/3033

ALAN BULLOCK: Hitler, A Study in Tyranny. ° *Illus.* TB/1123

E. H. CARR: The Twenty Years' Crisis, 1919-1939: *An Introduction to the Study of International Relations* ° TB/1122

GORDON A. CRAIG: From Bismarck to Adenauer: *Aspects of German Statecraft. Revised Edition* TB/1171

WALTER L. DORN: Competition for Empire, 1740-1763. * *Illus.* TB/3032

CARL J. FRIEDRICH: The Age of the Baroque, 1610-1660. * *Illus.* TB/3004

RENÉ FUELOEP-MILLER: The Mind and Face of Bolshevism: *An Examination of Cultural Life in Soviet Russia. New Epilogue by the Author* TB/1188

M. DOROTHY GEORGE: London Life in the Eighteenth Century TB/1182

LEO GERSHOY: From Despotism to Revolution, 1763-1789. * *Illus.* TB/3017

C. C. GILLISPIE: Genesis and Geology: *The Decades before Darwin* § TB/51

ALBERT GOODWIN: The French Revolution TB/1064

ALBERT GUERARD: France in the Classical Age: *The Life and Death of an Ideal* TB/1183

CARLTON J. H. HAYES: A Generation of Materialism, 1871-1900. * *Illus.* TB/3039

J. H. HEXTER: Reappraisals in History: *New Views on History and Society in Early Modern Europe* TB/1100

A. R. HUMPHREYS: The Augustan World: *Society, Thought, and Letters in Eighteenth Century England* TB/1105

ALDOUS HUXLEY: The Devils of Loudun: *A Study in the Psychology of Power Politics and Mystical Religion in the France of Cardinal Richelieu* § ° TB/60

DAN N. JACOBS, Ed.: The New Communist Manifesto and Related Documents. *Third edition, revised* TB/1078

HANS KOHN, Ed.: The Mind of Modern Russia: *Historical and Political Thought of Russia's Great Age* TB/1065

KINGSLEY MARTIN: French Liberal Thought in the Eighteenth Century: *A Study of Political Ideas from Bayle to Condorcet* TB/1114

SIR LEWIS NAMIER: Personalities and Powers: *Selected Essays* TB/1186

SIR LEWIS NAMIER: Vanished Supremacies: *Essays on European History, 1812-1918* ° TB/1088

JOHN U. NEF: Western Civilization Since the Renaissance: *Peace, War, Industry, and the Arts* TB/1113

FREDERICK L. NUSSBAUM: The Triumph of Science and Reason, 1660-1685. * *Illus.* TB/3009

JOHN PLAMENATZ: German Marxism and Russian Communism. ° *New Preface by the Author* TB/1189

RAYMOND W. POSTGATE, Ed.: Revolution from 1789 to 1906: *Selected Documents* TB/1063

PENFIELD ROBERTS: The Quest for Security, 1715-1740. * *Illus.* TB/3016

PRISCILLA ROBERTSON: Revolutions of 1848: *A Social History* TB/1025

ALBERT SOREL: Europe Under the Old Regime. *Translated by Francis H. Herrick* TB/1121

N. N. SUKHANOV: The Russian Revolution, 1917: *Eyewitness Account. Edited by Joel Carmichael* Vol. I TB/1066; Vol. II TB/1067

A. J. P. TAYLOR: The Habsburg Monarchy, 1809-1918: *A History of the Austrian Empire and Austria-Hungary* ° TB/1187

JOHN B. WOLF: The Emergence of the Great Powers, 1685-1715. * *Illus.* TB/3010

JOHN B. WOLF: France: 1814-1919: *The Rise of a Liberal-Democratic Society* TB/3019

Intellectual History

HERSCHEL BAKER: The Image of Man: *A Study of the Idea of Human Dignity in Classical Antiquity, the Middle Ages, and the Renaissance* TB/1047

R. R. BOLGAR: The Classical Heritage and Its Beneficiaries: *From the Carolingian Age to the End of the Renaissance* TB/1125

J. BRONOWSKI & BRUCE MAZLISH: The Western Intellectual Tradition: *From Leonardo to Hegel* TB/3001

ERNST CASSIRER: The Individual and the Cosmos in Renaissance Philosophy. *Translated with an Introduction by Mario Domandi* TB/1097

NORMAN COHN: The Pursuit of the Millennium: *Revolutionary Messianism in medieval and Reformation Europe and its bearing on modern Leftist and Rightist totalitarian movements* TB/1037

Literature, Poetry, The Novel & Criticism

Myth, Symbol & Folklore

Philosophy

EDMUND HUSSERL: Phenomenology and the Crisis of Philosophy. *Translated with an Introduction by Quentin Lauer* TB/1170

IMMANUEL KANT: The Doctrine of Virtue, *being Part II of The Metaphysic of Morals. Translated with Notes and Introduction by Mary J. Gregor. Foreword by H. J. Paton* TB/110

IMMANUEL KANT: Groundwork of the Metaphysic of Morals. *Translated and analyzed by H. J. Paton* TB/1159

IMMANUEL KANT: Lectures on Ethics. § *Introduction by Lewis W. Beck* TB/105

QUENTIN LAUER: Phenomenology: *Its Genesis and Prospect* TB/1169

GEORGE A. MORGAN: What Nietzsche Means TB/1198

MICHAEL POLANYI: Personal Knowledge: *Towards a Post-Critical Philosophy* TB/1158

WILLARD VAN ORMAN QUINE: Elementary Logic. *Revised Edition* TB/577

WILLARD VAN ORMAN QUINE: From a Logical Point of View: *Logico-Philosophical Essays* TB/566

BERTRAND RUSSELL et al.: The Philosophy of Bertrand Russell. *Edited by Paul Arthur Schilpp*
Vol. I TB/1095; Vol. II TB/1096

L. S. STEBBING: A Modern Introduction to Logic TB/538

ALFRED NORTH WHITEHEAD: Process and Reality: *An Essay in Cosmology* TB/1033

WILHELM WINDELBAND: A History of Philosophy
Vol. I: *Greek, Roman, Medieval* TB/38
Vol. II: *Renaissance, Enlightenment, Modern* TB/39

Philosophy of History

NICOLAS BERDYAEV: The Beginning and the End § TB/14

NICOLAS BERDYAEV: The Destiny of Man TB/61

WILHELM DILTHEY: Pattern and Meaning in History: *Thoughts on History and Society. ° Edited with an Introduction by H. P. Rickman* TB/1075

RAYMOND KLIBANSKY & H. J. PATON, Eds.: Philosophy and History: *The Ernst Cassirer Festschrift. Illus.* TB/1115

MILTON C. NAHM: Genius and Creativity: *An Essay in the History of Ideas* TB/1196

JOSE ORTEGA Y GASSET: The Modern Theme. *Introduction by Jose Ferrater Mora* TB/1038

KARL R. POPPER: The Poverty of Historicism ° TB/1126

W. H. WALSH: Philosophy of History: *An Introduction* TB/1020

Political Science & Government

JEREMY BENTHAM: The Handbook of Political Fallacies: *Introduction by Crane Brinton* TB/1069

KENNETH E. BOULDING: Conflict and Defense: *A General Theory* TB/3024

CRANE BRINTON: English Political Thought in the Nineteenth Century TB/1071

EDWARD S. CORWIN: American Constitutional History: *Essays edited by Alpheus T. Mason and Gerald Garvey* TB/1136

ROBERT DAHL & CHARLES E. LINDBLOM: Politics, Economics, and Welfare: *Planning and Politico-Economic Systems Resolved into Basic Social Processes* TB/3037

JOHN NEVILLE FIGGIS: The Divine Right of Kings. *Introduction by G. R. Elton* TB/1191

JOHN NEVILLE FIGGIS: Political Thought from Gerson to Grotius: *1414-1625: Seven Studies. Introduction by Garrett Mattingly* TB/1032

F. L. GANSHOF: Feudalism TB/1058

G. P. GOOCH: English Democratic Ideas in Seventeenth Century TB/1006

J. H. HEXTER: More's Utopia: *The Biography of an Idea. New Epilogue by the Author* TB/1195

ROBERT H. JACKSON: The Supreme Court in the American System of Government TB/1106

DAN N. JACOBS, Ed.: The New Communist Manifesto *and Related Documents* TB/1078

DAN N. JACOBS & HANS BAERWALD, Eds.: Chinese Communism: *Selected Documents* TB/3031

ROBERT GREEN MCCLOSKEY: American Conservatism in the Age of Enterprise, 1865-1910 TB/1137

KINGSLEY MARTIN: French Liberal Thought in the Eighteenth Century: *Political Ideas from Bayle to Condorcet* TB/1114

JOHN STUART MILL: On Bentham and Coleridge. *Introduction by F. R. Leavis* TB/1070

JOHN B. MORRALL: Political Thought in Medieval Times TB/1076

JOHN PLAMENATZ: German Marxism and Russian Communism. ° *New Preface by the Author* TB/1189

KARL R. POPPER: The Open Society and Its Enemies
Vol. I: *The Spell of Plato* TB/1101
Vol. II: *The High Tide of Prophecy: Hegel, Marx, and the Aftermath* TB/1102

HENRI DE SAINT-SIMON: Social Organization, The Science of Man, and Other Writings. *Edited and Translated by Felix Markham* TB/1152

JOSEPH A. SCHUMPETER: Capitalism, Socialism and Democracy TB/3008

CHARLES H. SHINN: Mining Camps: *A Study in American Frontier Government. ‡ Edited by Rodman W. Paul* TB/3062

Psychology

ALFRED ADLER: The Individual Psychology of Alfred Adler. *Edited by Heinz L. and Rowena R. Ansbacher* TB/1154

ALFRED ADLER: Problems of Neurosis. *Introduction by Heinz L. Ansbacher* TB/1145

ANTON T. BOISEN: The Exploration of the Inner World: *A Study of Mental Disorder and Religious Experience* TB/87

HERBERT FINGARETTE: The Self in Transformation: *Psychoanalysis, Philosophy and the Life of the Spirit.* ‖ TB/1177

SIGMUND FREUD: On Creativity and the Unconscious: *Papers on the Psychology of Art, Literature, Love, Religion.* § *Intro. by Benjamin Nelson* TB/45

C. JUDSON HERRICK: The Evolution of Human Nature TB/545

WILLIAM JAMES: Psychology: *The Briefer Course. Edited with an Intro. by Gordon Allport* TB/1034

C. G. JUNG: Psychological Reflections TB/2001

C. G. JUNG: Symbols of Transformation: *An Analysis of the Prelude to a Case of Schizophrenia. Illus.*
Vol. I: TB/2009; Vol. II TB/2010

C. G. JUNG & C. KERÉNYI: Essays on a Science of Mythology: *The Myths of the Divine Child and the Divine Maiden* TB/2014

JOHN T. MCNEILL: A History of the Cure of Souls TB/126

KARL MENNINGER: Theory of Psychoanalytic Technique TB/1144

ERICH NEUMANN: Amor and Psyche: *The Psychic Development of the Feminine* TB/2012

ERICH NEUMANN: The Archetypal World of Henry Moore.
107 illus.   TB/2020

ERICH NEUMANN: The Origins and History of Consciousness   Vol. I *Illus.* TB/2007; Vol. II TB/2008

C. P. OBERNDORF: A History of Psychoanalysis in America
                                                    TB/1147

RALPH BARTON PERRY: The Thought and Character of
William James: *Briefer Version*   TB/1156

JEAN PIAGET, BÄRBEL INHELDER, & ALINA SZEMINSKA: The
Child's Conception of Geometry °   TB/1146

JOHN H. SCHAAR: Escape from Authority: *The Perspectives of Erich Fromm*   TB/1155

Sociology

JACQUES BARZUN: Race: *A Study in Superstition. Revised
Edition*   TB/1172

BERNARD BERELSON, Ed.: The Behavioral Sciences Today
                                                    TB/1127

ABRAHAM CAHAN: The Rise of David Levinsky: *A docu-
mentary novel of social mobility in early twentieth
century America. Intro. by John Higham*   TB/1028

THOMAS C. COCHRAN: The Inner Revolution: *Essays on
the Social Sciences in History*   TB/1140

ALLISON DAVIS & JOHN DOLLARD: Children of Bondage:
*The Personality Development of Negro Youth in the
Urban South* |!   TB/3049

ST. CLAIR DRAKE & HORACE R. CAYTON: Black Metropolis:
*A Study of Negro Life in a Northern City. Revised
and Enlarged. Intro. by Everett C. Hughes*
                Vol. I TB/1086; Vol. II TB/1087

EMILE DURKHEIM et al.: Essays on Sociology and Philoso-
phy: *With Analyses of Durkheim's Life and Work.* ||
Edited by Kurt H. Wolff   TB/1151

LEON FESTINGER, HENRY W. RIECKEN & STANLEY SCHACHTER:
When Prophecy Fails: *A Social and Psychological Account of a Modern Group that Predicted the Destruc-
tion of the World* || TB/1132

ALVIN W. GOULDNER: Wildcat Strike: *A Study in Worker-
Management Relationships* || TB/1176

FRANCIS J. GRUND: Aristocracy in America: *Social Class
in the Formative Years of the New Nation*   TB/1001

KURT LEWIN: Field Theory in Social Science: *Selected
Theoretical Papers.* || Edited with a Foreword by
Dorwin Cartwright   TB/1135

R. M. MACIVER: Social Causation   TB/1153

ROBERT K. MERTON, LEONARD BROOM, LEONARD S. COTTRELL,
JR., Editors: Sociology Today: *Problems and Pros-
pects* || Vol. I TB/1173; Vol. II TB/1174

TALCOTT PARSONS & EDWARD A. SHILS, Editors: Toward
a General Theory of Action: *Theoretical Foundations
for the Social Sciences*   TB/1083

JOHN H. ROHRER & MUNRO S. EDMONSON, Eds.: The Eighth
Generation Grows Up: *Cultures and Personalities of
New Orleans Negroes* || TB/3050

ARNOLD ROSE: The Negro in America: *The Condensed
Version of Gunnar Myrdal's An American Dilemma*
                                                    TB/3048

KURT SAMUELSSON: Religion and Economic Action: *A
Critique of Max Weber's The Protestant Ethic and
the Spirit of Capitalism.* || ° *Trans. by E. G. French;
Ed. with Intro. by D. C. Coleman*   TB/1131

PITIRIM A. SOROKIN: Contemporary Sociological Theories.
Through the First Quarter of the 20th Century   TB/3046

MAURICE R. STEIN: The Eclipse of Community: *An Interpretation of American Studies*   TB/1128

FERDINAND TÖNNIES: Community and Society: *Gemein-
schaft und Gesellschaft. Translated and edited by
Charles P. Loomis*   TB/1116

W. LLOYD WARNER & Associates: Democracy in Jonesville: *A Study in Quality and Inequality*   TB/1129

W. LLOYD WARNER: Social Class in America: *The Evaluation of Status*   TB/1013

RELIGION

Ancient & Classical

J. H. BREASTED: Development of Religion and Thought in
Ancient Egypt. *Introduction by John A. Wilson*
                                                    TB/57

HENRI FRANKFORT: Ancient Egyptian Religion: *An Interpretation*   TB/77

G. RACHEL LEVY: Religious Conceptions of the Stone Age
and their Influence upon European Thought. *Illus.
Introduction by Henri Frankfort*   TB/106

MARTIN P. NILSSON: Greek Folk Religion. *Foreword by
Arthur Darby Nock*   TB/78

ALEXANDRE PIANKOFF: The Shrines of Tut-Ankh-Amon.
Edited by N. Rambova. 117 illus.   TB/2011

H. J. ROSE: Religion in Greece and Rome   TB/55

Biblical Thought & Literature

W. F. ALBRIGHT: The Biblical Period from Abraham to
Ezra   TB/102

C. K. BARRETT, Ed.: The New Testament Background:
Selected Documents   TB/86

C. H. DODD: The Authority of the Bible   TB/43

M. S. ENSLIN: Christian Beginnings   TB/5

M. S. ENSLIN: The Literature of the Christian Movement
                                                    TB/6

JOHN GRAY: Archaeology and the Old Testament World.
Illus.   TB/127

H. H. ROWLEY: The Growth of the Old Testament
                                                    TB/107

D. WINTON THOMAS, Ed.: Documents from Old Testament
Times   TB/85

The Judaic Tradition

MARTIN BUBER: Eclipse of God: *Studies in the Relation
Between Religion and Philosophy*   TB/12

MARTIN BUBER: Moses: *The Revelation and the Covenant*   TB/27

MARTIN BUBER: Pointing the Way. *Introduction by
Maurice S. Friedman*   TB/103

MARTIN BUBER: The Prophetic Faith   TB/73

MARTIN BUBER: Two Types of Faith: *the interpenetration
of Judaism and Christianity* °   TB/75

ERNST LUDWIG EHRLICH: A Concise History of Israel:
*From the Earliest Times to the Destruction of the
Temple in A.D. 70* °   TB/128

MAURICE S. FRIEDMAN: Martin Buber: *The Life of Dia-
logue*   TB/64

FLAVIUS JOSEPHUS: The Great Roman-Jewish War, *with
The Life of Josephus. Introduction by William R.
Farmer*   TB/74

T. J. MEEK: Hebrew Origins   TB/69

Christianity: Origins & Early Development

AUGUSTINE: An Augustine Synthesis. *Edited by Erich
Przywara*   TB/335

ADOLF DEISSMANN: Paul: *A Study in Social and Religious
History*   TB/15

7

Christianity: The Middle Ages and The Reformation

Christianity: The Protestant Tradition

Christianity: The Roman and Eastern Traditions

Oriental Religions: Far Eastern, Near Eastern

Philosophy of Religion

A. WOLF: A History of Science, Technology and Philosophy in the 16th and 17th Centuries. ⁰ *Illus.*
Vol. I TB/508; Vol. II TB/509
A. WOLF: A History of Science, Technology, and Philosophy in the Eighteenth Century. ⁰ *Illus.*
Vol. I TB/539; Vol. II TB/540

Mathematics

H. DAVENPORT: The Higher Arithmetic: *An Introduction to the Theory of Numbers* TB/526
H. G. FORDER: Geometry: *An Introduction* TB/548
GOTTLOB FREGE: The Foundations of Arithmetic: *A Logico-Mathematical Enquiry* TB/534
S. KÖRNER: The Philosophy of Mathematics: *An Introduction* TB/547
D. E. LITTLEWOOD: Skeleton Key of Mathematics: *A Simple Account of Complex Algebraic Problems* TB/525
GEORGE E. OWEN: Fundamentals of Scientific Mathematics TB/569
WILLARD VAN ORMAN QUINE: Mathematical Logic TB/558
O. G. SUTTON: Mathematics in Action. ⁰ *Foreword by James R. Newman. Illus.* TB/518
FREDERICK WAISMANN: Introduction to Mathematical Thinking. *Foreword by Karl Menger* TB/511

Philosophy of Science

R. B. BRAITHWAITE: Scientific Explanation TB/515
J. BRONOWSKI: Science and Human Values. *Revised and Enlarged Edition* TB/505
ALBERT EINSTEIN et al.: Albert Einstein: Philosopher-Scientist. *Edited by Paul A. Schilpp* Vol. I TB/502
Vol. II TB/503
WERNER HEISENBERG: Physics and Philosophy: *The Revolution in Modern Science* TB/549
JOHN MAYNARD KEYNES: A Treatise on Probability. ⁰ *Introduction by N. R. Hanson* TB/557

KARL R. POPPER: The Logic of Scientific Discovery TB/576
STEPHEN TOULMIN: Foresight and Understanding: *An Enquiry into the Aims of Science. Foreword by Jacques Barzun* TB/564
STEPHEN TOULMIN: The Philosophy of Science: *An Introduction* TB/513
G. J. WHITROW: The Natural Philosophy of Time ⁰ TB/563

Physics and Cosmology

DAVID BOHM: Causality and Chance in Modern Physics. *Foreword by Louis de Broglie* TB/536
P. W. BRIDGMAN: The Nature of Thermodynamics TB/537
P. W. BRIDGMAN: A Sophisticate's Primer of Relativity TB/575
A. C. CROMBIE, Ed.: Turning Point in Physics TB/535
C. V. DURELL: Readable Relativity. *Foreword by Freeman J. Dyson* TB/530
ARTHUR EDDINGTON: Space, Time and Gravitation: *An outline of the General Relativity Theory* TB/510
GEORGE GAMOW: Biography of Physics Σ TB/567
MAX JAMMER: Concepts of Force: *A Study in the Foundation of Dynamics* TB/550
MAX JAMMER: Concepts of Mass *in Classical and Modern Physics* TB/571
MAX JAMMER: Concepts of Space: *The History of Theories of Space in Physics. Foreword by Albert Einstein* TB/533
EDMUND WHITTAKER: History of the Theories of Aether and Electricity
Volume I: *The Classical Theories* TB/531
Volume II: *The Modern Theories* TB/532
G. J. WHITROW: The Structure and Evolution of the Universe: *An Introduction to Cosmology. Illus.* TB/504

A LETTER TO THE READER

Overseas, there is considerable belief
that we are a country of extreme conservatism and
that we cannot accommodate to social change.

Books about America in the hands of
readers abroad, can help change those ideas.

The U. S. Information Agency cannot,
by itself, meet the vast need for books about
the United States.

You can help.

Harper Torchbooks provides three packets
of books on American history, economics,
sociology, literature and politics to
help meet the need.

To send a packet of Torchbooks [*] overseas,
all you need do is send your check for $7 (which
includes cost of shipping) to Harper & Row.
The U. S. Information Agency will distribute the books to libraries, schools, and other
centers all over the world.

I ask every American to support this
program, part of a worldwide BOOKS USA campaign.

I ask you to share in the opportunity to
help tell others about America.

EDWARD R. MURROW
Director,
U. S. Information Agency

[*retailing at $10.85 to $12.00]

PACKET I: Twentieth Century America

Dulles/America's Rise to World Power, 1898-1954
Cochran/The American Business System, 1900-1955
Zabel, Editor/Literary Opinion in America (two volumes)
Drucker/The New Society: *The Anatomy of Industrial Order*
Fortune Editors/America in the Sixties: *The Economy and the Society*

PACKET II: American History

Billington/The Far Western Frontier, 1830-1860
Mowry/The Era of Theodore Roosevelt and the
    Birth of Modern America, 1900-1912
Faulkner/Politics, Reform, and Expansion, 1890-1900
Cochran & Miller/The Age of Enterprise: *A Social History of
    Industrial America*
Tyler/Freedom's Ferment: *American Social History from the
    Revolution to the Civil War*

PACKET III: American History

Hansen/The Atlantic Migration, 1607-1860
Degler/Out of Our Past: *The Forces that Shaped Modern America*
Probst, Editor/The Happy Republic: *A Reader in Tocqueville's America*
Alden/The American Revolution, 1775-1783
Wright/The Cultural Life of the American Colonies, 1607-1763

*Your gift will be acknowledged directly to you by the overseas recipient.
Simply fill out the coupon, detach and mail with your check or money order.*

HARPER & ROW, PUBLISHERS · BOOKS USA DEPT.
49 East 33rd Street, New York 16, N. Y.

Packet I ☐   Packet II ☐   Packet III ☐

Please send the BOOKS USA library packet(s) indicated above, in my
name, to the area checked below. Enclosed is my remittance in the
amount of _____ for _____ packet(s) at $7.00 each.

_____ Africa   _____ Latin America

_____ Far East   _____ Near East

Name_____

Address_____

_____

NOTE: This offer expires December 31, 1966.